A710

MODERN ECONOMICS

Jan Pen was born in 1921. He studied economics at Amsterdam University, where he received a doctorate in 1950. Until 1956 he worked in the Ministry of Economic Affairs, finally as Director of General Economic Policy. Since 1956 he has been Professor of Economics at Groningen University, and since 1960 he has been Visiting Professor of Macro-economics at the Free University, Brussels.

He has published several books in Dutch; for instance *The Joy of Economics* (1963) and *A Hard World* (1964). *The Wage Rate under Bargaining*, written in 1949, was translated and published by the Harvard University Press in 1959; the author is still not sure why. Together with Trevor S. Preston, M.A., he is now working on an English edition of *Harmony and Conflict*; it contains a good deal more sociology and a bit less economics than the present volume.

The author has travelled extensively between Groningen and The Hague, mostly by train. However, he prefers to stay at home. He also likes to make abstract paintings and to play boogie on the piano. The latter, the author says, is not generally appreciated, though his two sons say they like it.

J. PEN

MODERN ECONOMICS

TRANSLATED FROM THE DUTCH
BY
TREVOR S. PRESTON

PENGUIN BOOKS

Penguin Books Ltd, Harmondsworth, Middlesex, England
Penguin Books Inc., 3300 Clipper Mill Road, Baltimore, Md 21211, U.S.A.
Penguin Books Australia Ltd, Ringwood, Victoria, Australia

—

Moderne Economie first published by Uitgeverij Het Spectrum Utrecht 1958
Published in Pelican Books 1965
Reprinted 1966, 1967

—

—

Made and printed in Great Britain by
Hazell Watson & Viney Ltd, Aylesbury, Bucks
Set in Monotype Times Roman

Contents

CHAPTER I

Modern Economics is Neo-Keynesian

1 · WHAT IS MODERN ABOUT MODERN ECONOMICS?

The object of this book is to describe a number of the main aspects of modern economics. More precisely, its aim is to give the reader an impression of what is modern about modern economics by surveying the development of the subject in the last twenty-five years. This is really a rather precarious undertaking. For what is modern? We tend to describe as modern something that happens to have caught our eye, forgetting that our hobby-horses may have been ridden by others long before. For this reason it is as well to bear in mind that some economists do not rate the progress of their science particularly high. Half in jest, the proposition has occasionally been defended that every fancied new feature can already be found in the work of Alfred Marshall, the great exponent of the classical tradition, who published his *Principles of Economics* towards the end of the last century (1890).

And, apart from the question whether the modern aspects of a science can be easily picked out or not, the difficulty remains that many new finds are less important than they appear at the time. If we search only for what is modern, we run the risk of overlooking truths which have stood the test of time and which are more important than the passing whims of fashion.

But if I nevertheless go in search of the modern elements in economic thought, the reason and the justification for this are that I really do believe that there is something new about it. 'It's all in Marshall' is amusing and provocative, but it is not true. Marshall's view of the relations between important economic quantities such as consumption, investment, taxes, and national income differed from ours. The examination of these relations is called 'macro-economics'. In Marshall's view the national economy functioned differently from the way we see it. And this modification in economic theory, which for the greater part dates

9

from the 1930s, has meanwhile had sufficient time to prove its *raison d'être*. Modern macro-economics is not a whim of fashion, although of course it is not an eternal truth either.

There is a further special reason why I believe that it is important to discuss the modern aspects of present-day economics before a somewhat wider audience. In the development of various sciences there are phases in which it is not so much scientific progress that is urgently required as practical application of what the theoreticians have found. In my opinion economics is now in this phase. In the 1930s the situation was different. Then the theory seemed more or less to have come to a halt on a number of points. The theoreticians were at a loss to understand a world which, despite a great productive capacity, could see no possibility of satisfying fundamental human wants. Unemployment and overproduction formed riddles that economics was unable to solve. It was necessary to break new ground, and this was done. Among the various pioneers who might be mentioned, John Maynard Keynes (1883–1946) is of particular significance. More than anyone else he helped economics out of its impasse. Since then others have continued this work, and we now understand more than we did then.*

Nowadays what really matters is to fructify the theories developed by Keynes and his followers. They are admirably suited to this. Keynesian theory – opinions may still differ about its precise content – has a bearing on economic policy. It may have an uncommonly salutary effect on future prosperity. However, its application is not so simple. This can be achieved only by a great effort; we shall see later why this is. Now an important condition is that insight into economic relations does not remain confined to a small group of theoreticians; it must pervade all who are concerned with economic policy. In a democracy this means that everybody ought to have a certain knowledge of economic affairs. And in any case this knowledge must be possessed by journalists, by Members of Parliament, by businessmen, and by civil servants.

---

* In this book the newer ideas will be designated as Keynesianism. This term has the advantage that it constantly reminds us of Keynes's historic importance. However, the word is misleading to the extent that it appears to ascribe to one man what was the work of a number of people.

Experience shows that occasionally this knowledge is not all that it should be. Not in the field of 'older' economics; most of the lessons of earlier economists have penetrated a large section of the public. But the specifically modern ideas which are to form the subject of this book are still viewed askance by many practical people. The name Keynes has an unpleasant ring to some. His theory is sometimes associated with permanent inflation, with unsound state financing, with excessive government interference. This may be understandable to some extent – we shall try to find this out in the coming pages – but at the same time it does harm to the realization of a modern economic policy. Views can differ on the right content and the right form of this policy. But practically all experts are sure about one thing: modern economic policy must be founded on modern views. And these are views which have been directly or indirectly influenced by Keynesian thought.

We are now passing through a period of economic history in which the application of economic theories lags behind the development of these theories themselves. Too often restraining factors occur in politics. There are too many governments which, though aware of the recommendations made by modern macro-economics, cannot follow these recommendations because public opinion cannot keep proper pace with modern economics. And therefore every contribution, however small, to the propagation of these new ideas is useful. This is one of the reasons why an attempt will be made in this book to point to the typically modern aspects of economics.

What *are* these modern elements in the later theories? A number of them may be mentioned, of which I should like to spotlight two. The first is the influence of Keynes's work, from which there follows a new view of the working of the economic system, of macro-economic relations.

A second characteristic is the pursuit of quantification through the use of statistics and statistical techniques. This tendency is of course not a new one. In the year 1679 Sir William Petty endeavoured to launch a new science, which he called 'Political Arithmetic', and which had the object of collecting quantitative knowledge on economic, social, and political life. But in the last few decades the technique of measurement has increased so considerably, and the set of concepts required for a quantitative theory has been improved so greatly, that we may speak of a new and striking development. Moreover, it has been found that a number of important qualitative problems can only be solved quantitatively, through statistics. These problems are to be found particularly in the province of general economic equilibrium. Incidentally, in my opinion, there is a fairly close connexion between the development of the theory started by Keynes (which relates to this general equilibrium) and quantitative economics.

It is these two aspects – Keynesianism and the search for quantitative relations – which give economics its present-day look. Around them are grouped other 'modern' phenomena (for instance in wage, price, and money theories), but it is these that we wish to discuss in particular. The next sections give a provisional impression of them; they will be elaborated in the following chapters.

2 · KEYNESIANISM

The significance of Keynesianism is most apparent when it is compared with pre-Keynesian views; Keynes himself spoke of the 'classical' theory, and we shall follow his lead in this.* Now an essential point is that the classical theory, if I may exaggerate somewhat, had no place in its system for unemployment. That is to say, this system could interpret unemployment only as a consequence of overproduction of *specific* goods. Too much textile might be made because the textile industry had expanded too quickly; but in that case the result would only be local unemployment. General overproduction was considered to be out of the question.

The reason for this optimistic view was to be found in a relation which the 'classicists' designate as 'Say's Law' (after Jean Bap-

* The classical school of economics really begins with Adam Smith (1723–90) and his celebrated book *An Inquiry into the Nature and Causes of the Wealth of Nations* (1776). This school dominated economic thought in the nineteenth century, but underwent a series of modifications. In his criticism of the classicists Keynes was aiming not so much at Smith as at A. Marshall (1842–1924) and A. C. Pigou, who twenty-five years ago was professor of economics at Cambridge, successor as such to Marshall, and to a certain extent 'head' of the neo-classicists. Pigou long opposed the Keynesian modernism by the spoken and the written word.

tiste Say, who published his *'Traité d'économie politique'* in 1803). This law implies that the production and supply of products are in essence identical with the demand for other products. Supply as it were always creates its own demand. Total demand and total supply ought therefore always to be in equilibrium with one another. The total production can be absorbed by the market, and general overproduction is out of the question. Hence general unemployment is likewise impossible. Such unemployment as occurs is a manifestation of too large a supply of labour in a given sector of the market; the remedy is for these workers to acquire new skills and to find other work. What unemployment there is has a temporary and local character. The expression 'frictional unemployment' is used for this. General unemployment was not reconcilable with Say's Law.*

Right from the beginning many viewed with suspicion the optimism of this 'law'. Thomas Malthus, the early nineteenth-century clergyman who became famous for his gloomy population theory, did not trust this business. However, he was 'proved' wrong by his contemporary David Ricardo, the famous author of the classical rent theory, and Ricardo's authority was very great. Later 'classicists' borrowed the point of view that general overproduction was hardly conceivable, and they always managed to drown the doubters. These doubting Thomases included Marx, who predicted a general overproduction which would mean the downfall of capitalism. Although this downfall has still not happened in the Western world, Marx's theory had some validity on this point; it predicted an underconsumption which would paralyse productive capacity. Not until the thirties of this century did it become evident how far unemployment had to spread before official economics changed its point of view regarding the impossibility of general overproduction.

In those days views changed radically. In various countries plans were drawn up – and sometimes carried out – to get the national economy working again. Attempts were also made to give this policy a theoretical foundation. But the main stream of

---

* In this greatly abridged form Say's Law must strike the layman as a rather mystic affair. We shall return to it – see below, Chapter 11, section 1 – and then it will be seen that this relation is not mystic, nor is it difficult to grasp.

economic thought flowed on unimpaired. It was not until 1936 that Say's Law was finally discarded, and with it the basis of the classical system. This happened in *The General Theory of Employment, Interest and Money*, one of the most remarkable books ever written. John Maynard Keynes had studied mathematics and philosophy, had been brought up in the classical economic tradition, and had a great academic and practical knowledge of economics. He had already published a number of works that gave evidence of this. He taught in Cambridge, where no less a person than the great Marshall had introduced him, and he was the editor of the celebrated *Economic Journal*. Perhaps the special place of the General Theory in the development of the science is in part a consequence of the fact that its author was not someone launching his attack on these sacrosanct beliefs from outside, but someone who had been entirely *nourri dans le sérail*.

Keynes was anything but a bookish man, and he could not be accused of ignorance of worldly and commercial matters. He had been a civil servant, and at the end of the First World War he attended the Peace Conference as adviser to the British delegation, representing the Treasury. The Peace Treaty met with his disapproval, which he demonstrated by resigning and publishing his objections in a successful book (*The Economic Consequences of the Peace*, 1920), in which he predicted economic difficulties – which did not fail to materialize. He became the chairman of a life assurance company, which he brought to great prosperity. He was instrumental in merging the *Nation* with the *New Statesman*. He married the Russian ballet-dancer Lydia Lopokova, and was rich enough to help to finance the ballet and at the same time to build up a collection of paintings. His flair for playing the market stood him in good stead in this. This was doubtless not the reason why Keynes was appointed Director of the Bank of England – the appointment was rather due to his unremitting constructive concern with the country's monetary policy. His criticism of the conduct of affairs, especially the restoration of the Gold Standard by Winston Churchill in 1925, later proved sound. His opinion carried weight in government circles. When Lord Keynes – he had been meanwhile raised to the peerage – died in 1946, he left behind him a gap which none of his contemporaries could fill.

The Keynesian revolution – for that is how the new system was described by his followers – was therefore not launched by an impractical idealist, nor by a malcontent theoretician, nor by a bookish scholar. Nevertheless, the General Theory is not a pamphlet that can be read by an intelligent and interested layman. It is a scholarly work, difficult to understand, complicated in composition, interspersed with lengthy disquisitions on complex but not particularly relevant matters, couched in an esoteric jargon. It was written for fellow economists, and even they did not really know at first what to do with it. It was not until explanatory commentaries had been published by adepts and discussions held on obscure points that the tremendous importance of the new system began to penetrate. But by then the world of the economists proved in actual fact already to have been conquered. True, the Keynesian theory of macro-economic relations had undergone changes in the course of the discussions. The Neo-Keynesians depart from the original train of thought at a number of points. Some stay closer to the anti-classical orthodoxy than others.* But all economists have undergone the influence of the new way of thought, even the small sect that still professes to be anti-Keynesian.

It is a fortunate circumstance that the later theories are simpler than the original system of the General Theory. Modern macro-economics is not obscure or complicated; on the contrary, it is simple and direct; it has brought the science of economics closer to reality and also to some views which the layman holds on economic matters. In particular the worker's distrust of unemployment and the businessman's fear of a general slump have become much more comprehensible in the light of the modern theory. Keynes showed that there is every reason for this fear – unless the authorities are prepared to follow an active policy on this point. Although the nature of this policy is not yet under-

* An example of an orthodox Keynesian is A. P. Lerner (e.g. in *Economics of Employment*, 1951). Less unadulterated views can be found in P. A. Samuelson (e.g. *Economics*, 1948, 6th impr. 1964) and L. R. Klein (in, *inter alia, The Keynesian Revolution*, 1950). A remarkable point is that Samuelson calls the modern theory 'neo-classical'. He therefore appears to be of the opinion that classical theory (i.e. economics since Adam Smith) has absorbed and digested the Keynesian revolution. Personally I still prefer to contrast 'classical' with 'Keynesian', although in actual fact I agree with Samuelson.

stood by everybody, the Keynesian theory concerning overproduction appeals to the layman more than a theory which, on mass unemployment and stagnant markets, cannot think of anything much better than to pretend ignorance and to evoke Say's abstract law.

Modern economics is much more critical of this 'law'. Since Keynes we have been able to understand how it comes about that there can be too big a supply and too little a demand all round. The factors which lead to a general slump are now known in principle. They are disturbances of equilibrium originating in the relation between consumption, investment, taxes, and national income. The last concept has become a central one. Modern economics tries in particular to understand the size of the national income. The ins and outs of this matter will be discussed in following chapters. This much will be plain: knowledge of these disturbing factors is of great social importance. If we wish to be rid of depressions, of stagnating prosperity, and of the evil of unemployment, we must first know the factors leading to these things. Neo-Keynesian theory gives us this knowledge.

But that is not all. For, although Keynes's theory was originally drawn up to explain why demand for goods and services might be too small, it later proved also to lend itself very well to an understanding of the reverse situation, that of too great a demand, of inflation. Too often Keynesian economics is still described as the depression theory. It will become evident that it is equally the theory of inflation. To put it another way: it is a theory of the disturbance of economic equilibrium and of the ways of avoiding this. It is a method for analysing the factors which determine national income and for indicating the means of maximizing this income, and with it prosperity. It is more of a practical approach than a doctrinal theory, and the problems that are tackled are vital. This gives Keynesianism a practical importance that can hardly be overestimated.

3 · QUANTITATIVE ECONOMICS

Economics is a science with many facets, which can be practised in greatly differing ways. One way is to take a few simple properties of man and society as your starting point, and to try to arrive at an understanding of relations by reasoning logically. This is the deductive method. Let me give an example. It is assumed that entrepreneurs aim at maximum profit. It follows from this that if possible they will use less of an expensive factor of production than of a cheap one. If the price of a factor of production, for instance labour, increases, then to achieve a given level of production less labour and more machinery will be used.

This deductive reasoning operates with quantities. The price of labour – the wage – is a quantity, as is the extent to which labour is demanded – employment. The reasoning tries to establish a connexion between wage and employment, and is therefore to a certain extent quantitative. But it tells us nothing about *how great* a reduction of employment results from a wage increase. Will the effect be large? Or small?

Deductive reasoning presents several dangers. In the first place it is tempting to create the impression by a convincing argument that a certain reaction will be quantitatively important. By applying purely literary artifices an attempt is made to extract more from the method than it contains. But all the rhetoric in the world cannot answer the question whether employment will react *materially* to a wage increase or not. That is a matter of figures and statistics. The deductive method must be supplemented by that of observation of reality in figures – the inductive method. Only then can you arrive at quantitative conclusions.

A more important shortcoming of the deductive method is that it is insufficient in those cases in which a number of forces are acting in opposition. Let us re-examine the example of wages given above. A wage increase, says the deductive method, leads to labour being replaced by other factors of production. It might be added to this that higher wages lead to higher prices, so that sales decrease. This also reduces employment. Both reactions operate in the same direction. But the deductive method also tells us that higher wages lead to the workers having more purchasing power, i.e. to greater sales of the products purchased by the workers. This reaction is opposed to the other two. What will the ultimate effect on employment be now? That depends on the balance of the three effects described. But the deductive method tells us nothing about the size of the three reactions, and even less about their total result. Will a wage increase add to or reduce employment? This is an important question, but deductive economics cannot answer it.

Now it so happens that in macro-economics, which thus examines the workings of the entire national economy, the multiple relation is the rule rather than the exception. This does not mean to say that we can do without the deductive method, but it does need supplementing by statistical techniques. If we scorn these, we easily tend to overestimate those factors in the system which we ourselves happen to consider important and which we push into the foreground through misleading rhetoric. Older economics offers many examples of this method, but the deficiency is still there, and must be remedied. Quantitative economics tries to do this. It has also acquired a certain importance for economic policy.

How does this quantitative method operate? In the simplest case it seeks the connexion between not more than two quantities. A well-known example is the connexion between the price of a good and the quantity sold. The deductive method teaches us that such a connexion will probably exist in the sense that a higher price leads to lower sales. Now data are collected on the trend of the price and the trend of the sales in time. In this way you get two time series. (Collecting the data is the statistician's task.) By comparing the two time series graphically with one another it can already be seen to some extent whether there is a correlation between the two. A sales peak would have to coincide in time with a drop in prices. If this checks exactly the correlation is described as perfect; the correlation coefficient in such a case is -1. If the variables had run parallel instead of being in opposition to one another, the perfect correlation would have been expressed by the figure $+1$. In the absence of any connexion the correlation coefficient is very small; it may even be 0.

Here quantitative economics makes grateful use of a mathematical technique which tracks down these relations: the correlation calculation. This amounts to the following: the connexion between one or more series – in this case the time series of sales and price – is expressed in the form of an equation, and this equation is checked against the facts. The deductive theory has for instance taught us that the sales of a product can be represented by a certain (but for the time being unknown) figure A, minus a certain influence a times the price p of that product, i.e. sales $= A - a.p$. This equation is called the demand function. We know the time series of sales and of the price, and the correlation calculation enables us to determine this equation. If our equation checks, we find a high correlation coefficient. At the same time the method of calculation tells us the value of a; this is extremely important, since it gives the extent of the effect that the price has on the sales. In general a is called the regression coefficient. The regression coefficients represent the structure of the equation, and they reflect the structure of the section of economic life examined.

However, one difficulty is that the connexion between economic quantities is often not as simple as this example suggests. Even the connexion between price and quantity sold is not as simple as stated here. For sales are also determined by other factors, such as the size of the national income, the prices of competitive products, and public taste. We may therefore find only an insignificant correlation between sales and price, since the connexion established by the demand function is cut across by the effect of the other factors, although a change in price would make its effect thoroughly felt if it occurred in isolation. In that case we must draw up a somewhat broader demand function, which also includes the above-mentioned variables such as national income, etc. If we possess the necessary time series we can apply the correlation calculation to this broader function too (multiple correlation). We then find for each of the 'explanatory variables' a regression coefficient which expresses the extent to which the variable concerned influences the combination of forces. This entire combination is quantitatively depicted by the regression equation.

Much of the quantitative method is directed towards knowledge of such regression equations; this branch of science gives our insight a concrete, quantitative form. The figures that occur in the equation are not chosen at random. They are based on our experience of reality, i.e. on the statistical time series, which in some cases go back far into history. It is important to put the latter fact on record, since some laymen are under the impression that quantitative economics plays with shadowy numbers which are the children of the fertile brains of armchair economists;

consequently the application of such numbers is regarded as unrealistic, dangerous, unworldly. But in actual fact this method, which is also called econometrics, aims at deriving the maximum of benefit from past events and trends.

Econometrics must not be confused with mathematical economics; the latter is usually pure deductive theory cast in mathematical form. If numbers occur in it, they are more or less made up. Econometrics, on the other hand, is not purely deductive; it is born of the marriage between economic theory and statistical analysis. The statistical mother of econometrics ensures that the child keeps its feet firmly on the ground.

There is a further misunderstanding against which I should like to sound a note of warning. It is often assumed that quantitative economics, if not obscure, is at any rate difficult, being extremely mathematical. And it is true that the active practice of econometrics does demand a great deal of mathematical knowledge. But we can understand the results without penetrating all the secrets of the correlation calculation, or without having any knowledge of logarithmic and exponential functions. Even the tangent is avoided in this book – not in actual fact, of course, for if a quantity increases and another also increases as a result, we are already concerned with a tangent. But the word is not used, to show that we can do without it.

The regression equation, on the other hand, is something that we cannot do without. It is short and sweet, concrete, simple. It designates those factors that determine a phenomenon, and indicates how great the effect of each of the factors is. This is so great an advantage that the reader must overcome any aversion he may have to $Z = aX + bY$. Z is determined by X and Y. The connexion is given by the theory. The statisticians have collected time series of X, Y, and Z. The econometrists have correlated, studied correlation coefficients with a critical eye, and found everything in order. They have presented us with the regression coefficients a and b that the economists could not provide. We must be grateful for this quantitative knowledge, and we must not turn away with the false modesty or the indolent antipathy encountered in some circles – even among economists.

This quantitative economics is of particular value for understanding somewhat more complicated economic relations. It is precisely in macro-economics that a network of forces occurs that in part reinforce one another and in part are opposed to one another. A typical example is the Keynesian system, which tries to describe the relations between consumption, investment, national income, employment, taxes, imports, and exports. These relations can all be understood quantitatively. That is why Neo-Keynesian and quantitative economics hit it off so well. And that is why, in my opinion, this conjuncture determines the present-day look of economics.

One of those who contributed a good deal to this coalescence of the two trends is the Dutch economist J. Tinbergen. He was one of the first who (at the request of the League of Nations) drew up a large-scale 'model' of a national economy and verified this quantitatively against reality.* This made him one of the predecessors of an entire school, and in this sense he may be regarded as a pioneer of modern economics. The name R. Frisch (Oslo) must also be mentioned. Keynes had little faith in the method applied by Tinbergen and Frisch; his scepticism did not do the theory any good. If he had grasped the significance of quantitative economics at an earlier date, his system might perhaps not have the same reputation of 'depression economics'. We shall revert to this matter in greater detail on page 56.

4 · A CHANGE IN ECONOMICS

I am now coming to a disputable proposition. It is this: in the last twenty-five years the focus of economics has shifted. In the decades before Keynes economists did not worry very much about the size of the national income. It was believed that its size was determined by a country's productive capacity. The latter had of course to be increased as much as possible, but if that was done there were no particular difficulties left as regards sales. After all, the latter were attended to by Say's Law, which says that supply always leads to an adequate demand.

An economist who thinks along those lines concentrates his attention on economic growth and also on the question whether the right goods are being produced within the framework of national production. According to classical thought general

* Cf. the monumental *Statistical Testing of Business Cycle Theories*, 1939.

overproduction is not possible, though particular overproduction, i.e. of one particular good, is. For pre-Keynesian theory it was therefore a major problem whether the proportions in which the goods were produced tallied with the demand for these goods.

This is in fact a remarkable problem. For the entrepreneurs are free to take their decisions. They decide what is going to be produced. They are guided by the market – but how exactly? Since Adam Smith (1776) the economists have studied this process. The argument is that the price system is the compass that must keep production on the right course. Price relationships must ensure that the consumer's wishes are translated into a production pattern. This argument has been developed by generations of theoreticians, and price theory has become one of the most refined chapters of economics.

But with refinement doubt entered. About fifty years ago many were of the opinion that the price system, if not faultless, was nevertheless a mechanism that functioned most satisfactorily. The optimum theorem implies that the pattern of production assumes exactly that form which the consumers desire. Later the realization grew that this applies only if the prices come about in perfect competition, i.e. a situation in which none of the suppliers can independently exert any influence on the price. The price is then 'formed' by anonymous forces, not 'made' by men. If the price is influenced by the entrepreneurs, i.e. if there is a price policy, we do not have perfect competition and then, as modern price theory teaches us, the production pattern need no longer be optimum. Now experience shows that most prices are more or less 'made' by the entrepreneurs. This is the case with a branded article, especially when there are only a few suppliers. And it is also the case when the entrepreneurs have entered into open or implicit agreements with one another. It is even the case when the suppliers are afraid that a price reduction may lead to a price war, so that they prefer to maintain a certain inelasticity of prices. In all these instances the optimum theorem proves invalid.

As stated above, considerable attention has been devoted to this problem. If you choose at random a textbook from the 1930s, you will find that most of the chapters deal with this kind of thing. This train of thought is to a considerable extent microeconomic, i.e. it relates to the reactions of individual buyers and suppliers, and it notes what happens on special markets. Such books also devote a good deal of attention to the more macro-economically oriented theory of money and banks, and the theory of international trade, but price theory forms the bulk of the work. The theory of the distribution of income was usually regarded as a pendant to price theory, since when all is said and done incomes are prices too: prices of factors of production such as labour, capital, land. The business cycle theory, which attempts to explain economic fluctuations, was generally viewed as an addendum.

This interest in the mechanics of price was connected with the idea that the make-up of society's pattern of production really formed a more interesting problem than its size did. This is the characteristically 'classical' idea.

After Keynes this changed. True, price theory is still an extreme-ly important part of economics. Nobody denies that the price system has an essential task in guiding production along the right lines. In fact much new work has been done in this field in recent years. The optimum theorem has been more closely examined, the theory of markets has been extended, and quanti-tative knowledge has been collected on the relations between prices, costs, supply, and demand. The modern theory of im-perfect competition is about as old as the Keynesian theory of macro-economic equilibrium. Both were developed in the 1930s.

But price theory has been overshadowed, though it must be admitted that it is still flourishing. The full light now falls on the theory of national income and of balanced growth. When Malthus wrote at the beginning of the nineteenth century in a letter to Ricardo that the size of national production was causing him concern, he received the answer that the size of national pro-duction was more or less a datum for economics, and that the main problem related to distribution of that income. Official economics agreed with Ricardo. Admittedly, there were always dissenting opinions, but they did not predominate. This has changed in the last twenty-five years. If you open a modern economics textbook and diligently count the chapters, you will find that the theory of national income and the macro-economic problems connected with it are usually given much more space than price theory. This is most obvious in revised editions of somewhat older textbooks. In each new edition the macro-economic part is expanded somewhat. Sometimes the integration of traditional and modern theory is successful; sometimes it remains an unsatisfactory whole.*

In my opinion this shift in economists' interest is quite correct. It may be of importance to the prosperity of the community that the right goods are produced, that the consumers' wishes as they are manifested on the market are complied with by the entrepreneurs, and that the price system performs properly in this matter; but the really pressing problems do not lie there. Even the important relation between the public and the private sector, which can easily be distorted in a growing or 'affluent' economy (J. K. Galbraith), seems to me to be secondary compared with the growth itself. Prosperity is more strongly influenced, for good or for ill, by the size of the national income. Other macro-economic phenomena, such as inflation and deflation, the balance of payments, taxes, economic growth, are of more decisive importance to the fortunes of Western civilization than the question whether too much of one good and too little of another might not perhaps be produced as a result of monopolistic price determination. Consequently it is macro-economic theory that forms the basis of much of the policy followed in the various countries.

This book will be further concerned with these macro-economic problems, which have been called the Keynesian problems so far; it will try to give a survey of them, couched as far as possible in everyday terms. It therefore deliberately omits large sections of modern economics. The reader will search in vain for a picture of price theory; he will be unable to acquaint himself with the classical theory of the international division of labour (the theory of comparative costs); and he will find no explanation of the

---

* The much-used *Elements of Modern Economics* by A. L. Meyers (1st ed., 1937) has been frequently revised, but still has an old-fashioned structure and does not give sufficient insight into macro-economics. The integration has been more successful in F. Benham, *Economics* (1st ed., 1938, 5th ed., 1955), although here and there it gives a strange impression of Keynes, and the title of the General Theory is curiously distorted by Benham. Of the older works, K. E. Boulding, *Economic Analysis*, is one of the best; the first edition in 1941 did not yet have a separate section for the theory of national income, but the third edition (1955) does have one, and is up to date.

traditional theory of monetary arrangements.* Even the theory of distribution, which is near to my heart, will be dealt with only incidentally, viz. when the part played by labour in the national income and wage inflation are being discussed. And there are many other such topics which certainly form part of modern economics but have found no place in this book. The following pages will attempt to outline the modern macro-economic approach: Neo-Keynesian, quantitative economics and its importance to economic policy.

5 · THE SET-UP OF THIS BOOK

This book has been written for the 'general reader'. This brings us to a delicate point. I am convinced that the Keynesian theory can be explained to the non-expert. He can understand what it is about. Of course there are technical details that are difficult; but even these, as regards their purport and general importance, can be more or less put in such a way that the 'layman' gets an impression of what is going on.

This optimism is not shared by everybody. Some non-economists distrust the expert. They suspect economics of being an occult science, and the use of mathematics by some economists helps to strengthen this misconception. For it *is* a misconception: the aim of economics is to make real processes understandable, and after all it is successful in its task only if the essence of its reasoning can be stated in a comprehensible fashion.

But some economists are also averse to 'popularization'. They make a sharp distinction between the expert and the layman. I do not like this. There are such things as gradual transitions, and there is such a thing as an ascending scale of expert knowledge. The man in the street practises economics, whether he wants to or not. Of course he may be unaware of some facts and relations. But even Keynes sometimes made mistakes. And some laymen have had sounder views on certain economic topics, such as the danger of general overproduction, than the official economics of the day. Of course I do not mean that everybody who is a lazy or a sloppy thinker should now fling himself eagerly upon econo-

* A suitable source of such information is for instance P. A. Samuelson, *Economics*, (6th ed., 1964).

mics, but I do mean that this subject should not be reserved for a small self-appointed group.

These pages are therefore meant for a large public, but they must be read in a peaceful, relaxed atmosphere. This means that the book is not suitable for dipping into. Anybody who reads it in such a fashion will find it indigestible. Unless he is an economist, in which case he can permit himself to take a quick look at what I think of the quantity theory (not much, as it happens) and leave the rest of the book unread. But the 'general reader' will have to begin at the beginning and then follow the numbering of the pages faithfully. Otherwise he will soon join the ranks of those who consider economics an occult science.

The chapters follow a deliberate system. This has been inspired by the idea that sooner or later we must combine the various parts of the macro-economic theory to form one balanced whole. There may really not be any loose ends. To achieve this a certain 'model' has been considered from the beginning, and my readers would do well to keep an eye on this. A model is a description of an economic system by means of separate relations which fit together logically (I shall revert to this in greater detail in Chapter IV). These relations are often expressed by equations, that is to say by mathematical functions. For instance, we may think that production depends on productive capacity; that is then an element of the model. We may also be of the opinion that production depends on the demand for goods; that is another element of the model. Both elements are important; they represent the central ideas of 'classical' and 'Keynesian' theory respectively. These two elements will first be separately explained in Chapters II and III. We have then laid the foundation for everything that is to follow: the fundamental difference between the 'old' and the 'new' macro-economics. In Chapter IV both elements are summarized in a simple (and above all non-'mathematical') system of equations, which in turn may be represented by a simple graph. We thus arrive at Neo-Keynesian theory. But in its original form this is still too primitive. For it only shows how consumption, savings, investment, and the productivity of labour in combination determine national income, production, and employment. Important social phenomena have been left out of consideration here. The model is too simple.

We therefore add further relations one by one. The first group of relations relates to foreign trade (Chapter v). The second is concerned with the government's budget (Chapter vi). The third has to do with the role played by money – it will become evident that there is a rather considerable difference of opinion between economists on this point, and we shall therefore be treading controversial paths. Chapter vii, in which this matter is dealt with, might perhaps also be of interest to some economists, since an attempt is made in it at a synthesis of 'old' and 'new' monetary theory. Then it is investigated how prices are fitted into the model (Chapter viii) and what the situation is regarding wages (Chapter ix). A separate chapter on economic growth follows (Chapter x). With all this behind us, our model is complete (Chapter xi). We can then consider it as a whole, and draw various conclusions in Chapter xii.

Of course I have given some thought to the manner in which the apparently complicated nature of modern economics can best be simplified. One of the ways of doing this is to keep on confronting the reader with alternative lines of thought, by saying: we can view this relation as follows, but also in this way. This method stimulates thought. But it also easily creates the impression that there is a great deal of bitter controversy among modern economists. And that is not so. There are shades of difference, and also disputed points, but these are subordinate all the same. There is general agreement about a number of main aspects of Neo-Keynesianism; so great, in fact, that Samuelson, as we saw above, proceeded to identify the Neo-Keynesians with the Neo-Classicists. From a didactic point of view this goes too far for me, but it nevertheless nicely symbolizes the great unanimity of thought that is beginning to prevail among economists.

And yet this book will stress a number of differences of opinion. This is unavoidable, for we want to find out what is modern about modern economics. We must therefore contrast the 'old' with the 'new'.

The differences in outlook which will come to the fore are in the main the following. In the first place there is the difference in approach between classical and Keynesian theory. Classical thought in its doctrinal form has been vanquished as far as economists are concerned. But it still lurks in many who have not drained the cup of economics as thoroughly as the economists. Did Keynes not say that the practicians base their views on theories held twenty-five years ago? This is true today, and it hampers popularization of the subject.

A second difference of opinion – if it may so be described – exists among the Keynesians themselves. Some have stayed closer to Keynes's original theory than others. Consequently a difference between orthodox Keynesians and Neo-Keynesians will occasionally emerge from the following pages.

Then there is a controversy which comes particularly to the fore in Chapter VII and relates to monetary theory. What position does money occupy in the community? Nowadays theoreticians, who are all in a certain sense Neo-Keynesians, tend to squabble about this to some extent. I have gone into this matter in some considerable detail because I found it interesting and also because money theory has long been somewhat overrated. The Stock Exchange, the banks, the Bank Rate all present real problems, but I thought that I would oblige the reader by demonstrating that these matters are less important to economic life than many monetary theorists seem to believe. But in the light of history this fraternal quarrel is merely a subtle difference.

However, there is a practical difference of opinion which I consider most important. Some believe that the authorities should pursue an active policy directed towards economic growth. They do not wish to submit to the once so notorious collapses of economic life, to depressions, unemployment, and poverty. Others adopt a pessimistic attitude to this, on the strength of their theoretical views. They give up too easily. Now they are the ones with whom I wish to do battle. A civilized society cannot tolerate a depression paralysing economic life any more than it should allow inflation to lead to social disruption. Some defeatists mean well, but a number of unfortunate experiences in the past have made them take a gloomy view of things. Others are malicious. They identify modern economics with an attack on free society, or at least with a distinct political system. I hope that the following pages will prove them wrong.

CHAPTER II

Productive Capacity Determines National Income: The Classical Theory

1 · SAY'S LAW

In the last chapter incidental mention was already made of the fact that the 'classical' theory believed that the productive capacity of a country determines how much will be produced. An economy produces as much as it can. This is the maximum real national income. On the one hand the classicists were more or less heedless of the possibility of less being produced, since they trusted that no great difficulties would occur in selling the goods produced. On the other hand they were not always alive to the possibility that a larger sale of goods might lead to a greater increase in productive capacity. Economic stagnation, retarded and also accelerated economic growth remained in the background; these are the very points that are elucidated by modern economics.

The confidence that the market makes it possible to sell all of the national product stems from Say's Law. As stated above, this amounts to the fact that a supplier only supplies goods because he demands other goods. Put in this way, this 'law' sounds rather mysterious. However, there is another way of putting it which is used more often nowadays, and which makes matters clearer. This new description originates with the circulation of purchasing power. This idea is first found among the eighteenth-century physiocrats. They noted how the product of agriculture was urged along by the national economy. Owing to the fact that this view was rather distorted, the circulation theory was long in discredit. It began to enjoy a new vogue at about the same time as Keynesianism; in particular national bookkeeping (see Chapter XI) contributed to this.

The simplest picture of the circular flow of goods and income is given below. The upper rectangle represents business. On the right-hand side the national product emerges; we shall assume for the moment that this consists entirely of consumer goods. These make their way to the households, which are represented by the lower rectangle. Arrow C represents this flow of goods.

Meanwhile the households have also supplied something to business: the factors of production such as labour, savings, land. In return for these they receive every week, every month, or every year a money income. The sum of these incomes forms the

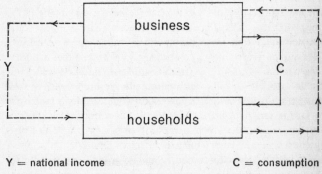

Y = national income   C = consumption

Fig. 1: The simplest form of the circulation

national income, the central quantity in modern economics. This quantity is represented in the figure as an arrow Y; since it is a flow of money, it has been drawn as a broken line.

Now an important point that must be borne in mind in the whole of macro-economics is that the real national product in business is linked to the national money income. And not only do the flow of goods and the flow of money come into being jointly; they are also quantitatively equal. For the value of the national product is equal to the sum of wages, interest, rents, and profits, that is to say the total price that the product must fetch on the market when it is marketed. But the same flow of money leaves business to the left of the diagram. It may be that the flows of money and goods are not entirely synchronized, but over a somewhat longer period they are in principle the same. Consequently, national income (or the national product) can also be measured in two ways: by observing the flow of goods on the markets (in doing so care must be taken not to count the same thing twice: the corn that the pigs eat must not be counted again) and by observing the money incomes of the recipients of income. Both measurements check one another. Such cross-checks are frequently applied in quantitative economics; they enhance the reliability of the statistics.

This therefore means that the households receive exactly the amount of money that they need to buy the national product.* The flow of money Y flows back from the households to business; the entrepreneurs receive in the form of revenue what they have spent on the factors of production, including the profit. National income and national expenditure are constantly transformed into one another. The line C represents consumptive expenditure. The modern version of Say's Law stresses this fact. If the households again and again spend the income they have received, the entrepreneurs have no difficulties with sales.

This is an important point. It shows how an increase in production creates the money income that can buy the extra production.

Of course this train of thought may not be applied microeconomically. If a shoe manufacturer produces a new model, in so doing he creates a money income for the factors of production, but this money is of course not necessarily spent on shoes. If the newly manufactured shoes are not bought, the consumers have received money to buy something else. The overproduction of shoes is then identical with the underproduction of other goods. A general overproduction cannot come about in this way. That is exactly what Say's Law means.

This way of presenting matters at once makes it clear where the weak spot of this law must be sought. True, the consumers have received enough money, but it is highly questionable whether they will also spend it to a sufficient extent. For instance, if they were to save instead of consuming, the entrepreneurs would find that part of the national product remained unsold. Keynes therefore launched his attack on the classical system from

---

* The sophisticated reader is invited to forget for the moment that business income may be saved by firms, that machines are bought every now and then but are used continually, and similar dynamic complications.

savings. Needless to say, it may not be derived from this that saving always leads to overproduction; this will be discussed in the following chapters. At this juncture the suspicion will merely be voiced that Say's Law displays a weak link.

And yet this 'law' is not as meaningless as some assume, under the influence of Keynes. Say's Law forms a good argument against the pessimism of those who see a general increase in production leading to a slump. For instance, many are afraid of the expansion of production in the underdeveloped countries. They fear that the world will presently be flooded with products. But they forget that this greater production automatically leads to a greater money income which, provided that it is spent in the right way, creates the market for the greater flow of goods. This does not mean to say that disturbances cannot occur, but these are anything but a necessary consequence of the expansion of productive capacity. Supply does in fact tend to create its own demand.

A related form of pessimism is somewhat more complicated. Some see a danger in the increasing productivity. If the same factors of production keep on making more and more products – for instance by automation – the flow of goods increases, but incomes remain what they were. And therefore an increase in production might lead to economic stagnation and unemployment.

But this pessimism, too, is based on a fallacy. For if the flow of goods broadens, the price of these goods must drop. The business firms, as a result of the increase in production, need less of the factors of production to make one unit product. When prices are lower the increased product can be purchased by the same money income. But what happens if the prices do not go down, despite the lower costs? In that case profits may increase, so that Say's Law continues to be obeyed, unless a disturbance in the spending of the money income has meanwhile occurred because profits are less likely to be spent than wages. In that case a drop in sales is probable, but this is not the result of the increase in productivity, but of the disturbance in the distribution of income, and the relatively high savings of those whose income is derived from profit. Increased productivity can lead to specific unemployment, which may be painful, but not to general unemployment. This macro-unemployment is almost always the result of a disturbed money flow.*

Classical theory ignores the latter disturbances, unlike Keynesian theory; it disregards what the recipients of income do with their money. However, it has a sound view of the genesis of incomes. Let us follow this theory for a moment, and assume that all additional production also leads to an additional market. In that case the size of the national product is determined by productive capacity. What else should be said about this?

2 · THE PRODUCTIVITY OF LABOUR DETERMINES PROSPERITY

A country's productive capacity is determined by a mass of factors differing greatly in nature. To make sense of them, they must be arranged in a certain way. This will be attempted below.

The starting-point is that according to Say's Law total production depends partly on the factors of production present – the quantity and the quality of labour; the stock of capital goods such as machinery, factories, roads, schools; the nature of the soil and the climate – and partly on the productivity of these factors of production. Productivity is defined as the ratio between the national product and the quantities of factors of production present. But this national product is extremely heterogeneous – it comprises shoes as well as newly built houses, road-building and the production of non-material goods, such as 'government services' (e.g. legal security and education). An attempt has to be made to solve this difficulty by reducing all products to a common denominator – money – and then making corrections afterwards for changes in the value of money. In this way an indication of the real income or the volume of production is obtained. In the second place the factors of production are also heterogeneous. The work of the office clerk, of the small shopkeeper, of the farmer, can if necessary be reduced via a sum of money to a common denominator with the productive services

* Or, in underdeveloped regions, because there is a shortage of complementary factors of production, that is to say of capital goods. See for this Chapter x.

– also expressed in money – of capital and of land. But figures obtained in this way have little point.

Consequently another method is preferably followed. We do not divide national production by the entire mass of production factors, but by the volume of only one factor, although this in itself is again fairly heterogeneous. Labour is often taken as this factor, but capital could also be taken. In the first case you find the productivity of labour, in the second case the productivity of capital. The productivity of labour is therefore defined as the national product divided by the amount of labour. It is a very rough and ready measure, but not unimportant.*

Strictly speaking, therefore, the concepts productivity of labour and productivity of capital are on a par. Now the strange fact occurs that they are of entirely different significance to the prosperity of a country. The productivity of labour has a decisive and immediate effect on welfare; the productivity of capital hardly has any direct effect. This may appear to be a strange paradox, but it is easily solved.

The prosperity of a country is determined to a considerable extent not by the total national product, but by the national product per head of the population. China has in total a greater product than Belgium, but there are relatively too many Chinese who want to share in this product; per head the average Belgian is at least twenty times better off materially than the average Chinese. Prosperity therefore depends on the national product divided by the number of mouths to be fed. The productivity of labour is identical with the national product divided by the number of pairs of hands. The ratio between the number of mouths and the number of pairs of hands is often more or less constant. It might even be thought that both numbers are identical. But that is not so: the working population is smaller than the consuming population. One can therefore at most assume that prosperity and the productivity of labour are in a fairly constant relation to one another. Not exactly constant, for if more women go out to work or if the school-leaving age or the pensionable age is changed, this relation also changes. It is determined by mainly sociological and institutional factors; at least, as long as Say's

* More subtle definitions making allowance for working hours will not be considered here.

34

Law holds good and there is no unemployment. But if a slump occurs, and the ratio between the number of people who want to work and the number actually employed changes, the ratio of labour productivity to prosperity is upset. Prosperity is then less than follows from the productivity of labour. The latter is the case examined by Keynes; he even believed that a higher productivity of labour would almost certainly lead to less welfare, because the risk of unemployment would be greater at higher levels of the national income.

But, given Say's Law, we see that it is the productivity of labour that determines prosperity to a considerable extent. This cannot be said of the productivity of capital. A country may have a rather high productivity of capital and still be very poor. It is possible that underdeveloped countries use the little capital they possess in such a way that it has a fairly high productivity per unit invested. But this does not mean to say that these countries are highly prosperous. The productivity of labour will be low, and in that case a high productivity of capital does not help much.*

A central element of the problem of prosperity is therefore labour productivity. The great international differences in prosperity – in the order of magnitude of one to twenty or more! – are correlated with this quantity. What determines the height of this productivity index? Before the factors are mentioned which are important in this respect, a warning may be uttered against a misunderstanding that ascribes fluctuations in the productivity of labour to fluctuations in the efforts or the skill of the worker. These personal properties are of course of influence, but their factual importance is overshadowed by more important factors. For we must remember that the definition of the concept 'labour productivity' means that the national product is divided by employment. If machines are added which make more product with less labour, the productivity of labour increases without the worker doing anything about it; in fact he will often not need to

---

* This does not mean to say that the productivity of capital is unimportant. A high productivity of capital makes investment attractive, and the investments determine the stock of capital goods, which in turn helps to determine the productivity of labour. This point will be taken up in the chapter on economic growth.

exert himself as much. Only in special cases – say a tennis player – is labour productivity directly correlated with the 'worker's' efforts and capacities.

In outline, the factors that determine the productivity of labour can be classified as follows:

(a) *The quality of labour*. This does not mean the extent to which the worker exerts himself as much as his skill, his knowledge, and his training. These qualities can be created only by a considerable 'investment' in human beings made either at school, in business, or in social intercourse generally. The production of knowledge is becoming more and more important. This is especially true in a rich and diversified country, where the mass media, the arts, administrative services and such play a big role in economic life. A special kind of labour must be specifically mentioned: that of the entrepreneur. He takes the initiative in production and organizes operations. He is the central figure in the dynamics of the economy.

(b) *The nature and the extent of the stock of capital goods*. Here we are concerned not only with the machinery and plant in business enterprises, but also with what is known as the infrastructure: the roads, the means of communication, the schools, which are provided to a considerable extent by government. All these provisions are the result of investments in the past. These investments and those in human labour supplement one another. (But ... what determines the size of the investments? This problem will engage us later.)

(c) *Technology*. This factor is an obvious one, but an unexpected problem occurs: its influence is difficult to separate from that of an improved quality of human labour and of more capital. Some statisticians believe that the whole of technical progress is 'embodied', i.e. is manifested in a growing stock of instruments of production. In their view investment is the 'vehicle' of technical progress. Others (such as S. Kuznets) are of the opinion that at least part of technical progress is 'disembodied' and can take place irrespective of the volume of investment. The discussion, which started in the 1950s, is far from closed.

(d) *Natural conditions*. Historically speaking these are extremely important; however, there is reason to assume that their importance is gradually declining. Production is becoming less dependent on natural conditions, in particular because of the development of new sources of energy (nuclear power). Nor is the local availability of raw materials a guarantee of a high productivity of labour. I have the impression that the importance of natural factors is overestimated in many popular views. For instance, the idea is still occasionally put forward that a country which is poor in natural resources cannot be rich; this may have been true once upon a time, but it is not nowadays.

(e) *The division of labour.* Ever since Adam Smith visited a pin factory in the eighteenth century and was struck there by the enormous increase in productivity which followed from the division of labour, this matter has had a place in every economic manual. There would be no reason to dwell on it, were it not that in the last twenty-five years attention has been arrested by a number of problems of a quantitative nature arising from the external division of labour (i.e. the division of labour among industries). Specialization in production naturally makes a complicated movement of goods necessary between firms and industries. These supplies from industry to industry have been measured by means of an enormous statistical apparatus. This investigation – called input–output analysis – has brought a number of interesting problems to the fore, and one of these is connected with productivity itself. These supplies must be well keyed to one another if production is to run smoothly. Difficulties in the production of a certain good give rise to repercussions elsewhere, which manifest themselves in low productivity. If only from a military point of view it is therefore desirable to know the ramifications of the division of labour, so as to foresee what will happen to the national product if for instance supplies of oil dry up, if a large number of aircraft are ordered for military purposes, or if large-scale disarmament should ever take place. But it has also proved useful to get to know the flow of goods so as to be able to programme. This programming technique forms one of the new branches of quantitative economics. It is also coming increasingly to the fore in business economics.

(f) *The efficiency of the firms.* This is of course connected with all the above factors, and especially with the ability of entrepreneurs. The engagement of the links in the internal production process, the route that the product follows through the firm, labour relations, the atmosphere in the firm, all these are matters which are being studied more intensively nowadays than formerly. The results of this work and the techniques resulting from it are sometimes surprising. It proves to be possible to increase the productivity in a firm by quite a considerable proportion – often by twenty-five per cent or more – by applying the right working methods and creating the right human relations. In this matter industry requires the advice of specially trained experts, who are therefore worth their weight in gold to national prosperity – a scale on which they are sometimes paid. Their work is often encouraged by the authorities in the countries of Western Europe within the framework of what is called productivity policy.

The purpose of the above classification is merely to list the circumstances that determine prosperity as long as Say's Law holds good. In the course of this outline we have on several occasions come across an activity which proves to be fundamental to the productivity of labour and which therefore deserves closer consideration. It is investment: increasing the productive capacity by acquiring new instruments of production.

3 · THE CAPACITY EFFECT AND THE INCOME EFFECT OF INVESTMENTS

In classical theory – for that is the subject of this chapter – the importance of investments to the national income was at all times recognized.* But only in the sense that investments increase productive capacity. The classicists did not make very much allowance for the fact that investments also have an entirely different result, viz. the creation of a money income. Nowadays it is said of them that they saw the capacity effect, but not the income effect.

The income effect means the following. If the entrepreneurs decide to build new factories or if the authorities construct a

* Investment here means the production of new capital goods. It must not be confused with the purchase of securities – investment in the other sense – and still less with not using income for consumption – saving, in other words. In Keynesian theory a sharp distinction must be made above all between investing in the sense of buying capital goods and investing in the sense of buying securities. It is a pity that English uses the same word for these two activities.

road, the factors of production are employed in doing this. They receive for this an income. With that income they can buy consumer goods – but these goods have not been produced. For the income has originated in the production of lathes and paving stones. If the recipients of the income wish to spend the whole of it on consumer goods, they will find that these are not available. To put it another way: there is too great a demand on the market for consumer goods. The income effect of the investments must therefore be compensated for by the decision to abstain from consumption: the recipients of the income must save. We shall have to consider this relation between saving and investing later, for it forms a keystone of Keynesian economics. But let us begin by explaining the classical view of it.

Since the classicists believed in Say's Law and always considered a sufficiently large market to be present, the machinery of production is in their theory always fully employed. There is no unused capacity. If an entrepreneur wishes to expand his production, he can do so only in one of two ways, either by increasing productivity or by withdrawing factors of production from other purposes to which they are being put. More shoes means less of something else. In macro-economic terms, more investment means less consumption.

An entrepreneur who wants to invest must have the necessary financial resources at hand. These are furnished to him by the savers: households and firms, and probably also by his own business. The households have received an income from production, but they do not spend this fully on consumer goods. They save, with the immediate aim of building up capital, but at the same time they help the entrepreneur. Without savings the latter cannot finance his business. (The bank can if necessary create credit, but this only helps the investor temporarily. In the long run he must consolidate from real savings.)

But not only do the saving households provide the financial resources by saving; they also make investment possible because, by their abstention from buying, they release the factors of production that can presently be employed in making capital goods. In the classical view saving is in a double respect the necessary preliminary to the real formation of capital. Savings and investments are in equilibrium with one another; the rate of interest

MODERN ECONOMICS

attends to that. But saving is primary and investment secondary.

In this line of thought, which is almost diametrically opposed to the Keynesian one, the national money income remains constant. It is not influenced by investing. True, investing has an income effect – the classicists would not have denied that – but investing has been preceded by a drop in consumption. This of course also has an income effect, and these two neutralize one another. In the classical interpretation the production of capital goods replaces the production of consumer goods. Total production and total income remain the same. Consequently, in the classical reasoning there is little point in indicating an income effect of investments. It is a foregone conclusion that this effect will be compensated.

The full loading of plant and full employment, which form the economic milieu to which classical theory relates, have a further effect on investments. Productive capacity can be increased only if the consumers are prepared to abstain from purchases for consumption. If they do not abstain, and there is nevertheless a great urge to invest, a tense situation occurs. The investors and the consumers are as it were fighting for the scarce factors of production. This fight has been very vividly described by F. A. von Hayek.* We may therefore call this accentuated scarcity of the factors of production the Hayek situation. In such a case there is really inflation. Sometimes the investors win, and then large projects are embarked upon, but there are too few consumer goods. Sometimes it is the consumers who win: in that case an over-investment crisis threatens, not because there is no market, but because the factors of production are taken out of the hands of the investors. In both cases an acute shortage of capital threatens, a special variant which is the reflection of the scarcity of factors of production. It manifests itself in two characteristic ways: in the first place the rate of interest goes up, and secondly we see that large projects are abandoned uncompleted. After this special type of depression we see no empty factories, no unemployed workers – we see half-finished factories.

In this argument, which by no means need be unrealistic in all circumstances, saving is almost identical with economic progress,

* *Prices and Production*, 1931.

and consuming hampers the latter. Saving increases productive capacity, and consuming checks this increase. This order of things was radically changed by orthodox Keynesian theory. Of course, here too investment leads to a greater productive capacity, but it is problematic whether saving always leads to increased investment. I shall be discussing this in the next chapter.

4 · THE CLASSICAL SYSTEM

In the earlier part of this chapter I have pointed to a number of elements of the classical argument, and at the same time to demonstrate that this view of economic life has a certain aesthetic attraction, I should like to add a few remarks. The main topic that I have in mind is the part played by the price system.

I have already said above that economics is traditionally interested in price theory. Behind this lies the idea that the price system brings the consumers' wishes to the notice of the entrepreneurs, so that they adjust their production in accordance with the customers' preferences. This is the theory which finds popular expression in the saying 'the customer is always right'. And it is the same train of thought that classical theory also follows with regard to macro-economic problems.

For in classical theory national income is given by productivity. The question is how this given real income is to be divided between consumer goods and investment goods. This division determines the ratio between immediate consumption and future consumption.

In the classical system this ratio is determined by the consumers. For the entrepreneurs can invest only if money has first been saved. The savers – and here the households were envisaged – therefore determine how much can be invested. If too much is invested, money capital begins to get more scarce, the rate of interest (the price of the money capital) rises, and the entrepreneur has to abandon his ambitious plans, since they are no longer remunerative at a higher rate of interest. Here, therefore, it is the consumer who lends force to his wishes via the price mechanism. This train of thought is entirely in accordance with the importance which economics in general attaches to prices.

This matter may also be considered from another angle. Say's

Law, in the classical argument, makes overproduction impossible and ensures that there is always a sufficiently large market to keep the productive forces employed. True, part of the income is not spent on consumer goods, but the factors of production thus released are employed in the production of capital goods. Since all savings are invested, the circulation is complete. But let us assume for a moment that, all the same, too much is suddenly saved. Savings increase; in a fit of absent-mindedness the entre-preneurs have neglected to start the corresponding investments. In that case the circular flow of income and expenditure could be interrupted. But if savings threaten to become greater than in-vestments, the rate of interest at which the entrepreneurs can borrow capital drops. This increases the possibilities of profit and encourages the entrepreneur to expand again. In this way the mechanism of the capital market is brought into operation again. Production always stays pressed against the ceiling of the avail-able factors of production.

The classicists apply the same reasoning to another factor of production, labour. Let us suppose that as the result of the equilibrium mechanism operating rather stiffly some unemploy-ment has occurred. This is at variance with the system, but even in the classical view reality may occasionally allow of minor aberrations from the theory. We thus have insufficient employ-ment, caused by 'rigidities'. But in that case the price of labour falls (unless the unions prevent this). At the lower wage it again becomes remunerative to employ the labour. Thus here, too, price flexibility ensures maximum production. The price system is the 'feedback', the automatic regulator that not only ensures that bicycles, toothpaste, and sugar beet are produced in the right proportions, but also creates the right ratio between con-sumption and investment, and *en passant* also creates full em-ployment and a maximum national income.

Reasoning in this way, we may conclude that the classical system is founded on three pillars. The first is Say's Law, which ensures that there is a sufficient market. The second is the scar-city of the factors of production and the natural expansivity of the entrepreneurs. Battle is waged, so to speak, for the factors of production. And the third pillar is the price system. Its operation, and above all the movement of wages and the rate of interest, controls the size of the investments. This automatism settles the battle between the entrepreneurs for the factors of production. The consumer is the master; it is he who decides how quickly the stock of capital goods will grow, how the present and the future can be brought into equilibrium with each other.

It is an impressive system. Not only does it contain logical elements; it also leads to a practical view of economic life. It supplies us with the arguments against political controls, against a planned society forcibly imposed from above, neither of which makes any allowance for the consumers' interests. Experience shows that in dictatorships a burden may be imposed on the population owing to the fact that current consumption has been made too small, for the purpose of meeting expansive objectives. This would not be possible in a country with free price determination; in such a country the consumers would manage to appropriate factors of production to a greater extent. In this respect classical theory not only gives us a valuable insight but also leads to a political conclusion that is concordant with democracy.

The classical train of thought also stimulates empirical research, which concentrates on the development of productive capacity and in particular on the relation between total output on the one hand and various combinations of labour and capital on the other. The latter relation is called the production function. In the 1930s the Americans Cobb and Douglas devised a production function of a specific mathematical form which implies that labour and capital can easily replace each other in the productive process. Since the late 1950s the work of R. M. Solow of the Massachusetts Institute of Technology has aroused a new interest in this function, and various mathematical forms have been tested. Substitution of labour and capital proved to be less easy than under the Cobb–Douglas assumptions. The econometrists also proved that the historical increase in labour productivity is not so much a matter of more capital as of technical progress – which came as a shock to many economists. A tremendous amount of highly complicated research on these matters is in full swing; the implications of this neo-classical revival are not yet clear.* But this much is certain: the classical

* The literature consists mainly of difficult articles in *The Review of*

system is not a dusty museum piece but part and parcel of modern economics.

But other aspects of the system are weak and misleading. The confidence in Say's Law is misplaced. Unemployment can most certainly occur if nothing is done about it. Classical theory does not lead to a compensating policy. And the worst of it is that pre-Keynesian economics tends towards a false conclusion regarding the causes of unemployment. Adherents of the classical school maintained in the 1930s that unemployment had to be attributed to too high wages, i.e. to union interference with the labour market; and they believed that wage cuts were the most obvious means of putting a stop to the depression.* This is a fallacy, or at best a half truth. For it is forgotten that lower wages may lead to lower consumption, as a result of which the market, which is small enough as it is, shrinks still further. This point will be taken up in a separate chapter on wages. In that chapter classical and Keynesian ways part rather sharply.

In anticipation of my further conclusions, I may state at this early juncture that the classical approach gives a correct analysis of a certain economic situation, viz. that in which total expenditure tallies with productive capacity. If the sale of goods and services runs so smoothly that the whole machinery of production remains in operation, if there are no disturbances in circulation in the sense that the consumers do not spend enough of the income they have received, if the factors of production are really scarce – but without there being inflation – then the classical theory applies. It therefore analyses a special case, but one that is of great importance, especially since economic policy has been trying to realize this situation. For an analysis of situations in which the circulation has been disturbed Keynesian theory is called for. Let us now try to prove this proposition.

Economic Studies and *The Review of Economics and Statistics*. A particularly redoubtable research team: Arrow–Chenery–Minhas–Solow.

* Most clearly in L. von Mises, *Die Ursachen der Wirtschaftskrise*, 1931. Incidentally, prices were sometimes given the blame as well as wages. It was held that price rigidity could cause a depression. This, too, is hardly true, and in any case extremely exaggerated.

CHAPTER III

Total Expenditure Determines National Income: Keynes's Theory

1 · THE BREAKING OF SAY'S LAW

Both Keynes and the classicists proceed from the idea that the national product, upon its creation, gives rise to the creation of a money income that can exactly buy this product. It *can* buy the goods. But in answering the question whether it *will* do so, the old and the new theories part company.

To grasp what is going on here, and to appreciate the heart of modern macro-economics, the reader must closely follow the coming argument. A number of symbols will be used in it, but I promise that this will not end in 'mathematics'. About all that is going to happen is addition and subtraction. It is, however, necessary to bear the following figure in mind. It is a somewhat more extensive variant of the circulation diagram on page 30.

The national product appears from business at the top right of the diagram. Its size is P. This flow of goods (represented by a solid line) starts out but then divides into two parts. The larger part, consisting of consumer goods, makes for the households. This is C. A smaller part returns to business; it is that part of the production that serves to increase the stock of capital goods. This is I (investment).

These two flows of goods must be paid for. From the households to business a flow of money runs that is represented by a broken line, likewise of a size C. The flow of goods and the flow of money are quantitatively equal; they have to be, because both flows meet on the market for consumer goods.* To make a distinction between the flows – of course they are entirely different in nature – we speak of C (*goods*) and C (*expenditure*).

The same holds good for the investments. There too a flow of money and a flow of goods keep each other in equilibrium. This

---

* Supplying on credit can only effect a small time-lag in payment which is immaterial here.

splitting-off of *P* is shown in the top right-hand corner as a small circulation. The broken line is *I* (*expenditure*).

Whilst *P* leaves business, a flow of money *Y*, the national income, goes from business to the households. $P = Y$, that is to say quantitatively, for in essence these are again two entirely different things; a flow of potatoes, milling machines, or trucks

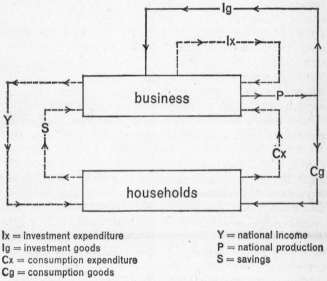

Ix = investment expenditure
Ig = investment goods
Cx = consumption expenditure
Cg = consumption goods

Y = national income
P = national production
S = savings

Fig. 2: Income and expenditure

is something quite different from a flow of money. The latter is drawn as a broken line.

Now this *Y* ends up with the households. In this simple circular flow they can only adopt one of two courses with it (later a larger number of possibilities will be put forward). They can consume the income or they can abstain from consumption. The latter is called saving. The flow of money for consumption is again called *C*, the total sum of savings *S*. *C* makes for the business firms, and *S* remains behind with the households. True, this money also goes to business, but it does not enter there in the form of a return but in that of a loan. Loans do not constitute incomes. They do

46

not appear on the profit and loss account. Consequently, it makes a considerable difference to the entrepreneurs as to whether they get Y back again in the form of S or of C.

The total receipts of the entrepreneurs are therefore $C + I$. The latter is the amount that they receive from their fellow-entrepreneurs who have bought machines and other capital goods. Since these have to be produced by business, the entrepreneurs spend Y and receive in return $C + I$. The households receive Y and spend C. S is retained and later invested. This is the picture of the circulation on which Keynesians and classicists agree. The question now is, how can a Keynesian breach of Say's Law occur?

We saw that $P = Y$. We also know that $P = C + I$. (This is the division of the product among two kinds of goods.) But Y, which is equal to P, is divided by the consumers among C and S. (This is the apportionment of the income among consumption expenditure and savings.) That is to say, $C + I = C + S$. Or $I = S$.

At first sight there does not seem to be anything sensational about this. Even the classicists knew that savings are equal to investments. But there is a great difference. In the classical view money was first saved and later invested. Investment was impossible before the savers had performed their task. But Keynes arrives at his celebrated $I = S$ without this reasoning. The mechanism that lies behind this equality looks entirely different in Keynes's theory.*

It looks as follows. Suppose that at a given moment the households wish to save a greater part of their income than formerly. That is to say, C (*expenditure*) decreases. The receipts of the business firms, $C + I$, therefore also decrease. This is the first consequence. But at that moment, $C + I$ threatens to become smaller

---

* We found $I = S$ by simple subtraction; in that case there are no mechanisms, only definitions. This way of proving that $I = S$ holds good if the income received by business $(C + I)$ equals the income received by the households $(C + S)$; in other words, under static conditions. If income grows or shrinks it is necessary to take time-lags into account; I and S are no longer equal by definition. In that case there is a mechanism at work that makes them equal. This point is only raised here for insiders. It led to an enormous discussion in the first years after the appearance of the General Theory, but has almost disappeared by now.

than Y. In that case there is a loss, or at least a reduction of profit. Since the profits are included in the national money income Y, at the same moment Y becomes smaller. This can happen in itself without production contracting. But the possibility of the latter happening is also great. In that case unemployment becomes probable. The money income decreases further and as a result the households receive less money. The result of their increased thrift is thus a smaller income! This compels them to cut down on their consumptive expenditure. In this way the receipts of the firms are again less than they already were, and once again a loss or a reduction in profit threatens. The dwindling money income cannot but lead to smaller savings – for saving is a luxury which cannot survive a drop in income. The process of contraction thus continues until the receipts of business firms are again equal to their expenditure. Or, to put it differently, until $C + I$ equals $C + S$. That is to say, until S has again become equal to I.

Here lies the starting point of Keynesian theory. If the savers proceed to save more, total expenditure decreases. As a result national income decreases – for that arises from total expenditure. If national income is lower, less is saved. In this way the equality of I and S, which for a moment threatened to vanish, is restored. The equilibrium between these two quantities is established by the variation of income, production, and employment. The rate of interest, which in the classical view provided the equilibrium, does not occur in this story.

Of course the classicists would have an answer to this. They would point out that an increase in savings does not lead to a contraction of expenditure but to greater investment, so that the total of the business firms' receipts $C + I$ remains unaffected. The Keynesians counter this with the following argument. In many cases the entrepreneurs will not react to the increased thrift with larger investments. Why should they? Investing means creating a greater productive capacity. There is no future in this if the households have just decided to cut down on their consumption. On the contrary, we may be thankful that investments remain at the same level. It is also conceivable that they will decline – and then the circular flow is completely disturbed, for in that case the total expenditure of business declines still further through the reduced sales of the engineering industry (see below, the

48

savings paradox). As a matter of fact, in the Keynesian line of thought the greater thrift of the households does not lead to greater savings balances. These disappear again for the very reason that income declines. Consequently there are no surplus savings that can be invested. They have disappeared with the drop in national income.

At this stage it is too early to decide who is right. The essential thing is that the Keynesians have detached the decision about the size of I from the supply of savings. It is true that savings are equal to investment, but that is because national income controls the size of the savings. Y adjusts itself. National income and therefore national production are not given quantities determined by productive capacity; they fluctuate, and they do so in such a way that savings become exactly equal to investments. The latter are primary: savings proceed from investments via the size of the national income. As a result of this the national income may occasionally work out far too small. We then see unused productive capacity and unemployment. This is exactly the opposite of the classicists' world.

This relation can also be approached from another angle. Suppose that at a given moment a wave of optimism floods business. Although consumption is constant the entrepreneurs consider that it would be a good and profitable idea to increase productive capacity. They order from their colleagues in the engineering industry a number of lathes, shoemaking machines, agricultural implements, and other forms of equipment.* The sale of capital goods increases, as does production of them. Assume that there is still unemployed labour in those branches of industry. As a result these men find work. They receive an income that they did not have at first. The profits in the capital goods industry also increase. In other words, national income increases. This comes as a pleasant surprise to the households. They therefore proceed to consume more. Now something strange happens: the expectations of the investing entrepreneurs, which at first were perhaps based on nothing better than a certain unfounded optimism, are

---

* The classicists would ask: how do the entrepreneurs get the financial resources to finance this? But note: in the Keynesian theory these resources appear as a consequence of investment, provided that the slightest start can be made, e.g. by bank credit.

fulfilled. Through their orders the investors have created the income that leads to the consumptive expenditure which will proceed to justify their increased productive capacity. Everyone is happy about this course of events. So are the producers of shoes, propelling pencils, and chewing gum, for they see their sales increasing. Perhaps they in turn also invest more, so that income and consumption further increase. We clearly see here the cumulative process known under the name of multiplier effect.

Here too the question arises: Will this process continue until the national economy finally explodes in an orgy of consumptive and investment expenditure? No. Because the increased income will lead not only to additional consumption, but also to additional savings. S accumulates, in such a manner that the increase in I is compensated in the long run. The additional investments have led via the increased national income to additional savings. And also exactly enough savings have been formed to help finance the investments. At this point the incomes of the firms, $C + I$, are equal to the expenditure $C + S$. Total expenditure is in equilibrium with national income. But the latter has increased, as has production, as has employment. Through the expansion of the circulation some unused productive capacity has again come into operation.

Anyone who comprehends this process no longer believes in Say's Law. He will no longer unquestioningly accept that there will always be a market for the total production. True, in the first instance the income required for this is created; but if this income is not consumptively spent to a sufficient extent, the flow of money and production will begin to contract. Overproduction will threaten.* The entrepreneurs rectify this by cutting down on production – but in that case the factors of production are no longer fully employed. There is no question of the entrepreneurs fighting in all circumstances for the factors of production. They

---

* I should like to point out at this stage that there is also a trend in modern economics that considers Say's Law to be broken in another way. It notes the withdrawal of money from circulation, which happens by the increasing of cash holdings ('hoarding'). This way of thinking is not necessarily at variance with that which has been followed here, but it does often lead to a somewhat different view of things. I shall come back to this.

may do, but not necessarily so. It is therefore not productive capacity that determines the real national income; total expenditure forms the determinant. Productive capacity is only a ceiling. Usually, the more orthodox Keynesians say, economic life is far below that ceiling. Idle machines and unemployment are normal phenomena if we do nothing about them. Some followers of Keynes consider economic stagnation to be the constant threat to the national economy.

It is highly problematic whether the older Keynesians, and also Keynes himself, are right about this. Their pessimism on this point has been abandoned by a later generation of Keynesians. But this does not detract from the fact that the relation of the macro-economic quantities as given above is accepted in broad outline by the Neo-Keynesians. They follow the circulation idea and, with certain variants, regard national income as the quantity that establishes equilibrium in the system. This is characteristic of all Neo-Keynesians: Y is not a given quantity emanating from productive capacity. National income is determined by a combination of investment and consumption, which we shall call total expenditure.

2 · THE PROPENSITY TO SAVE AND THE MULTIPLIER

We have now seen a number of the main features of Keynes's theory, and we must next study his train of thought somewhat more closely. This can be done by examining two quantities which played a large though still somewhat concealed part in the above, viz. the propensity to save and the multiplier.

What is the propensity to save? It is that part of national income that is saved. We shall call this quantity s. The propensity to save is a percentage. It may for instance be 10, or 15. More than 25 is improbable. Side by side with the propensity to save is the propensity to consume; this is designated by c and is equal to $1 - s$. These concepts do not really appear in classical theory, for in the latter national income is a datum. That is to say, an increase in the propensity to save *pari passu* means an increase in savings. Both quantities run exactly parallel, and there is little point in introducing the propensity to save alongside savings S as a separate concept. Nor does the propensity to consume have a special place in classical reasoning.

In the modern approach, on the other hand, the distinction between s and S in particular is very important. For we saw in the preceding section that S equals I. According to orthodox Keynesianism (we shall be giving a more moderate view later), the size of savings is considered to be determined by the size of investments. Strangely enough, therefore, the savers have no say in the volume of savings! They are at the mercy of the fluctuations in national income. This looks at first sight like an absurd idea. For we have also drawn the conclusion that total expenditure is of vital importance to national income. And this expenditure is partly determined by the households. They decide what part of their income will flow on in the form of consumptive expenditure and what part will remain behind in the form of savings. This free and independent decision on the division of income is a privilege of the recipient of that income in a democratic society.

And in fact the recipient of income does decide for himself how he will divide his income among clothes, food, gramophone records, and savings. He is free in his choice. He or she independently determines his or her own propensity to save. But in so doing he has not yet determined how much he will save! For the volume of his savings is the product of his propensity to save and his income. Saving is to a certain extent a luxury – as is the buying of records – a luxury that depends on income. Viewed macro-economically, income turns out to depend precisely on . . . the propensity to save! This is the heart of Keynesian theory, which we should now like to explain again, this time by means of the new concepts.

The savers determine the propensity to save and the entrepreneurs determine the volume of investment. Whatever the propensity to save proves to be, savings must, according to the circulation theory, equal investments. The quantity that creates this equality is, as we have seen, national income. It adjusts itself in such a way that $I = S$. Now, how large is that national income in that state of equilibrium? Exactly so large that the product of the propensity to save (determined freely and independently by the savers) and of national income equals the investments. In 'mathematical' terms: Y becomes so large that I equals $s \cdot Y$.

Here I and s are given, so that Y is determined: $Y = \dfrac{I}{s}$. National income is the quotient of investments and the propensity to save. If the investments in a country amount to five thousand million pounds, and the propensity to save has been fixed by the income-earners at $1/7$, national income will proceed to be thirty-five thousand million pounds. This is the heart of Keynesian theory in a nutshell.*

From this relation it becomes clear what effect the recipients of income exert on the circulation. They fix the percentage that they wish to save. But by so doing they at the same time, in unconscious combination with the investors, fix national income. Since national income has a decisive effect on the volume of savings, afterwards exactly those savings come about that match the investments. The propensity to save has determined not so much the volume of savings as the national income. The effect of the decision to save is therefore enormous in the Keynesian system; but it is quite a different effect from what the savers themselves think. They do not know what they are doing. Perhaps through exaggerated thrift they are opening the door to a depression which perforce breaks them of the saving habit. Keynesian theory gives people control of their own fate – but they do not know it.

This obscure relation between the various aspects can be understood in another way. We can check what the position is with regard to the multiplier effect, which was touched upon in the preceding section. In this effect we encounter exactly the same quantities.

Let us assume that the entrepreneurs extend their productive capacity at a given moment. They give an 'investment impulse', to use the Keynesian jargon. This impulse is the income effect of the new investments. The circular flow swells on the left-hand side. The households get the extra income; part of it they use for consumption (a fraction c) and part for savings (a fraction s;

* The reader must grasp this proposition, but not learn it by heart. For it applies only to the simple circulation that we have in mind at present. In reality things are more complicated; we shall be concerned with this later. In fact the multiplier is much smaller. And it is not simply 'given'; the multiplier may depend on the national income and on other factors. This sounds very unpleasant to those who are looking for a Great Constant.

$c + s = 1$). The part spent on consumption returns to business; it is an increase in revenue. If we call the investment impulse ΔI, then the households that receive this additional income spend a sum equal to $c\Delta I$. This again returns to business in the form of extra revenues. Consequently $c\Delta I$ is spent again on the factors of production, and as a result assumes the form of a second increment of income. Part of this, determined by the propensity to consume, is spent again on consumer goods. In the second round of the multiplier, therefore, a sum $c^2\Delta I$ makes its way to the business enterprises. In the third round this is $c^3\Delta I$. The multiplier process continues to work in this way. Ultimately national income has increased by a sum which is equal to all these extra impulses together. This total increase amounts in the first place to ΔI (primary effect) and then to $c\Delta I + c^2\Delta I + c^3\Delta I$, etc. Perhaps at first sight it might seem as if this infinitely long series displays an infinitely great sum, and that the multiplier process keeps on stirring up expenditure, an idea that occasionally passes through the minds of some enthusiastic laymen when they philosophize about the effect of (for instance) public works. But in actual fact the process of passing on and receiving income gradually peters out. For c is less than 1, so that c^2, c^3, etc., become steadily less. After the first impulse smaller and smaller ones follow. The impulses approach zero, and the increase in national income has a finite value. But nevertheless the increase in Y is greater than the original investment impulse. The ratio between the two is called the multiplier. It is defined as $\dfrac{\Delta Y}{\Delta I}$, and represents the proportion by which an additional investment causes national income to swell via income effects.

Now how large is this multiplier?

To understand this we must bear in mind that the multiplier effect ceases to operate if in the course of the increase in income a new equilibrium is found. This is the case as soon as the consumers have been able to save so much that S has become equal to I. The increase in investments, ΔI, has then 'leaked away' in its entirety in the form of savings. $\Delta I = \Delta S$. In this situation the entrepreneurs again receive as much from their customers as they put into circulation as incomes. The circulation is again in equilibrium. By bearing this in mind we can determine the size of the multiplier. For we know that ΔS must be equal to $s\Delta Y$. Consequently, in the final situation ΔI equals $s\Delta Y$. It follows from this that the multiplier, which we have defined as $\dfrac{\Delta Y}{\Delta I}$, must equal $\dfrac{1}{s}$. Or, to put it in another way, must equal $\dfrac{1}{1-c}$. The multiplier equals the reciprocal of the propensity to save.*

The doctrine of the multiplier can once more be described as the heart of Keynesianism. Perhaps the reader has gradually come to the conclusion that this theory contains a little too many hearts. But that is not so. Everything that has been said in this and the last section is a constant repetition of one and the same thing. The same economic event, viz. the income-creating effect of consumption and investment, has been approached from various angles. The story changes, the terms are different, but the essence remains the same. The question is always: how big is national income? And the answer is always: so big that savings equal investments, or, to put it differently, so big that the multiplier has provided sufficient savings, or, in yet other terms, so big that total revenues are sufficient to cover the total expenditure of business, or finally, so big that the circular flows of money and goods are in equilibrium. This is the Keynesian mechanism.

It is definitely important. However, its quantitative importance can easily be exaggerated. I should like to warn the reader against a misunderstanding which is encountered among some adepts of the modern theory. They have grasped that the multiplier equals $\dfrac{1}{s}$; and they also know that the marginal propensity to save s may lie somewhere between 10 and 20 per cent. This leads them to estimate that the multiplier is about 7. That is to say that building a factory that costs a million pounds would cause the potential sales of business to increase by no less than seven million. This idea leads to a sort of Baron Munchausen economics: a national

---

* In actual fact this propensity to save must be related to the part of income added or marginal income. We must not have the average propensity to save $\dfrac{S}{Y}$ but the marginal propensity to save $\dfrac{\Delta S}{\Delta Y}$. In the following pages the letter s is to be understood as this marginal quantity.

economy could pull itself up out of a depression by its own boot-straps. This view of things is misleading, for two reasons.

The first reason is that we have introduced here a simple form of circulation in which purchasing power leaks away in only one direction: savings. But in reality there are two other leaks, viz. taxes and imports from abroad. We shall come back to these. They lead to the multiplier being much smaller than would appear at first sight.

The second reason is theoretically rather complicated. It is connected with the fact that the multiplier operates in time. The new revenues which are the result of the income effects are not present forthwith. The Keynesian process of income accretion and additional consumption takes time. If only a single investment impulse occurs, income will not be lastingly raised to a higher level. 'Pump-priming' is therefore a misleading expression. If national income is to expand permanently, the investment level must be permanently raised. Incidentally, this can quite easily be the case if the additional consumption which occurs in the course of the multiplier process encourages the entrepreneurs to maintain or even increase the new investment level.

The fact that the multiplier operates in time also has the result that S does not immediately become equal to I. There is a time-lag. In the interim the entrepreneur will have to do his financing with other means than current savings. This gap can be filled by bank credit, to which we shall return in Chapter VII.

In the General Theory the stress tends to fall on the constant equality of I and S. There has been a good deal of discussion about this. Now more stress is laid on the time-lag. This can be done by what is called period analysis (D. H. Robertson and the Stockholm School), which follows the movement of Y, C, and S in time. Tables can be drawn up showing all this. I prefer to leave these exercises to those who fancy such things.

3 · IS KEYNESIANISM DEPRESSION ECONOMICS?

The development of modern economics, and in particular that of the political conclusions that can be drawn from it, has been harmed by the fact that many have characterized Keynes's theory as a special depression theory, a theory of idle machinery and unemployment. It would be dangerous, it is reasoned, to apply this theory to other situations, for instance inflationary ones, for it was not constructed for these.

This criticism is understandable. Keynes himself gave rise to it to some extent, and some of his followers in particular have promoted this belief. They were impressed by a theoretical system that was able to explain a low income. Classical theory believed that national income would always be maintained at such a high level by Say's Law that productive capacity would be fully utilized. The General Theory had shown that a lower national income was also possible. And more than that; national income could freeze at a low level, without any chance of recovery. Say's Law had been put out of operation, and the hope that a surplus of savings would lead to a revival of investments via a lower rate of interest had vanished. In the Depression, according to the Keynesian view, there *were* no surplus savings at all; as a result of the drop in national income these had disappeared, shrunk, been lost, just as national income had shrunk to a considerable extent. The circulation was just ticking over; there were no sales because there was no income, and there was no income because there were no sales. Moreover, this vicious circle was no abstraction, no pessimistic view of the future, but the reality of the 1930s. Small wonder that the Keynesians believed that their theory not only explained the Depression, but also predicted it for many years to come. Economists thought that they had discovered the forces that brought about a permanent slump.

Keynes himself developed a special theory on these forces in the General Theory. He was of the opinion that the propensity to save which, if it is too high, summons up depression and unemployment, would display a steadily rising trend. He based this belief on the fact that a higher income leads to a greater propensity to save. Rich people save a greater percentage of their income than poor people. The same holds good for rich countries. Rising prosperity and a growing national income form a threat to themselves. Our prosperity spells our downfall: poverty in the midst of plenty. To put it in technical terms: the marginal propensity to save increases with income. A further expression that ties up with what was said above about the fundamental determinations of prosperity: the higher the productivity of labour, the higher unemployment will be. The fruits of progress are spoilt by the monetary disturbances in the circulation.

This special relation between income and propensity to save is, however, doubtful when taken as a general law. Keynes had arrived at it by deduction, and in this respect he reasoned like an old-fashioned economist of the abstract school. He believed that pure logic, if at least it started from wide observation of reality, could lead to quantitative conclusions. This is a mistake, fostered by the special situation in the 1930s. The Keynesian system is a strictly logical structure. But it cannot express an opinion on the value of concrete quantities. These have to be filled in later. We need quantitative economics for this – a scientific technique about which Keynes was all too sceptical, to the detriment of his system, for now he incorporated an element – too great a propensity to save – which in later years proved hardly tenable.

For it is by no means the case that the propensity to save must be greater in the event of a larger income than in the event of a smaller one. The invalidity of this proposition is already apparent from a comparison of the incomes of different people. Some income-earners in the middle classes find it more difficult to save than those members of the income classes immediately below the middle classes. And macro-economically, too, we can sometimes observe things that are at variance with Keynes's view. The year 1956 gave a characteristic example of the converse in the Netherlands as did the year 1959 in the United Kingdom. In each year the national income of the country concerned increased enormously, but this did not make people any more thrifty; on the contrary. There were reasons for this which are irrelevant here, but which in any case were more complicated than the over-simplification that a higher percentage of savings results from a higher income. This oversimplification has contributed towards Keynesianism being wrongfully labelled the theory of 'depression economics'.

There was a further reason. One of Keynes's most influential followers, the American Alvin Hansen, developed an alarming theory about the permanent depression. He foresaw not only too great a propensity to save, but also a constant abatement of investments. Population growth would come to a stop, which was supposed to discourage capital outlay. True, technology would not stand still, but it would lead to increasingly compact and thus more limited investments. (Hansen thought that an instance of this lay in the switch from railways to airfields, which have a smaller income effect.) The entrepreneurs would become increasingly disheartened. Hansen's view was depression economics with a vengeance. This was, however, not due to the logic of the Keynesian system, but to the special premises that Hansen had incorporated in his theory. An insufficient distinction has been made between these two things – the logic and the figures. The opponents of this stagnation theory, as it is called, have used Hansen's pessimistic theory as an argument against modern macro-economics. Events were on their side to the extent that the post-war period in the Western world displayed the exact opposite of stagnation. However, their criticism of Keynes is misplaced, for Keynesian logic and the depression theory are two different things.

Despite the fact that Keynes personally had little faith in capitalism's ability to maintain a decent level of employment, his theory can be very well applied to a situation in which the factors of production are all in operation. That is also the reason why the General Theory of Employment, Interest, and Money is rightly called General. Keynes reproached the classicists with having dealt only with the special case of non-inflationary full employment. But there exists also the Hayek situation.

In the unemployment situation many economic activities have to be judged differently. The latter applies particularly to saving. The classicists saw saving as a fine and useful activity. It promotes the acquisition of property, and it increases productive capacity and with this future prosperity. Individual benefit and society's benefit coincide – one of the most comforting aspects of the classical system. But then Keynes comes along to tell us that saving is harmful. It reduces sales, slows economic life down to a jog-trot, and leads to unemployment, whilst moreover savings do not even increase as a result of it. Saving becomes suspect.

But this applies only if there are productive forces which are unused. If there should be a real scarcity of factors of production – which Keynes considers not very probable, at least in peace-time – the classical view holds good. In that case investment is possible only if the recipients of income are prepared to sacrifice part of consumption. *A fortiori* this is true in an inflationary situation. We can also put it in this way: in the Hayek situation consumption and capital formation are competing for the factors of production. In the depression consumption supports investment; they are not rivals, but help one another in that one supplies the sales for the other.

The General Theory therefore confronts us with two worlds: one in which unemployment prevails and machinery is used only in part, and another in which full loading of machinery and full employment predominate. In the first world national income is smaller than the productivity of labour allows; in the second the productivity of labour forms the factor determining prosperity. The Keynesian theory can grasp both worlds; but at first it believed that the former world would be the more probable one. Now this view of probability is dubious. For in fact the deductive theory cannot by itself teach us whether a certain national economy will yield a large or a small national income. The Keynesian system of thought merely arranges the variables that lead to a given result. Some of these variables have an expansive effect on the circulation: these are investments and consumption. Other variables – the propensity to save – have a contractive effect. The way in which they keep each other in equilibrium can be shown in the form of a general theory, but this equilibrium can be quantified only if we know the figures. We have here an example of what has been said in Chapter I about the shortcomings of the deductive theory and of the necessity of quantitative economics. This is all the more cogent because the economic system that we have described above is extremely simple in its set-up. It has been stripped of imports and exports, of taxes and of government expenditure. No allowance has been made for the fact that investments are not given but, as regards size, might sometimes react on consumption. To use the language of the next chapter, an extremely simple model has been used. If we introduce more variables – and this is necessary if we really want to give Neo-Keynesian theory – the force field of opposed expansive and contractive factors becomes more complex. At the same time the need for quantification becomes greater. Only when we know the concrete figures can we say whether an economy is growing or shrinking, whether it is threatening to become bogged down in depressive stagnation or to soar up an inflationary spiral.

However, quantification presupposes a conveniently arranged theory. This is something that we do not yet have. The Keynesianism discussed in this chapter is still too elementary. Things will improve somewhat in the next chapter.

4 · IS HOARDING OR SAVING THE CAUSE OF UNEMPLOYMENT?

I have written this section for three kinds of readers. In the first place it is intended for those who read a book from cover to cover, irrespective of the appeal of the chapters. In the second place it is meant for those who when reading the preceding pages have occasionally thought to themselves: 'Oh well, we knew that already; of course a depression can come about if people don't keep money moving about. If we hoard unemployment follows.' This idea is rather misleading, and it is really a pity that it is so popular. In the third place this section might perhaps claim the attention of those who consider a difference of opinion among Neo-Keynesians, a kind of family row in other words, interesting. Let me add that what is stated in the following pages is a subjective view. Opinions about it can differ considerably.

In the above the word 'money' did not appear when the breaking of Say's Law was discussed. Keynes has a money theory, but it operates in quite a different corner of his economic system: interest theory, which we shall not go into further in this book. The disturbance in the circulation is of course a disturbance in the flow of money, but it does not come about because people do or do not do something special with that money. In particular the consumers do not aim at retaining more money than before. They do not hoard. They do save, but that is something different. For the saver does not need to be a hoarder. Usually he buys securities, or banks the money, or loans it out. In any case it is not necessarily his intention to increase his cash holding.

In the Keynesian train of thought the disturbance in the circulation comes about particularly because the recipients of income proceed to save more. They abstain from consumption. The latter embarrasses the entrepreneurs, since they see their sales decreasing. The drop in sales reduces national income, as a result of which savings stay at their old level. 'Hoarding' does not enter into the picture.

But there is a school of modern economists that sees this matter differently. They say the following: if the savers save more, they retain more money. They ought really to give this at once to the entrepreneurs, who ought to spend the money on capital goods. If this happened, there would not be any question of the circulation being interrupted, for investments would increase to the same extent as savings, and total expenditure $C + I$ would remain constant. However, so reason these economists, we often see that investments do not immediately increase (in this they agree with Keynes). But this means that savings have been held in the form of money. At some point the path from saver to investor has become blocked; there the money is piling up, and there the breaking of Say's Law begins.

In itself this reasoning is not incorrect. It is true that the additional savings, even if it is not their purpose to increase cash holdings, will sometimes lead to a certain hoarding. But it is dangerous to pay too much attention to this. For then it is so easy to arrive at the widespread misunderstanding that in a depression large cash holdings are formed which are the *cause* of business activity shrinking. These cash holdings are then supposed to represent the savings that were not invested. But that is not so. It would be so if the savings were constantly greater than the investments, if there was a great discrepancy between S and I. But this discrepancy cannot continue to exist.* It destroys itself. As long as S threatens to become greater than I, the money flow is not in equilibrium, and savings shrink.

In my train of thought the dynamic discrepancy between S and I is small and temporary. And therefore hoarding is, too. It is more of a minor phenomenon attendant upon economic contraction than the cause of it.

This subject, which is one of considerable dispute, may safely form a subject for study for the more ingenious theoretician. But it should not be stressed in a simple theory such as the one given

---

* That is, in the model under discussion. If a government sector and international trade are introduced S and I may differ. This will be discussed later.

here. Indeed, a warning must be uttered against this, for it is tempting to assign to hoarding a greater role than it deserves.

There are two reasons for this. The first is that older macro-economics always paid a good deal of attention to the phenomenon of money. It had been discovered that bankers can make money – something that some older bankers themselves do not yet seem to believe (they think that they only lend money that they have received from others). We shall come back to this curious matter in a later chapter. However, one thing that is certain is that the economists were impressed by this power of the banks, and that they tried to explain a whole series of phenomena in this light. In so doing they assigned a very great importance to the independent effect exerted by money. This has led to many people having a strange view of capitalistic society.

The second reason why hoarding is often considered more important as a causal factor than it is lies in the fact that in a depression money is in fact very easy. True, the unemployed are poor, the middle classes have financial worries, and the large entrepreneurs see themselves confronted with declining sales and perhaps losses, but there is still plenty of money about – in the hands of the *rentiers*. But this is not because they have hoarded part of their income or because they have set out in some other way to withdraw money from circulation. The cause is rather that national production has shrunk, whilst the community's stock of money has not decreased *pari passu*. The capital market has become liquid – not because S is greater than I, but because wealth-owners prefer to keep their already existing wealth in the form of money than to invest it in securities which, it appears, can easily drop in value on the Stock Exchange. A wealth-owner who fears this fall in price is sometimes called a 'bear'; this animal reappears on the scene in the chapter on monetary theory. If desired, this liquidity preference of the bears may be described as 'hoarding', if it is only borne in mind that this is not directly concerned with the disturbance of the circulation by the withdrawal of money from the sphere of transactions. The circulation has been disturbed by saving, i.e. by a reduction in consumption. Compared with this, the increase of liquidities hardly plays a separate causal role.

I have discussed this matter separately, not because there are

considerable differences of opinion about it among economists –
the discussions relate to subtleties – but because hoarding plays
an exaggerated part in many amateur theories on the depression,
just as, conversely, the phenomenon of money gets too much
blame for inflationary developments. This makes matters need-
lessly complicated. It also puts the blame for unemployment on
the wrong people, such as wealth-owners or bankers. And finally
this train of thought may arrest the progress of a deliberate
stabilization policy.

We shall come back to the part that money plays in economic
life (see page 131). It may already be remarked that models from
which the money factor is absent are incomplete. They have also
led on occasion to incorrect forecasts. Something more will be
said about this in the concluding section of the next chapter. We
shall see there that the 'monetary' factor must be fitted into our
system. We shall try to do this in the chapter: 'Old and New in
the Theory of Money'. But it will be seen in that chapter that
many of the older theoreticians overestimate the significance of
money. In my opinion money theory should occupy a more
modest place in economics than it did formerly.

CHAPTER IV

How do we Build a Model?

1 · LOGICAL AND QUANTITATIVE MODELS

The word 'model' is becoming a vogue word in economics. There is no objection to this as such; the drawback is that economists do not always mean the same thing when they use it. Sometimes the word relates to the subject that is going to be studied; in that case model means a somewhat stylized part of economic reality. I do not wish to follow this usage. Sometimes the term is used to designate a purely logical relation. One speaks of a model and means a theory. We might call this a logical model. Then we have the real quantitative models. In these not only is a certain logical relation indicated, but certain magnitudes are also placed in an interrelation that is quantifiable. The model is not a genuine model until all these magnitudes have been put in such a form that the figures could be filled in by an econometrist who is expert enough and who possesses sufficient statistical data. The logical models precede the quantitative ones. We are really concerned here with exactly the same contrast as was discussed above under the theme of deductive versus quantitative economics. Quantitative economics is based on deduction, but not on deduction alone; it is also founded on quantification via statistics.

However, it can do no harm first to cast the Keynesian model in its logical form once again and to compare it with the classical model. Then it will be the turn of the quantitative models.

The classicists start from productive capacity. This is fully employed and thus determines production and national income. The recipients of income decide what part of the income will be consumed and what part will be saved. The savings so determined fix the investments. In the somewhat longer run the latter influence productive capacity and in that way national income.

In schematic form the classical reasoning looks like this:
productive capacity → production = national income → savings → investments → productive capacity.

The Keynesian scheme is different in appearance:

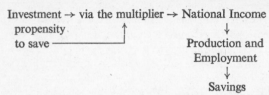

A comparison of the two schemes clearly reveals the difference between the two trains of thought. In classical theory investments come after savings, and savings in turn come after productive capacity. In Keynesian theory investments precede the causal chain, they are as it were a datum which, together with another datum, viz. the propensity to save, determines national income. Savings follow on behind; they form a passive remainder, which has to be there to tone down the income effects of investments but which barely plays any part in the causal chain. Production is also a resultant, as is employment; this is, of course, at variance with classical theory, in which production is practically in the forefront and is only gradually increased by changes in productive capacity.

These logical 'models' can help us to depict things in an orderly manner. In particular they give a picture of the way in which data are used as a starting point, and of the path followed to arrive at the quantities to be explained (the independent and the dependent quantities). But they are not complete. For instance, they do not show that the equilibrium between S and I in classical theory is established by the rate of interest, which brings the demand for capital for investment purposes into line with the supply of capital from savers. In Keynesian theory this equilibrium is also established, but in quite a different way: there national income adjusts itself, so that savings, given the propensity to save, are brought into line with investments. It will be clear that this is an important point: it matters a good deal to a community whether the equilibrium between saving and investing is brought about by the movement of the rate of interest or by the movement of the national income. A rise or fall in the rate of interest is noticed by the *rentiers*, by the Stock Exchange, by the bankers, in short by the world of small and big finance. It is by no means an unimportant phenomenon, but nevertheless it is a limited one.

Movement of the national income, on the other hand, is felt by everyone. The reduction in income hits big businessmen, the workers, the farmers, and the middle classes; they are all dragged through a depression to reconcile a certain value of the propensity to save with a certain level of investment. If the quantities work out in a somewhat different relation to each other, the community prospers. This mechanism is therefore much wider in scope than the fluctuation in the rate of interest. It is now time to specify these trains of thought more exactly by means of a quantitative model. Such a model may be complicated, and frighten off the non-mathematician; the equations may also be of extreme simplicity. The Keynesian theory as outlined above offers an example of the latter type.

2 · THE SIMPLE KEYNESIAN MODEL

The equations that we need are, in words, the following. There are three of them.

No. 1. *National income equals the sum of consumption expenditure and investment.* (This is an outcome of the proposition that $Y = P$; see section 1 of the previous chapter.)

No. 2. *Consumption depends on national income.* In the previous chapter we have designated the relation between consumption and income as the (average) propensity to consume. Let us take the simplest case, that in which the relation between the growth of the income and the extra consumption resulting from it is constant; this relation is the marginal propensity to consume. Part of income is 'autonomous', that is, it does not depend on current income. In that case the average propensity to consume drops as income rises. This is the case discussed by Keynes. It is still insufficiently realistic, but can do excellent service as a first approach.

No. 3. *Investments are given.* This means that they do not depend on the other variables in the model, especially total expenditure. This is a fairly improbable assumption, one that we shall have to change later. We shall have to consider further the question of which factors determine investments. This will be done in the next section.

This simple set-up gives us our model. There are three equations, of differing nature. The first is a simple sum; it represents an equality, without quantities being involved other than the variables that we want to find out: $Y = C + I$. The second is a 'regression equation'; it can take the form $C = A + cY$. The coefficient c represents the extent to which Y is influenced by C; in general such a quantity is called a regression coefficient. In this case the regression coefficient is called the marginal propensity to consume. The third equation ($I = I_0$) is hardly a real equation; it is merely a piece of notation to say that we do not bother to analyse the variable I.

These three equations determine the three quantities that we want to know. National income is fixed, as are consumption, savings, and, of course, investment.

A pleasant feature of this model is that it can be represented in the form of a graph that gives a clear summary of Keynes's theory. The graph shown in Fig. 3, or at least the top part of it, is therefore held in great esteem by the Neo-Keynesians.

On the horizontal axis national income Y has been plotted. This is a money flow; its size is what we want to find. On the top part of the vertical axis we have the sum of consumption and investment. This sum $C + I$ represents the total production of, and expenditure on, goods and services. In Keynes's theory $C + I$ and Y are equal, as emerges from the first equation. This first equation will be represented in the figure by a line which passes through the origin at an angle of 45° to the axes. For every point of this line $Y = C + I$. The point of equilibrium will therefore have to lie on this line in any case.

Next the line $C = A + cY$ is drawn: the consumption function. This is a straight line that intersects the 45° line. At the point of intersection consumption equals Y; at this point, therefore, the whole income is consumed; nothing is saved (and nothing is invested). The national economy is 'stationary' here. It moves constantly in the same channels; productive capacity does not expand. Left of the point of intersection capital is eaten into: savings are negative. Right of the point of intersection the national economy begins to save. The savings are represented by the difference between the 45° line and the consumption line.

To arrive at the total expenditure, the sum invested I must be added to the consumption function. The curve is shifted in an

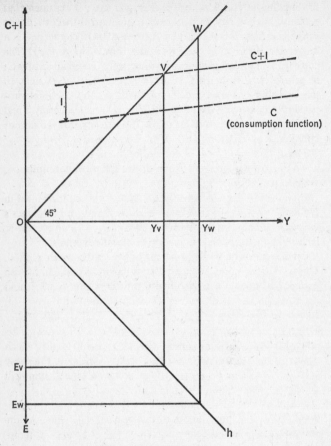

Fig. 3: The simple model

upward direction over a distance I. In this way we find the total expenditure function $C + I$. This gives the total expenditure in relation to the national income.

The point of intersection V of this total expenditure function and the 45° line is the Keynesian point of equilibrium. There the entrepreneurs get back exactly the sum that they spend on the factors of production, including their profit. There is no reason for swelling or shrinking of the flow of money and goods. The national income has been determined. It is represented in the graph by OY_v. No other point can exist (permanently), for it implies a discrepancy between receipts and expenditure of business.

There is consequently only one size of national income possible: that size at which this income generates exactly as much expenditure as its own size. A national income that evokes less expenditure than its own size shrinks. A national income that evokes more expenditure than its own size expands. The circulation is at rest only at V. This is the essence of Keynesian theory.

The size of the income OY_v is not related to the community's productive capacity. It may work out smaller than would be possible with the available working population and the level of labour productivity. This is represented in the graph by extending the vertical axis downwards. On this is plotted E, employment. The relation between E and Y is a straight line in the fourth quadrant, given by h. The gradient of this line is determined by the productivity of labour, which we have defined as national product (national income) divided by the quantity of labour used: $\dfrac{Y}{E}$. Accordingly as labour productivity lies higher, the straight h becomes increasingly horizontal.

This h line helps us to determine whether total expenditure on goods and services does or does not yield a satisfactory national income. We produce the perpendicular VY_v downwards, and go to the left from the point of intersection with the labour productivity line. There we find a point E_v. This is the employment that results from the model. But perhaps this is too small, in the sense that unemployment ensues. Let OE_w represent full employment, the point at which the whole working population is employed (apart from frictional unemployment, seasonal unemployment, and the like). By returning to the Y axis via the h line, we find the national income that would be needed for the state of full employment. It is the most desirable result that our model could show. In the state of affairs that we have depicted, employment is too small. Unemployment is E_vE_w. National income is also too small: Y_vY_w has never come about. Why not? Because the total expenditure was too small. It was only VY_v.

To yield an optimum national income it should have been WY_w. V is thus the False Equilibrium, W the True Equilibrium. The False Equilibrium, the cause of unemployment and of the too small national income, is in turn caused by $C + I$ having a deficiency of $WY_w - VY_v$. We call this the deficiency of demand or the deflationary gap.* By assuming a different position of the $C + I$ curve the model would have produced an inflationary gap. These gaps are the villains of the piece; if a happy ending is to be achieved, they have to be got out of the way. In our story this is the task of the government. Keynesian policy means eliminating a gap between actual spending and the socially desired amount of spending. We shall come back to this later.

In this model the factors are given which determine national money income. But in the meantime a number of related problems have been solved. One of these is the definition of the concepts inflation and deflation. The Keynesians speak of inflation if V lies to the right of W; this is an inflationary *situation*. (Inflation can also be defined as a *process*: this is the case if V lies to the right of W and moves farther to the right. A movement to the right that has not yet reached W is then called reflation. A deflationary process occurs if V, already to the left of W, moves to the left; if V is to the right of W, and the movement is towards W, this is called disinflation; the inflationary gap becomes smaller. In each case the criterion is therefore whether the total expenditure $C + I$ brings the point of full employment closer or not.)

These definitions are rather narrow; they are concerned only with employment, but nevertheless they make a very useful first approximation. (We shall have an opportunity later to make the objectives of economic policy more realistic.) The remarkable thing is that this Keynesian inflation and deflation seem to be entirely detached from increases and decreases of the quantity of money, the very things with which they are associated in com-

* This term is also used in a different sense, viz. to mean the primary impulse required to eliminate a given total deficiency of demand. It is so used by, for instance, P. A. Samuelson. This gap is smaller than ours; the ratio between the two is equal to the multiplier. I prefer my own definition, since in practice the total deficiency of demand is easier to calculate than the impulses which are supposed to be able to eliminate it. For in practice the multiplier cannot be exactly calculated.

mon usage. Here inflation is not too much money but too much expenditure. These resemble each other, but they are not the same. We shall now shelve this matter until we come to the theory of money (Chapter VII).

This is a suitable moment to ask ourselves what exactly the difference is between the classical and the Keynesian models. Classical theory can also be depicted in a graph like the one we have drawn. Whilst the result in Keynesian theory is an income that does not give full employment (the latter happens only by chance), the classical reasoning will always lead to the income OY_w. Why is this?

We already know that there are two reasons for this. The first is Say's Law. This entails that the flow is in equilibrium at every point on the 45° line or, in other words, that the $C + I$ line of expenditure coincides with the OW production line. Every size of production creates the equivalent total expenditure, and can therefore be maintained. (In Keynes's theory there is only one size of production that does this, viz. that indicated by the point of intersection of the $C + I$ function and the 45° line.) And since every size of production in the classical view is a bull's eye, macro-economically speaking, there is no reason for underloading the machinery of production. There is no reason for an inflationary or a deflationary gap. But should this occur for a moment, the price system, and especially the working of the rate of interest and the wage level, will ensure that economic life glides effortlessly to point W. The price system therefore supplies the second classical reason for reaching W. On the 45° line there are no resistances to restrain this movement. In the Keynesian system this restraint exists: it is the $C + I$ line. This intersects the 45° line. In the classical theory both lines coincide.

A further striking point is that in the determination of the Keynesian point V the price system does not occur, nor do wages, nor does interest as the establisher of equilibrium between I and S.*

* It will emerge from the following section that the rate of interest has a marked effect in orthodox Keynesian theory, but that this effect is of a different nature. In Keynes's opinion the rate of interest does influence investment, but does not serve to create equilibrium between S and I – the movement of the national income attends to that.

It is definitely no law of the Medes and Persians that a Keynesian model such as the one we are now discussing must yield a deflationary situation. If we move the line $C + I$ a little upwards and thus start from a strong urge to consume and a marked tendency to invest, the point of intersection with the 45° line moves to the right. National income increases. An efficacious method of achieving this in the graph is not so much to move the total expenditure line vertically upwards as to rotate it. If this line assumes an angle that lies in the neighbourhood of 45°, the point of intersection V can suddenly move strongly to the right. (This is a case which will engage our attention again when we discuss the stability of national income, see p. 79.) The income then increases vigorously; V, the False Equilibrium, moves to the right of the True Equilibrium; via the h line we then end up at a point on the E axis that lies 'below' E_w. This means that there is a greater demand for labour than the working population can satisfy. The national money income is then too great and tensions occur in the national economy. More goods are demanded than business can make. This is an inflationary gap, which can be graphically analysed in exactly the same way as the deflationary gap.

It is again evident from the latter that Keynesian theory is not only useful for explaining depression and unemployment. The reasoning can also serve to describe and to explain inflation. Everything depends on the position and the location of the $C + I$ line. It is now time to consider this material problem somewhat more deeply.*

* The attentive reader may perhaps feel that the Keynesian theory contained in this model is different from the one explained in the last chapter. Concepts and propositions that played a central part there, such as the multiplier, the propensity to save, and the equality of S and I, have not turned up. But in this respect the graph is a puzzle picture. Everything is there, but you don't see it right away. If you look closely you will see that the marginal propensity to consume is represented by the gradient of the consumption function in relation to the Y axis, so that the propensity to save must also be given. (Incidentally, we can best depict the latter quantity graphically by using a somewhat different figure, which shows the income on the horizontal axis and the difference between the consumption function and the 45° line on the vertical axis. This is a twin brother of our graph; it also shows the multiplier somewhat better.) In our drawing $S = I$ is immediately apparent; this equality is realized exclusively at V.

The question of what determines expenditure on capital goods has been touched upon now and again above, but has not yet been answered. In the classical system the answer was simple: savings, in their turn determined by the savers, give the extent to which the stock of capital goods will increase, the rate of interest supplying the right signals. In orthodox Keynesianism this relation has been entirely abandoned. For investments determine savings, and not the other way round. Though it remains to be seen whether this is true as it stands. We shall come back to this.

Keynes himself had a very concrete theory about the determinants of I. If the entrepreneurs are considering buying new machinery, they have in mind a certain additional profit that is to result from this. By capitalizing these profits of successive years the value of the new capital good to the enterprise is found. In this capitalization the rate of interest plays a big part; the higher the rate of interest at which you capitalize, the lower the value. Now it is always possible to point to a certain rate of interest that makes the value of the additional capital good equal to its cost. Keynes calls this rate of interest the marginal efficiency of capital, in my opinion a somewhat artificial term which often gives rise to confusion with related concepts. And Keynes's investment theory amounts to the fact that the entrepreneur will buy the capital good in question if its marginal efficiency is higher than the rate of interest at which he can borrow money.

But in Keynes's theory this rate of interest is not determined by the supply and demand of savings (after all, S and I are equal), but by people's liquidity preference and the quantity of money. Thus the quantity of money influences investments via the rate of interest. Keynes borrowed this strategic effect of the monetary factor from a Swedish economist, K. Wicksell (c. 1900). Many Neo-Keynesians do not follow him in this. They consider total expenditure and its movements more important to I than the financial sphere.

The argument that the rate of interest determines the size of I is not illogical, but it seems hardly realistic. In fact the rate of interest probably plays a minor role: one of the reasons for this is self-financing out of profits, a matter for which insufficient allowance is made in orthodox Keynesian theory. It has been one of the first fruits of quantitative economics, and in particular of the investigation performed by Tinbergen,* that the rate of interest has proceeded to play a somewhat more modest part in economic thought. The influence of interest had been over-estimated not only by Keynes but also by various classical and other authors.

The marginal efficiency of capital no longer plays an important role in economics. It is one of the aspects of the General Theory that has not been able to hold its own. But in one respect it has brought an old truth to our notice again. Investments are to a considerable extent determined by expectations for the future, and therefore by psychological factors. For this very reason the prevalent mood among entrepreneurs is of tremendous importance to economic equilibrium. If they take an optimistic view of things and buy more capital goods, there is a good chance that the income effects which this will evoke will prove them right. The expectations for the future tend to realize themselves via the flow of goods and money. This psychological influence may be a reason simply to accept investments in the model as given.

But this is a makeshift solution. Entrepreneurs do not act on whims; the determinants of investment lie not only in the psychological but also, and in particular, in the sober sphere of business. Expectations with regard to future sales are the entrepreneur's guide.

The effect of sales on capital outlay entails a complication. At first sight it does not seem implausible that a 10 per cent rise in sales must lead to a 10 per cent increase in productive capacity, and therefore also to a 10 per cent increase in investment. But this is not so; the increase in investment tends to be greater.

This remarkable thing can best be explained by starting from the difference between investment for replacements and invest-ment for expansion. In the normal course of business, machinery is constantly being written off and replaced. This leads to a level of gross investment that is needed to keep up the stock of capital goods. Part of the sales of the capital goods industry is based on this. Now to this part are added the investments for expansion.

* *Statistical Testing of Business Cycle Theories*, 1939.

They can give the sales of machinery a strange look. Let me illustrate this by an example.

Let us suppose that a shoe factory makes 100,000 pairs of shoes a year. It has ten machines at work, each of which lasts ten years. Their age is spread uniformly over the years, so that every year one machine is replaced. The engineering firm that makes these machines therefore sells one a year. Now the sales of shoes increase by 10,000 pairs, or 10 per cent. To meet this additional demand one new machine is purchased. The sales of the engineering firm now rise from one to two shoemaking machines; an increase of no less than 100 per cent. The percentage by which the sales have increased has increased tenfold in passing from the shoes to the machines. This is known as the acceleration principle. Accurately formulated, it implies that investment is proportional not to sales but to the increase in sales:

$$I = a.\Delta(C + I).$$

This is the investment equation which we would have to include in our model if the acceleration principle effectively described reality. What the surprising result would be is described in the next section.

However, the acceleration principle, though remarkable, is not quite realistic. The entrepreneurs do not react entirely in this spirit. Productive capacity is not as rigid as the acceleration principle assumes. In actual fact the increases in consumption do spread in intensified fashion to the investment activity, but this intensification is not as accentuated as the acceleration principle assumes. If there is overcapacity, the principle does not work at all. The acceleration principle is moderated by a certain flexibility. This may be expressed in an equation which implies that investments are determined by the difference between the stock of capital goods desired by the entrepreneurs and the actual stock. The former then depends in turn on the expected expansion of sales. The regression coefficients of this equation show how lively the acceleration will be; it may be great or small, according to circumstances. Such a relation is called the flexible accelerator.*

* R. M. Goodwin, 'Secular and Cyclical Aspects of the Multiplier and the Accelerator', in: *Income, Employment and Public Policy, Essays in Honor of Alvin Hansen*, 1948.

But another view of the investment equation is possible. We have let the expansion depend on the volume of expected sales. But it can also rightly be said that profits determine investments. Profit is the aim and forms the incentive; moreover, the profit normally serves to finance a great deal of the investments. There is not a single sound firm that relies in all circumstances on the capital market if expansion is envisaged. A new share issue means that the old shareholders get less of a return on their money. Financing from reserves is often considered safer, solider, sounder. Statistical surveys confirm this rule. It was found for the United States that two thirds of the gross investments by big business were financed by retention of profits. The figure for the Netherlands is even higher; in the 1950s the self-financing percentage for corporations was approximately 90 per cent. And it was about the same for small firms. After all, the trading middle classes have to do their financing from their own savings. They can hardly fall back on the capital market, and they do not benefit from the Keynesian proposition that every I yields its own S.

The investment equation will therefore perhaps have to include profits, too. In his above-mentioned investigation for the United States Tinbergen paid particular attention to the generation of profit. He got good correlations. But this does not necessarily mean that sales are of no importance.

The conclusions which can be drawn from the importance of savings by enterprises are not only relevant to the investment equation. They could change our view of the macro-economic relation. The Keynesian idea that savings form a purely passive quantity at the far end of the causal chain (see section 1 of this chapter) is only a half-truth. It is true that S is determined by Y, and thus by I; but at the same time S again determines the size of the investments in many cases. In this respect the classicists are not as far wrong as some Keynesians thought. Nor is this denied by the Neo-Keynesians.

The savings of enterprises and their effect on investment influence our view of the circulation in two other respects. In the first place we see that saving is an activity not only of the households, but also of the firms. It occurs not only 'at the bottom of the circular flow' but also 'at the top'. And in the present institutional circumstances it is there that the most profuse source of savings is to be found, besides that of the collective investors such as the life insurance companies and pension funds. The firms retain part of their net income, in exactly the same way as consumers do. All of this has to be included in the propensity to save.

A second important consequence of the manner in which the size of the investments is determined concerns the savings paradox. Keynesian theory had discovered a strange contradiction in saving. People save to acquire savings – but it does not help them. By so doing they reduce their income, and the savings balances remain what they are. That is to say, in the most favourable case, for orthodox Keynesianism may take an even gloomier view of things. After all, the sales of consumer goods have dropped, and this will have its repercussions on investments – perhaps even according to the acceleration principle. Then the circulation shrinks still further, and savings decline. This is the savings paradox: more saving leads to smaller savings.

Now that we have considered the determinants of investment in somewhat greater detail, we know that in practice this paradox is not as bad as it looks. There are savings that lead direct to investments. To put this in another way: there are investments that cannot be made before saving has taken place. The origin of this lies in micro-economic situations. On the macro-economic plane the savings will put in an appearance, but this is no help to the grocer who wants to buy a delivery van. By observing the micro-economic situation we come closer to classical theory. This does not entirely do away with the savings paradox, but the contradiction is no longer as acute. Only quantitative results can say for certain whether the savings paradox has been done away with or not. And if it proves to exist, it must be removed by the government's macro-economic policy.

It will be evident from the above that the form of the investment equation is still the subject of study. This also applies to the consumption equation, by the way. New explanatory variables can always be added and tested. What in fact has to be done is to split the investment equation into a number of sub-equations, since the investments consist of different parts. In this way allowance can be made for the fact that part of I is not so much induced by the growth of sales as governed by the progress of technology (autonomous investments). There is also some point in detaching investments in raw materials (which are sometimes speculative, and then depend on the expected price movement) from those in machinery. Then it is obvious to place housing in a separate equation; it has often played an important role in inflation and deflation, but its explanatory variables are of a special nature (growth of the population, government measures). This principle – splitting up equations – is very important. It can make our insight more realistic, it 'opens up' the model, and as a result it stimulates the thought and the progress of economic science. We shall come back to this later on.

4 · THE STABILITY OF NATIONAL INCOME

A question of practical importance is to what extent national income is sensitive to changes in the determining variables and in their interrelation. If the equilibrium is sensitive, there is a considerable danger of fluctuations in prosperity. We then live in an unstable world, in which we are constantly threatened with inflation and deflation.

This sensitivity can be read off from the graph shown in Fig. 4. It is manifested by the angle at which the total expenditure curve intersects the 45° line. If this angle is a fairly wide one there is a good chance of the system standing firm. It is rather like a cyclist who wants to ride on the pavement. To get up there he should preferably take the kerb at right angles. If he takes it at too narrow an angle, he scrapes along it, and then it cannot be said for certain where he will end up on the pavement. He may even fall.

A number of things may be said *a priori* about the angle between the $C + I$ line and the equilibrium line. In the earlier figure we drew the total expenditure curve fairly flat, so that an obvious equilibrium was created. As investments were taken as a constant in that figure, this means that the marginal propensity to save is high. However, it can also be quite well imagined that the consumption line originally runs fairly close to the 45° line – the recipients of income in that case have no scope for saving – and curves away somewhat to the right at a higher income. The curvature of the consumption function then introduces stability into the system. This form of stability has attracted the attention of the prophets of stagnation; they deduced from it that the national income would be stable, but at too low a level.

But total expenditure is not determined by consumption alone. Investments must be added to the C line. If these are independent of the other variables in the model, as we first assumed, addition of these investments makes no difference to stability. This is the 'total expenditure 1' curve in the figure. But now note what

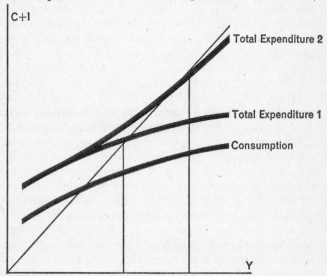

Fig. 4. The stability of equilibrium.

happens if not only consumption but also investments depend on total expenditure. In that case we do not even need to believe in the genuine acceleration principle to find a $C + I$ line that scrapes along the equilibrium line. In the diagram this situation is represented by the 'total expenditure 2' line. We can clearly see how investments operate as a destabilizer. The total expenditure line $C + I$ curves increasingly up and away from the C line, and adopts an angle of almost 45° to the horizontal axis. It is even conceivable that this angle reaches 45° or even exceeds it. Then something most peculiar happens: there is no longer any point of intersection with the equilibrium line. The model 'explodes'. The national money income exceeds all bounds, demand is no

80

longer checked (at least in *this* model). We have a situation of unbridled inflation.

It might be as well to point out to the reader now that this uncontrollable inflation is the result of only two things: the form of the consumption function and the investment function. Together they drive the demand for goods and services beyond the bounds of productive capacity. This much is certain, that this inflation in our model is not the fault of the government for having excessively inflated the supply of money. Nor are the bankers to blame for having given credit rashly. Even less is it due to price-raisers, profit-makers, stock-jobbers, or other mysterious figures. None of these scapegoats of the inflation process is around. There are only recipients of income who for once see no point in a high propensity to save (which they are fully entitled to do), and there is a certain relation between total expenditure and investment. It is nobody's 'fault'. We shall return in the chapter on money theory to this question of guilt, which is of course important to daily life and to economic policy.

This interplay of two functions has been pushed very much to the fore by a number of later Keynesians. Since then it has been known as the 'interaction of the multiplier and the acceleration principle'. The process can also be very well described in words, quite vividly in fact. Let us assume that at a given moment consumption increases because people have become somewhat less thrifty. The entrepreneurs see their sales increase, and react to this by buying more machines. To the normal orders which they place with the engineering industry for the purpose of replacing worn-out machinery are added the extra orders – the production of capital goods therefore increases by a multiple of the original increase in consumption. But we know that an increase in production is translated into an increased income for the factors of production. The households proceed to spend part of that income – and that again causes sales to increase. Once again the entrepreneurs do good business, and again they decide to increase capital outlay. This investment comes on top of the previous one, which is perhaps still having its effect. And in this way acceleration and multiplier reinforce each other reciprocally.

However, the opposite can also happen. If economic life has been at rest for some time, there is a chance that the expansion investments will not be made as readily as they were. The entrepreneurs will confine themselves to replacing their worn-out machinery. They may not have a very gloomy view of the future; it is sufficient if they prefer to await developments. The consequence is that the sales of the capital goods industry decrease sharply. The drop in production makes itself felt in the incomes of the factors of production in the engineering and building industries. And this then means less consumption. In this way the drop in sales makes its effect felt throughout the economy. The acceleration principle has done its dirty work, and the multiplier ensures that the deflationary effect spreads. Then the accelerator begins to work again. And so the system slips into the depths of a depression.

We thus see that a model consisting of a consumption function and an investment function can easily become unstable. It goes almost without saying that those who discovered this were struck by their find and began to think that the interaction of the two functions describes a realistic process. I doubt that. For the model that we are now considering is much too simple. We are far from having a complete picture of the stabilizers and the destabilizers that have been 'built in'. Reality is more complicated, and we shall have to examine why.

I should like to mention a further important factor. A model such as our present one derives its significance from the fact that the relations used are comparatively stable. Their result may be unstable, but the regression coefficients of the consumption and the investment function remain the same. If they do not, and the functions on which the reasoning has been built up begin to vanish, the model becomes shaky; it loses its usefulness and also its theoretical foundation.

However, the stability of our consumption function is not beyond suspicion. In other words it is not certain that every value of the national income is also matched by a certain well-fixed value of consumption. It may also sometimes happen that consumption changes in size while national income does not give cause for this.

A single change in saving habits or, in the terms of the model, a shift or twist of the consumption curve, does not interfere with our reasoning. The very advantage of the model is that we can investigate the effect of such a change. But if fluctuations in the ratio between extra income and extra consumption become the rule, if the marginal propensity to consume can no longer be relied on, our model cannot be used any more. It is then too primitive. In that case new explanatory variables will have to be included in the consumption equation. Some of them are obvious ones. Take for instance the growth in population: babies are expensive and big families are small savers. Another factor is the distribution of income: the more uniform this is, the higher the propensity to consume will be. However, these factors have a gradual effect. In the short term consumption may vary for two reasons which both form serious complications in their own way.

The first complication lies in the durable consumer goods. Purchase of these can be postponed. This means that not only the income itself but also, and in particular, the expected income in the near future proceeds to play a part in the extent of consumption. The latter variable can be inserted in the model. But then 'psychological factors' may play a role in the postponement or the acceleration of spending on durable goods. From the theoretical point of view this is dreadful. G. Katona, author of *The Powerful Consumer* (1960), for this reason does not believe in the possibility of setting up a properly stable model. This problem is not at all solved yet. My suggestion would be to extract the durable consumer goods such as cars, furniture, television sets, refrigerators, etc., from the general consumption function and to place them in a special equation. This probably displays a special affinity with the investment equation: there too there is a reaction to expectations for the future regarding the growth of income. The problem is not solved in this way, but it is isolated for further study.

A second complication concerns the money factor. The short history of the construction of models has already yielded an instance of the difficulties that may be encountered in this respect. At the end of the Second World War American economists understandably worried about the post-war economic situation. They feared that the disappearance of the armaments contracts might start off a multiplier process that would then be intensified by acceleration. Entirely in the spirit of the above reasoning they had ventured to make predictions on the basis of an econometric model, and they feared a slump. This did not happen. Not only did the total demand not drop, but it actually increased. The point of equilibrium V did not shift to the left, but to the right. It was not so much unemployment that proved to be the big problem; inflation reared its ugly head.

The model had therefore not yielded the right results. How did this come about? The reason probably lies in the situation in which consumers found themselves at the end of the war. They had had to abstain from consumption for the last few years. The war was over – the consumers wanted something a little more cheerful. The propensity to consume rose.

In itself this was not yet at variance with the essence of the model – at most with the value entered for the regression coefficients. For it was obvious to believe that an understandable and unique change in the propensity to consume was occurring here. But upon reflection matters proved to be more complicated. For the consumers did not only have their psychological reasons for desiring a somewhat higher consumption. They also had the financial resources to do so. The war had led to people having large cash holdings. These liquidities did not only make consumption possible: they encouraged it as well. Much of the additional consumption originated from the spending of increased cash holdings.

Now this is unpleasant for our model. On the one hand the influence of cash holdings is difficult to predict. What will the consumers do if they have money in their pockets? Will they perhaps try to collect still more money? Or will they get rid of it at some unpredictable moment by greater consumption? Or will they perhaps spend it on securities? The position of the consumption curve becomes less certain, the model becomes less stable. It cannot be said whether the income will become more stable or more unstable as a result. In 1946 cash holdings in the United States were a stabilizer, in 1956 they were a destabilizer in the Netherlands; the increase in consumption led to a somewhat increased inflation.

Another unpleasant aspect of these cash holdings is of a more theoretical nature. It proves that the presence of abnormal liquidities among the consumers may be relevant to consumption. But that influence has not been included among our variables.

Many modern economists consider this to be a serious drawback of the simple Keynesian model. Money plays no part in it. We shall go into this matter more fully later, since it has led to interesting differences of opinion among the Neo-Keynesians.

It follows from all this that the simple straight line from the Keynesian figure cannot contain a usable consumption equation. Come to that, this is quite obvious if you make a sample calculation in which the equation has for instance the form $C = 0.4\ Y + 30$. At an income of 100, C is then 70 and S is therefore 30. But if the national income grows to for instance 200 – which with the present growth figures can happen in about twenty years – the result is most strange: $C = 110$ and $S = 90$. The average propensity to save is 45 per cent; this is exceedingly high. In the long run, therefore, allowance will have to be made for a structural increase in the propensity to consume. But how? That is an unsolved problem.

And so the consumption function gives rise to numerous questions. That is precisely one of its pleasant aspects: it stimulates research. In the last few years a series of attempts have been made at a more exact explanation. For instance, M. Friedman has tried to establish a fixed connexion between consumption and that part of the income that the households regard as permanent. The fluctuating parts of the income, i.e. the extras, are said to display no fixed propensity to consume. Such investigations are experimental; the last word has not yet been spoken.

In this uncomplicated book we do not wish to try to describe in detail the above refinements, the more so because the three-equation model reproduced above has other shortcomings that do demand our attention. To begin with, international trade does not appear in our model, nor does the effect which government expenditure and taxation have on the circulation. These two sectors give rise to new equations. We shall now look into this.

CHAPTER V

The Impact of International Trade

1 · THE CLASSICAL VIEW OF THE BALANCE OF PAYMENTS

Since olden days economics has concerned itself with the phenomenon of international trade. In the thirties it looked as if a
well-rounded theory had been achieved in this field too – until
here, as well, Keynesianism elucidated new relations. The modern
views closely follow what was said above about the macro-
economic equilibrium. They regard the international movement
of goods and the income effects that are the result as part of the
circular flow. To grasp the significance of this it is as well to
confront the modern views with some older ones. In this field,
too, it may be said that some still adhere to pre-Keynesian one-
sidedness; it stands in the way of a correct insight into practical
problems, such as those of the equilibrium of the balance of
payments, of devaluation, of flexible rates of exchange, and the
like. (My critics will no doubt raise the point that my own reasoning suffers from post-Keynesian one-sidedness, and they may
be right.)

The older views originate in a discussion that began centuries
ago. The sixteenth- and seventeenth-century writers on economic
problems – the mercantilists – had a clear purpose in mind: they
wanted to make the country in which they lived a strong one. The
best way to strength was wealth – above all wealth in terms of
gold, since with gold mercenaries could be mustered and fleets
could be fitted out. How is gold to be obtained if the country has
no gold mines? The answer is foreign trade. By selling other
countries more goods than are imported from them a favourable
balance with these countries is created; this was once upon a time
covered in gold, and it still is today in a certain sense. The ratio
between imports and exports was called the balance of trade. It
was later realized that the gold balance with which the mercantilists were concerned was also affected by other items not directly

concerning trade: the proceeds of services, the interest on debts, and the like. All these items together, including the balance of trade, were subsequently given the name of balance of payments. This is therefore a list of transactions with other countries, over a given period (generally a year) which give rise to payments.* If the incoming payments are greater than the outgoing ones, the balance of payments is called favourable. In that case gold (or foreign currency) enters the country. In the opposite case – that is to say when the country, roughly speaking, buys more abroad than it exports – a drop in the gold stocks is the obvious consequence. The mercantilists therefore aimed at a favourable balance of payments. One of the ways in which they did this was to check imports of finished products as far as possible by import bans and the like. The Navigation Laws of the middle of the sixteenth century were also an attempt in this direction.

The mercantilistic view was combated by later writers. From Adam Smith onwards economists went to a good deal of trouble to make it clear that a favourable balance of payments cannot be maintained in the long run. For, so ran the criticism of mercantilism, if the balance of payments is favourable, and therefore gold pours into the country, the medium of payment (in this case the gold coin) will become abundant. More money means higher prices. The country that receives gold becomes an expensive country. But an expensive country prices itself out of foreign markets. It will lose its foreign customers to other, cheaper countries. And so exports decline to a level at which imports of gold are no longer necessary; the price level then comes to rest, and imports and exports are equal to one another. This is the classical theory of the equilibrium of the balance of payments. Exports cannot lastingly exceed imports; the prices attend to the equilibrium. In this train of thought an adverse balance of payments leads to the export of gold and a drop in prices; exports increase; and the deficit on the balance of payments cannot

* If we speak below of the balance of payments, we mean the current payments, i.e. excluding movements of gold and capital. The equilibrium of the balance of payments is equilibrium on current account (imports and exports, service transactions, donations, returns on capital, transferred profits). 'Export' is therefore a short way of saying 'all current transactions that bring in foreign exchange'; it should not be understood in its narrow sense of export of goods.

therefore be maintained any more than the surplus on the balance of payments.

The attentive reader will have encountered a typically classical idea in this. It is the price system that establishes equilibrium. We have also encountered this in the equilibrium between S and I, where the rate of interest – the price of capital – in the classical view attended to the equality, as in general the price of a good has the function of bringing supply and demand into line with one another. Small wonder, therefore, that the import and export argument fitted so well into classical theory. And small wonder, too, that the modern theory differs in its view of this as well.

Let us examine this classical equilibrium mechanism a little more closely. The first link in the reasoning is that gold enters the country because the balance of payments is favourable. (This is the mercantilistic aim.) The second link is the rise in the price level in the country receiving the gold. This link is rather weak, firstly because 'gold' is here put on a par with 'money', and this need not always be so. But there is more. As we shall see later, it is not necessary that a country in which the supply of money increases experiences a rise in its price level. It is also quite possible that the greater quantity of money stays inactive, so that the rise in prices does not happen. And it may also be that a greater demand for goods gives rise to a greater supply, so that prices remain the same for this reason. The latter can occur in particular if there are many unused instruments of production, if machines are standing idle and workers are unemployed. The import and export argument does not make much allowance for the latter situation. Quite logically, for it is part of classical theory, and classical theory does not recognize unemployment, since it has firm confidence in Say's Law.

An increase in prices is therefore not a certain, though a possible, consequence of a favourable balance of payments. But let us assume that the rise in prices really does occur. The country in question then becomes an expensive country compared with others. However, the foreigner is not directly concerned with the internal price level of the supplying country. He is concerned with the number of units of his own currency that he has to pay. And this is governed not only by the price of the supplying country, but also by the ratio between the prices of the two currencies.

This is the rate of exchange. The rate of exchange is therefore of just as much importance in determining whether exports are attractive or not as the price in the supplying country's own currency. The competitive position of a country on foreign markets depends on its own price level in relation to the prices of other countries, and on the rate of exchange. It is worth taking the trouble to remember this truth; it will stand us in good stead when we extend the model to form a realistic reproduction of reality.

The competitive position is therefore partly determined by the rate of exchange. This price ratio between the currencies is sometimes a fixed one – for instance under the Gold Standard, or under the present-day Bretton Woods Agreement, by which the various countries have engaged to ensure fixed rates of exchange – but sometimes it can fluctuate freely. This was the case for much of the 1930s. Such a freely varying rate of exchange again has a typical function in respect of the balance of payments. Thinking along classical lines, it is easy to decide that this special price is the establisher of equilibrium *par excellence*. Whilst older classicists, when combating the mercantilists, started from a variable price level and a fixed rate of exchange (they lived under the Gold Standard), the variable rate of exchange fits better into the later classical train of thought. Even nowadays it is often advocated as an excellent means of establishing equilibrium in the balance of payments. It is praised as a good way of promoting balanced foreign trade. I think that this is again a half truth, of which we must beware – but we shall first summarize the argument again.

The neo-classical equilibrium theory of the balance of payments, then, says that the rate of exchange tends to make imports and exports equal. If exports happen to be larger, the foreigners must make net payments to the exporting country, as a result of which the currency of that country, measured in other units of currency, becomes more expensive. In this way the competitive position of that country is weakened, and exports will again decline. Moreover, through the change in the rate of exchange, the country's imports have become cheaper. Its inhabitants will proceed to buy more foreign goods. As a result of this, imports increase. In this way the favourable balance of payments disappears again. The rate of exchange has led to a new equilibrium, even without further intervention of the price levels in the countries concerned.

It is a tempting theory. What is wrong with it? We can find this out by examining the circulatory effects of the balance of payments.

2 · THE INCOME EFFECT OF EXPORTS

The reader will doubtless recall from Chapter II that one of the remarkable differences between classical and Keynesian theory lies in the fact that the first makes no allowance for the income effect of investments and the second does. Investment means production of capital goods, i.e. the application of production factors which in return for their assistance receive an income. Classical theory does not need to pay particular attention to this – after all, one of its fundamental premises is full loading and full employment, so that labour and capital put to work by the investments had first to be diverted from other uses in which they were also earning an income. But in modern economics, where allowance is made for idleness of factors of production, the position is different. There investing leads to an investment impulse in the circulation, which spreads further via the multiplier.

Now this difference in outlook is directly concerned with the balance of payments. For in this respect there is a clear analogy between investing and exporting. In both cases instruments of production are used to make a product that does not reach the consumer, at least not the domestic consumer. And yet this consumer, as a recipient of income, has received the money created in the course of the production process. The worker, the entrepreneur, the furnisher of capital in the export industry earns his income: export has an income effect. But the product that they jointly produce withdraws from the circulation. It crosses the frontier and disappears. Domestic purchasing power continues to search for goods that are not there.

The income effect of exports is inflationary; it causes money income to swell. Will this lead to a disturbance? No – for at the same time goods are imported from abroad. These have been produced, have had an income effect, and have led to an extra demand – but this process was enacted over the frontier. If the import goods enter the country they arrive there without bringing the corresponding income with them. It is a good thing that exports provided this income. In this way the circulation is complete again. Exports attend to the income effect, imports attend to the matching goods.

We must bear this process in mind if we want to understand the Keynesian equilibrium mechanism of the balance of payments. We see a similar process occurring to that in saving and investing. The investments provide income, but not goods ready for consumption; the inflationary effect of this is neutralized by saving. S equals I; the multiplier sees to this or, to put it another way, the movement of national income. The latter fluctuates in such a way that saving and investment are brought into balance with one another. Exactly the same happens with regard to imports and exports. These can also be kept in equilibrium by national income and its fluctuations.

To form a clear picture of how this works, we must imagine a community in which there is no saving and no investing: a stationary economy. We shall call the exports of goods and services X (from eXports), and imports M (from iMports). The problem is the following: is there a tendency towards equilibrium between X and M and, if so, where does this come from?

Let us suppose that the balance of payments is in equilibrium at first, and that exports increase at a given moment owing to the fact that a new product is being made for which there is a ready market abroad. We shall call the additional exports ΔX. This additional production has an income effect; the additional income impulse $\Delta Y = \Delta X$. This sum goes to the households. They do not save (or so we have assumed) and therefore they can do only one of two things: buy domestic consumer goods or buy foreign ones. The ratio in which they divide their income among the two categories forms an important quantity in our reasoning. We call this quantity the (marginal) propensity to import, defined as the ratio between extra imports and extra national income. In letters: $m = \dfrac{\Delta M}{\Delta Y}$. Of the additional income ΔX an amount $m\Delta X$ therefore goes to the import goods; the rest $(1 - m)\Delta X$ is spent on the consumer goods produced by domestic business. The entrepreneurs therefore see their receipts increase by this amount. To meet the extra demand they must engage new factors of production who appropriate the amount of additional receipts, convert it into income, and return the sum $(1 - m)^2 \Delta X$ to business. Do you see the multiplier effect? The original income impulse from the export firms spreads through the whole system. Again and again a portion is diverted to imports. The process stops when all the extra income has leaked away abroad. In that case ΔM equals ΔX; imports and exports have both grown equally. The balance of payments, which at first had become favourable through the increase in exports, has again been brought into equilibrium.

The characteristic thing about this recovery of equilibrium is that the rate of exchange has nothing to do with it. Nor has, in our reasoning, any change in prices manifested itself. The equilibrium-restoring factor is national income. This quantity increased to such an extent that it caused higher imports which were ultimately equal to the increase in exports. When this had happened, the firms got back from the consumers that sum which they had spent on the factors of production. The circulation then continued along the same path without swelling or shrinking. But, compared with the original situation, national income, employment, and the use of existing machinery have increased.

How much has national income grown through the increase in exports? An answer can be given to this question that is entirely analogous to the answer that we gave to the question: when has Y grown enough to make S equal to I? The reasoning can follow two paths. The total increment in income equals $(1 - m) \Delta X + (1 - m)^2 \Delta X + (1 - m)^3 \Delta X$, etc. In this way we find the sum of a descending geometric series. The reader who considers this too scholarly an approach can take another route. He can bear in mind that the increment in income ΔY must be such that it makes ΔM equal to ΔX. There is consequently equilibrium at

$m \Delta Y = \Delta X$. From which it follows that $\Delta Y = \dfrac{\Delta X}{m}$. The growth

in national income equals the increase in exports divided by the propensity to import. We can also put it this way: the primary

income effect of exports must be multiplied by $\dfrac{1}{m}$ to find the total income effect. You will not be surprised to learn that this factor $\frac{1}{m}$ is the export multiplier. It is a quantity that is strictly analogous to the factor $\frac{1}{s}$ which we have encountered before, and which shows the amount by which national income increases as the result of an income impulse from increased investments.

This is the Keynesian equilibrium mechanism of the balance of payments. It is obviously something quite different from the classical view. Before further explaining this difference, let us have a look at a circular flow which is subjected not only to the influence of international trade but also to that of saving and investing. In other words, we are adding to the model that was set up in the preceding chapter in all too simple a form.

3 · THE MODEL BECOMES MORE COMPLETE

The results of the last section and those of the preceding chapter can now be combined. We are now starting on the assumption that three kinds of goods are produced by business: consumer goods, which make their way to the households; investment goods, which are sold by the one entrepreneur to the other, and export goods, which disappear over the frontier. This situation is shown in the following diagram. From total production a money income follows that equals $C + I + X$. This money income goes to the households (in so far as it does not remain in the enterprises as their own savings). These households can do three things with it: they can spend the income on home-produced consumer goods, they can spend it on consumer goods produced abroad, or they can save it and then invest it. It emerges from the circulation diagram that the income Y received is divided among C, M, and S.

The circulation is now in equilibrium if business receives as much in return from its customers as it has spent on income. In symbols: $C + I + X = C + S + M$. Or $I + X = S + M$. This equation replaces the oversimple $S = I$ from Chapters III and IV and the oversimple $X = M$ from the last section.

This equation again throws a new light on economic events.

We can see from it how the inflationary impulses from investments and exports have finally to be restrained by deflationary
purchasing power absorptions S and M. Only when the sum of
saving and importing has become large enough to offset the sum
of investing and exporting is national income at rest.

This important mechanism can be illustrated by means of the
multiplier process. Assume an increase in investment activity.

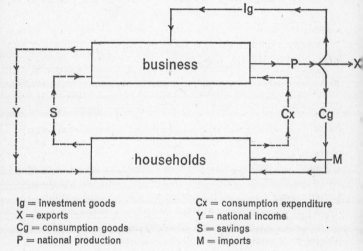

Ig = investment goods   Cx = consumption expenditure
X = exports   Y = national income
Cg = consumption goods   S = savings
P = national production   M = imports

Fig. 5: The circulation including foreign trade

The extra income that results from this finds its way to the households. Insofar as they spend it on additional consumer goods new
revenue is created. But part of the income will also leak away.
This can happen both through imports and through saving. We
therefore see that the extra investments can sometimes lead to
extra imports of consumer goods. It cannot be said in advance
how the extra money will be spent. Only the ultimate apportionment among imports and savings is certain: this is given by the
propensity to save and the propensity to import. Saving and
importing form the leak through which the original increment of
income resulting from investments has flowed away. But not only
the income effect of the investments must flow away through this

leak; the income effect of exports must also be compensated in this way.

In view of this we can now draw up a somewhat more realistic formula for the multiplier. We had originally found a multiplication factor that was equal to $\frac{1}{s}$. This gives an exaggerated impression of the total increase in income. Upon closer examination the double leak proves to lead to the multiplier being equal to $\frac{1}{s+m}$.

For the reader who wants to see this proved: $S + M = I + X$. Since $S = sY$ and $M = mY$, we have $I + X = (s + m)Y$, or $Y = \frac{I + X}{s + m}$. An impulse, either in investments or in exports, ultimately propagates itself in income in accordance with the factor $\frac{1}{s + m}$. Or: the multiplier equals the reciprocal of the sum of the leaks.*

Besides a better view of the multiplier we now have a more realistic outlook on the relation between savings and investments. From the simple Keynesian theory you might gain the impression that a shortage of capital can *never* occur. Every investment begets its 'own' nest-egg – although, for the individual, this marrying-up process may not be relevant. It may be that the savings are formed in an entirely different part of the economic system, so that the original investor cannot make use of them for his financing, but even in that case the savings have come into being all the same. However, it now proves that this naïve Keynesian belief is based on an illusion. A discrepancy can quite easily occur between I and S. Not only *can* it form, it probably *will*. And we can also state the exact size of this discrepancy. For we know that $I + X = S + M$. It follows from this that $I - S = M - X$. The 'savings deficit' is made good by the deficit on the balance of payments.

This somewhat surprising proposition does not only help us better to understand the relationship between saving and investing.

---

* I have assumed here that the average and the marginal propensities are the same.

It also gives us a new theory of the balance of payments. For we find that the balance of payments will be adverse according as more is invested and less saved. The two deficits on the balance of payments and on the capital market belong together like Narcissus and his reflection.

This Keynesian conclusion does not fit into the classical theory. A deficit on the balance of payments is in the classical view hardly within the bounds of possibility in the long run, and certainly not if there is a free rate of exchange. For the country will see its currency become cheap; the foreign customers will again be keen to buy the product of the country in question, and equilibrium of the balance of payments will again be established. But now we see that, whatever the rate of exchange, the balance of payments will permanently continue to display a deficit as long as a marked urge to invest is combined with a low propensity to save.

Anyone who considers the sixteenth- and seventeenth-century mercantilistic theory in this light has a greater appreciation of it than the classicists had. The mercantilists wanted to acquire gold by a favourable balance of payments; the classicists thought that this would not prove successful. Now it seems to us that it would. However, not via the policy of import barriers advocated by the old mercantilists, but by a deliberate regulation of the flow of goods and money. If a country wishes to collect gold, it must make sure that a slight deflation prevails. The savings surplus $S - I$ finds expression in the balance of payments as an export surplus. We could phrase this recommendation to mercantilistically-minded governments differently. We could say: restrict imports, but not by an obtrusive and difficult policy of tariffs or quotas. Do not do so via customs officials and government offices that divide a pre-set quantity of imports among the would-be buyers. Instead, do it via national income. Ensure that the flow of national income is hampered in such a way – we shall see in the next chapter what powerful means of doing this are available – that imports, which depend on Y, remain relatively small. Keeping down national income, in combination with the promotion of exports, proves to be an efficacious means of achieving a favourable balance of payments. But the gold thus obtained has its price. If great care is not taken it is bought with unemployment and idle machines, with too low a production for the home market and with too low a rate of economic growth. In short, with a depression.

However, it is not the sole advantage of the Keynesian theory of the balance of payments that neo-mercantilistic recommendations of dubious value can be derived from it. Its more useful side is that we learn from it why some countries in the post-war years were beset with a constant drain of foreign exchange. The reason for this lay particularly in too great imports, which themselves were caused by too large a national money income, which in its turn can be attributed for the greater part to the necessary expansion of productive capacity, which was inadequately compensated for in its income effects by savings. The ambitious investment programmes – vitally necessary for increasing productive capacity and the productivity of labour, and so increasing prosperity – did not match the insufficient thrift. Or, to put it differently, the sum of consumption and investments was too great. Exports did not go badly, but they were outdone by the imports resulting from the multiplier.*

This inflationary interaction can be understood by the theory outlined here. Consequently we cannot do without it if we are to see what happened in Europe after the war. But that is not the only positive side of modern macro-economics. It also gives us a realistic view of the importance of the rate of exchange. We shall now discuss this.

4 · THE RATE OF EXCHANGE DETHRONED?

It thus proves that the equilibrium of the balance of payments, and also its disequilibrium, can be explained without bringing price relations, and also the rate of exchange as a special price relation, into matters. M is made equal to X, or the sum of M and S is made equal to the sum of I and X, through the movement of

---

* There is, however, a complication. If a country tries to spend more than it can produce the relationship between extra imports and extra income may increase. The goods that cannot be produced are sucked into the economy from outside. In other words: the marginal propensity to import is not a constant; an inflationary gap causes this quantity to rise (and the multiplier to fall).

national income. The movement of prices seems to be completely detached from all this. Now does this mean that the rate of exchange is without the slightest importance for the balance of payments? This would be a premature conclusion. For in the above we have come across a relationship in which the rate of exchange does indeed appear. It is the relationship between exports and the factors which determine the size of these exports.

We may again state that exports depend on two factors. The first is the overall foreign demand. This is a quantity on which a country cannot exert much influence, although nowadays attempts are being made to control the international economic situation by joint consultation. If the size of the total foreign market is given, the question is what share a country will have in these total sales. This depends on the competitive position which that country occupies in respect of other countries, which is composed of three elements: the quality of the product (in relation to what other countries have to offer), the price level of exports in relation to the prices asked by the other countries, and the rate of exchange. In this respect we can therefore say that the rate of exchange helps to determine exports. As exports cause income effects at home, creating direct and indirect employment, income and prosperity, the rate of exchange is an important quantity for the community. It has definitely not been dethroned by the circulation theory, but has been given another place in the system.

A practical conclusion that can be drawn from this relates to the right level of the rate of exchange. The government controls this level. Not if there is a free, fluctuating rate of exchange – this is governed by supply and demand of the currency concerned – but in the event of a fixed rate such as we now have under the Bretton Woods Agreement. Since the governments have to fix this rate of their own currency, an important question arises: is the existing rate the right one? Must it be lowered? That is to say, must the foreign currencies become dearer? This is called devaluation.* Or must the home currency be revalued, that is to say must its price in respect of the foreign currencies be increased?

The answer to these questions, like all political answers, is not

* Not, therefore, to be confused with deflation: a shrinking of the circulation below the point at which the factors of production are in full use.

simple. It does not depend solely on the circulation diagram. But we can learn something from this diagram about answering this question. The first lesson is this: formerly it was believed, following in the footsteps of classical theory, that a deficit on the balance of payments would indicate that the country's own currency is too dear. A country with an adverse balance of payments must devalue to stop the drain of gold and foreign exchange. But this is a misconception. Such a country must not devalue in the first place; it must deflate. This is something quite different. It must ensure that expenditure becomes smaller and that the circulation contracts. Devaluation must be applied if exports stagnate, if unemployment and slackening of effort become endemic in the export sector. It then becomes time to strengthen the competitive position and to give business a helping hand by devaluation. Now flagging exports are not the same as a deficit on the balance of payments. True, the first can lead to the second. But this is not necessarily so. For it may be that a decline in exports leads to a multiplier process through which the income is affected to such an extent that imports shrink. In that case the equilibrium of the balance of payments is not disturbed, but employment decreases. Consequently, it may never be derived from the existence of an equilibrium on the balance of payments that the rate of exchange is at the right level. Even then devaluation may be called for to arouse the national economy out of its lethargy.

The above also implies opposition to the free rate of exchange. Some neo-classicists are proponents of a freely fluctuating rate of exchange determined by supply and demand. The basic idea here is that the equilibria of the balances of payment of the various countries are in that case established automatically. But this opinion is disputable. A country suffering from inflation will display a deficit on the balance of payments. The currency concerned will become abundant on a free market; after all, there is considerable supply, since the importers, who have too large a home market behind them, demand large quantities of foreign currency in exchange for the national medium of payment. The value of the country's own currency drops and drops on the free market; there is a lingering depreciation. As a result, exports will be promoted. But will the deficit on the balance of payments disappear? Not necessarily. For such a country, which is already in an inflationary situation, gets still more income effects to absorb. The swollen circulation has to put up with still more extra impulses from the export sector; the exporters, their workers, and shareholders spend more money than formerly, which spreads as a result of the multiplier. Perhaps inflation gallops even harder. And moreover – this is an aspect of the matter to which we shall return – the prices of import goods rise as a result of the devaluation. If this increase in prices hits a market which is already under tension, it will merely strengthen inflation. Perhaps commerce makes larger profits – and profits form incomes which are spent, which encourage investments which in turn evoke new income effects. The free rate of exchange can hurl the country that was previously in a tense (Hayek) situation into the chaos of an uncontrollable inflation. In that case it is a destabilizing factor, not one establishing equilibrium. The free rate of exchange would have been fatal to countries such as France under the Fourth Republic, and to a lesser extent to Britain, which have difficulty with their domestic circulatory equilibrium. At least, so it would seem to me; others think differently about it. Whether flexible rates of exchange are advisable or not is a rather controversial matter.

5 · THE INTERNATIONAL ECONOMY

The approach applied above may also be of use when examining the community of nations. True, we have concentrated on the national economy, but we have found that this is linked via imports and exports to other countries. The strategic relations are the following: the exports of a country depend above all on the income abroad; imports depend above all on the country's own national income. (As the country's own national income depends on exports, imports also depend on exports.) Now these relations lead to the international propagation of the trade cycle. When a deflationary disturbance occurs in a country, the incomes of the suppliers in other countries are threatened, which can continue to have its effect via the multiplier. In this way, therefore, the one country has a considerable interest in a balanced development in other countries.

This is not a new discovery, but it lends a new urgency to the desirability of international cooperation. Economists have long pointed out that prosperity is harmed when countries protect themselves against imports from other countries by import duties and quotas. Not only the prosperity of the supplying countries – but their own as well. A protectionist country everywhere damages the international division of labour, and consequently productivity. This classical train of thought is quite correct, and it is only a pity that the obstinacy with which economists defended it was often surpassed by the energy with which industrial and agricultural interests opposed it. But the modern circulation theory also shows that import duties and quantitative restrictions are not the only obstacles in the path of international trade. At least as serious are the disturbances in the pattern of trade caused by reductions in purchasing power. They can dislocate trade and harm prosperity even more than protectionism.

The threat that emanates from a retarded growth of the neighbour's income is felt more strongly by some countries than by others. A high ratio of X/Y easily leads to an ideology in which free trade, international cooperation, and a joint cyclical policy are regarded as urgent. This quotient, which is approximately equal to m, characterizes the economic openness of a country. The Netherlands, long a free trade country, has an m that is now about 55 per cent. Other countries have much lower quotients: the United States has one of less than 5 per cent, and for this reason alone it is understandable that the American ideology of free trade is occasionally criss-crossed by protectionist measures (for instance by bans on the importing of Swiss watches or Dutch cheese).

The parties most interested in an international trade which is not threatened by disturbances in purchasing power are the developing nations. Their gigantic problems, which are not otherwise dealt with in this book, become completely insoluble if their exports, vulnerable as they already are, are harmed by a recession in the world's purchasing power. The losses of foreign exchange that result can easily be several times greater than the foreign aid received. Even if there should be absolutely no other reason for a Neo-Keynesian policy than the needs of the developing countries, such a policy should still receive high priority.

European integration is also related to the problems outlined here. As the interlocking of the economies of Western Europe proceeds and the trade between the various countries grows, the interest that these countries have in each other's economic equilibrium becomes greater. It is simply not tolerable that one of the countries should let a depression seep through: this would place the partners in great difficulties. Conversely, an inflationary process also forms a danger, since an inflationary economy drains off too many imports without being able to pay for them in the long run; if M constantly remains higher than X, a country is compelled to take restrictive measures which are against the spirit of integration and which could ultimately destroy the common market.

Opinions may differ about the practical conclusions which must be drawn from the above. Some believe that the cyclical policy in the countries of Western Europe must be directed from a central point (Brussels), or at least they want to go very far with the international coordination of national policy. Others are of the opinion that the national cyclical policy can continue to exist, provided that it is followed in an effective way. Personally, I tend towards the latter view. Balanced international relations must be based on balances of payment in equilibrium, which in their turn can be traced back to domestic equilibria in the creation and the spending of the national income. Promoting the latter is the task of the national governments, who for that purpose select their own instruments as far as possible. Only if they fail in that policy must they be corrected by other countries and international bodies. To put it another way: strong international pressure groups must be created which advocate a sound economic policy.

It is now time to consider this political side more closely. To do so we must introduce into the circulation a component that so far has not been considered: the government. This will be done in the next chapter.

CHAPTER VI

The Role of the Budget

1 · GOVERNMENT EXPENDITURE, TAXES, AND NATIONAL INCOME

We started with a particularly simple flow of incomes and expenditure, in which only consumer goods were produced. After this, investment, i.e. the production of capital goods, was brought on the scene, and we found that with this complications entered which finally led to Keynesian theory. This was then applied to a third kind of goods: export goods. We are now coming to a fourth category which again is admirably suited to a Keynesian analysis. This category is formed by the 'products' of the government.

The word products is between inverted commas. The question whether the government does or does not produce anything has long been the subject of controversy and doubt. The nineteenth-century classicists – and this opinion was held in particular by J. B. Say – denied that government activity was productive. As the government unmistakably employs factors of production – especially labour – such a view leads to the conclusion that this is a pure waste, which must be restricted as much as possible. Even now the idea is often encountered that the government is really unproductive.

The idea is of course untenable. The government has a number of absolutely essential functions. To fulfil these it must employ productive forces. These have a certain productivity, and they produce something. The only question is what this 'something' is exactly. It is a peculiar and moreover heterogeneous product. Some parts of it are just as tangible as the products of business – the coal of the British National Coal Board (but this is not a proper example, for the mines can also be operated by private enterpreneurs). Part of the government's productive output is not tangible, but nevertheless is visible: services of roads, parks, national theatres. But the most characteristic are the extremely tenuous but nevertheless very real products such as legal security, well-regulated traffic, the right supply of money, a balance of payments in equilibrium and full employment, social security and social welfare, and the like. If all is well, these ethereal things are promoted or produced by the government. They form a 'product'. We do not need to philosophize further on this, except

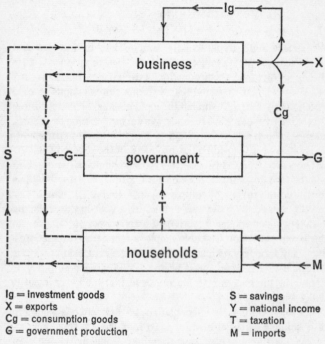

Ig = investment goods
X = exports
Cg = consumption goods
G = government production

S = savings
Y = national income
T = taxation
M = imports

Fig. 6: The circulation including foreign trade and the government economy

in one single respect. Much of government output is characterized by the property that it cannot be sold on the market to consumers. For only a minor part of the product can payment be demanded in the form of fees from those most directly concerned. This does not apply to the greater part; the product is not marketable. It is also called 'collective'. Payment has to be regulated in another way: via the levying of taxes.

The reader must bear these well-known matters in mind for a moment, for they are most relevant to Keynesian theory. While C flows to the households and meets half-way a flow of money heading for business, the government product, which we shall call G, goes differently. G leaves the government, which we therefore regard as a production economy (but which we draw separately in the figure, because it is so special) at the top right, but then does not make for the market for consumer goods. This flow of output is scattered far and wide; it is distributed for the general good, *urbi et orbi*, for the households and for business. But meanwhile a money income has been created, equal in size to G, which ends up in the hands of the factors of production. They cannot spend it on the government product, for that is not for sale. They therefore have too much money. If they were to spend it on consumer goods, there would be inflation.

This situation is the twin of the one which we have encountered with reference to exports. There too we have the making of a product that disappears. The recipients of income who have helped to create it cannot spend their income on the export goods, and they cannot fully spend it on consumer goods produced at home – for $C + X$ is of course larger than C. Too much spending seems unavoidable. But then imports come to the rescue and check this inflation. Something similar happens with the relation between saving and investing. There too we have a product that does not come on the market for consumer goods and an income that therefore cannot be spent on consumer goods. And there too we have a compensatory, deflationary flow of money: S. This striking analogy is the starting point of the modern theory of public finance.

The deflationary flow of money that must compensate for G is the taxation T.* T is drawn off by the tax authorities from the flow of income Y. It does not make much difference to circulation analysis where exactly this happens (though it most certainly does to other problems – such as the position of the taxpayers!). Various places are conceivable. In the figure only

---

* The Exchequer has other forms of income than real taxes; fees, fines, profits from state concerns. The first two categories are included in T; the state concerns are usually put under the business sector. For they produce a marketable product that is paid for over the counter.

one has been drawn: the income goes from business to the households, from where part of it is led to the Exchequer; this is the flow of money T.

Now the reasoning which we learned earlier can again be applied to these quantities. As long as the inflationary components I, X, and G – which create incomes but no consumer goods for the home market – cause national income to swell more than the deflationary components S, M, and T – which use up these incomes without affecting home demand – hold it down, the entrepreneurs will continue to receive more from the households and the investors than they spend. This surplus is again translated into income, and this increases the flow of money. National income is in equilibrium only when $I + X + G = S + M + T$. It becomes manifest that saving, importing, and paying taxes have the same effect on the circulation, however different they may be in their importance to the national economy or to individuals.

And a second proposition comes to the fore. The size of national income depends not only on saving and investing, but also on the other components. An extra impulse in investments creates not only savings, but also imports; and now we find that taxes may also result from it. The same applies to government expenditure. If this increases, one of four things happens: savings increase as a result, or imports, or consumption, or taxes. In practice all four happen, until such time as national income has once more found its equilibrium value. The circulation is then again at rest. The proportions in which the income effect is divided among the four uses to which income is put are given by the ratio between the propensity to save, the propensity to import, and the 'propensity to tax' or tax rate.

The latter is a new element; it is usually called 'tax burden'. There is an analogy with the propensity to save s and the propensity to import m. It is defined as $\dfrac{T}{Y}$. The marginal tax burden $t = \dfrac{\Delta T}{\Delta Y}$ shows how much taxes increase for a given change in Y.

These fractions are fixed by the recipients of income, but in a manner quite different from the way in which the propensities s

and m are fixed. They do this as citizens; via the electoral system, Parliament, and the Cabinet they ensure that t is expressed in fiscal laws. A noteworthy feature of this is that these laws do not provide for a given tax revenue T. Whilst in general the appropriation acts state how large government expenditure G may be, there is no such system regarding taxes. These come about via the effect of the multiplier. The law fixes the tax rates and T then follows from Y. Incidentally, the marginal tax burden is higher than the average; this comes from the progression. So t is not a constant but depends on Y.

Now that we have finally got the government inside the circulation, we can state the real value of the multiplier. Everything that has been said about it so far has been a preliminary exercise, which may have a misleading effect because it suggests to the reader much too high an estimate of the multiplier. In fact the following reasoning is the only complete one: if national income is in equilibrium, $I + X + G = S + M + T$. An income impulse given either by exports, or by government expenditure, or by investments, therefore leads to an increment of national income that is $\dfrac{1}{s + m + t}$ times as large. This is the multiplier. It is much smaller than the reader who has stopped at $\dfrac{1}{s}$ might think.

There are many remarkable views on taxes, some correct, others less so. One of these, which in my opinion is correct, should be mentioned here, because it is rarely heard: taxes do not form a burden for the community, and therefore the term tax burden is misleading. This sounds incredible. Everyone who has to pay tax sees as a result his spendable income decrease, and does this then not hold good for the whole?

The answer is no. This is best illustrated by assuming that one day taxes are suddenly abolished while G is maintained. In that case spendable incomes would increase, but if full employment had already been achieved, no extra real income would result. Tremendous over-expenditure would occur, which would drive up prices, to the detriment of those whose incomes would not rise so quickly. The burden would be shifted from the taxpayers to the victims of the increased prices. For in fact it is not taxes that cause a sacrifice to be made, but the use of the factors of production by the government; as a result of this the product is sacrificed that otherwise could have been made with that work and that capital. Against that cost we have the government product. Taxes do not form an extra burden, but are only an instrument for dividing the cost among the members of the community in a fairer manner than the increase in prices would otherwise have done, and at the same time they serve to keep the circulation of money within bounds. The fact that taxes do not form a sacrifice – unless they become so high that they harm the real income, which happens in a depression – is one of the curiosities and apparent paradoxes which characterize macro-economics. Taxes demonstrate once more that macro-economics and micro-economics must not be confused with one another.

2 · BUDGETARY EQUILIBRIUM

By budget we mean below the confrontation of T and G. We are therefore ignoring for a moment the fact that the appropriation acts contain only predictions of T and authorizations regarding G, whilst in the circulation this 'paper' side of the matter does not count as much as the actual development of the flow of money. We say that the budget is in equilibrium when $T = G$. This differs from the usage followed by some to the extent that tax revenue (in the broad sense, i.e. including other current government income) must equal *total* government expenditure; often the budget is said to be in equilibrium if T equals the 'current' part of G. According to some, government investments ought to or might be paid for out of loans, not out of taxes. Behind this there lies a profound difference of opinion about the way in which the government ought to finance its activities, a difference of opinion that will not be discussed until later. Let us say for the time being that we speak of budgetary equilibrium when there is no borrowing at all, but all expenditure is covered by current government income T. The national debt in that case is constant.

The position of this budgetary equilibrium in the Keynesian theory is a strange one. An illustration of this is to be found in a model which again is very simple in set-up; true, there is government expenditure and income, but we ignore foreign trade and also saving and investing. Production consists of consumer goods and government services. The recipient of income can do only two things with his income: consume or pay taxes. (A strange situation, but no stranger than a situation as discussed in our simple model: there, money was saved, but no taxes were paid. And taxes are even more difficult to think away than savings. But let us try it all the same and place ourselves in that strange world in which C and G form the national product.)

If it is decided in this simple model to increase government expenditure (for instance, new civil servants are engaged to alleviate the difficult existence of those civil servants already employed), whilst the fiscal laws remain unchanged, the uninitiated would predict a deficit on the budget. For G becomes larger than T. But the reader of these pages, who is gradually being transformed into a Keynesian, knows better. He sees how new income is created (the new civil servants, who have just left school and so have not been withdrawn from the production of consumer goods, receive a salary); he sees how this income is used to purchase consumer goods which were not demanded before; he sees the receipts of business increase, and with them national income; in short, he predicts a multiplier process. This will end when the new flow of income is compensated by the increment of tax revenue. We consequently see that the Treasury will attain a new equilibrium, although government expenditure has increased while the tax burden has remained constant. Only the Keynesian is not surprised by this. He knew that ΔG would lead to ΔT, just as (in the simple situation in which all that happens is consumption, saving and investing) ΔI leads to ΔS. This relation is already of practical importance in that it weakens a certain view of budgetary equilibrium. The idea has occasionally been put forward that equilibrium between government income and expenditure cannot have an inflationary effect. But that is not so, any more than it is true to say that $S = I$ provides a guarantee against inflation. For it is quite possible that the higher tax revenue has come about only by the grace of a swelling of income; a swelling of income which has perhaps brought national income to the right of the celebrated point W from Fig. 3 (p. 69). In that case that was an inflationary swelling of income. Likewise a balanced budget is no guarantee against too large or too small national expenditure.

Let us now return to the more realistic representation of the circulation of money, in which business and the government together produce consumer goods, export goods, investment goods, and government services. Will there also be an automatic tendency towards a balanced budget in this? The answer is in the negative: for we know only that the sum of taxes, imports, and savings will equal the sum of government expenditure, exports, and investments. But the system does not establish any particular equalities between S and I (capital market), M and X (balance of payments), and T and G (budget). These equalities can be disturbed one by one, while the total system is nevertheless in equilibrium. And more than that: the disturbance of the one equilibrium leads to a disturbance of equilibrium elsewhere. Applied to that part of the system with which we are concerned in this chapter, this means that the budget will get out of balance if $S + M$ does not equal $I + X$. If there is a lot of saving and a lot of importing, the tax revenue drops. If there is a lot of investing and a lot of exporting, it rises, without anything necessarily having happened to the tax burden.

We can also turn this way of thinking round. What does a balanced budget mean? It means that the sum of savings and imports is equal to the sum of investments and exports. Is it desirable for the budget to be in equilibrium? We do not know; at least it is not evident from this relation. For why should an equilibrium between these two sums be so desirable? If budgetary equilibrium is an aim worth striving after, it is certainly not due to this relation! From the point of view of economic balance, the equality of government income and government expenditure is of no particular importance.

In classical theory, which still governs many minds, this is quite different. There the balanced budget is a golden rule, which may be departed from only in so far as productive investments are financed by long-term loans (or, in exceptional cases, in so far as surpluses are created by means of which the national debt is redeemed). This, too, is understandable. For the national economy that the classicists had in mind is characterized by full use of the productive forces. Moreover, in that economy there is equilibrium of the balance of payments; the rate of exchange attends to that. And there is equilibrium between saving and investing; the rate of interest attends to that. In these circumstances government expenditure must also be covered by government income. If tax revenue is less than government expenditure, inflation rears its ugly head (unless the government drains off so much capital from private investments that the latter decrease). The particular equilibria between X and M on the one hand and S and I on the other hand render necessary such a government policy that T equals G.

The Keynesian theory does not believe in all these particular relations. For in fact they need not be realized. The total of taxes, savings, and imports is brought into equilibrium with the total of the inflationary components by the multiplier. This overall equilibrium does not imply a balanced budget.

And yet Keynesian theory, like the classical one, lays down rules for the budget. It is these rules that form the essence of Keynesian policy. In their more orthodox form they are known by the name of Functional Finance: a term which some politicians, late adherents of the classical school, unknowing adepts of the theory of particular equilibria, identify with (at choice): pernicious modernism, irresponsible extravagance, too much power in the hands of the authorities, the fanaticism of intellectuals with their heads in the clouds, the imposition of an excessive burden on later generations by a national debt run wild, inflation, opening the door to a depression, chaos, communism, and dictatorship. Let us have a look at this.

3 · FUNCTIONAL FINANCE

The essence of the new rules for public finance can best be understood if for a moment we ignore international trade, which in any case did not play an important part in the original Keynesianism. The overall demand for goods and services is then made up of consumption expenditure, investment, and government expenditure, $C + I + G$. The production resulting from this must be such that it exactly occupies the available productive capacity, no more and no less. The equilibrium must satisfy the requirement that the point W in Fig. 3 (p. 69) is reached: the True

Equilibrium, also characterized by the absence of inflation and deflation. The national money income is then at its best level. This point does not come into being of its own accord; it is not a 'natural' equilibrium. The government has to create it. There are two instruments available for doing so: government expenditure and the tax burden. These quantities must be so manipulated that the national economy displays an optimum total expenditure. This manipulating of public finance is called Functional Finance. This expression comes from one of Keynes's most fervent followers, A. P. Lerner,* who has repeatedly advocated this policy.

There are thus two instruments: t and G. Since it is confusing to discuss both of them at the same time, we shall assume for a moment that the tax burden is given, and that the circulation is therefore regulated by varying government expenditure. This was also the idea that most occupied Keynes himself; the extent of government expenditure could be varied by performing or postponing public works. An old idea – it already occurs in the nineteenth century – but one that has acquired a theoretical foundation through the new macro-economics.

The extent of government expenditure needed for full employment can be established without difficulty by means of our simple model. The equilibrium in the model is determined by $C + I$ (see page 69). If this sum of private expenditure and investment after deduction of tax is too small to yield full employment, G must fill the gap. But not all of the gap; there is also a multiplier. G should be made equal to the deficit in expenditure divided by the multiplier.

On the other side, the total tax revenue is equal to the average tax burden times Y and it is improbable that this amount equals G; this would be so only by chance. The budget will therefore not be balanced. In the case that we have in mind there is a deficit on the budget. If Members of Parliament should criticize the Chancellor of the Exchequer for this, he can refer to the rules of Functional Finance. However, he must be prepared for a question which will also have entered the reader's thoughts: what about the increase in the national debt that results from this budgetary deficit? Is this increase an innocent one, or even desirable? Or

* In his article 'Functional Finance and the Federal Debt', in: *Social Research*, 1943.

does it threaten the national economy in some way or the other? We shall try to answer these questions in the next section, just as ministers sometimes ask for notice of a question.

Meanwhile we can consider the case in which $C + I$ does not yield a deflationary situation but an inflationary one. Negative government expenditure is hard to conceive of; we must seek the recovery of equilibrium in the taxes. Let us start from a given government expenditure G.

The problem then is to get rid of the inflationary gap. This can be done by drawing off income by extra taxes. This will lead to a budgetary surplus that makes up for the overexpenditure.

Up to now t and G have been examined separately. But the new rules for public finance have the most point if they are applied to the income side and the expenditure side together. For instance, a depression can be eliminated by a combination of tax cuts, which cause $C + I$ to increase, and increased expenditure. The aim, the right size of $C + I + G$, can then be more easily achieved than by manipulating t and G separately.

This is Functional Finance in outline. No budgetary equilibrium, but a deliberate manipulation of t and G which compensates for the surplus or deficit of the expenditure of households and business. The government no longer aims at a balanced budget, but at a balanced national economy. Public finance becomes the great regulator of activity.

But is this possible just like that? Does an unbalanced budget not mean that there is danger of inflation? This question is too complicated to be fully answered at this stage. For complications can arise from the national debt and the stock of money, subjects with which we have not yet dealt. But we can even now refute the popular misconception that a deficit on the budget must *per se* lead to inflation. As long as the equilibrium lies to the left of W (Fig. 3, p. 69) and too little is being spent, a certain degree of reflation is desirable. This is precisely the aim of Functional Finance: reflation, increased expenditure, increased production, the re-employment of productive forces. Activity must be so encouraged that it arrives precisely at the point W. If it goes any further, there is inflation, and Functional Finance must again come to the assistance to combat this evil. Precision work is therefore demanded of the government, and we may shortly ask ourselves whether governments are capable of doing this. But in this more theoretical stage of the reasoning there is no harm in this. The aim of Functional Finance is to prevent inflation, not to invoke it.

The new rules also give us a new look at the function of taxes. It is obvious to assume that these serve to fill the Exchequer, and to make it possible for the Chancellor of the Exchequer to put at the disposal of his colleagues in office the funds required for government expenditure. But this view is too unsophisticated for the Keynesians. Taxes serve to keep total expenditure within bounds. The government can always get hold of money – by borrowing and if necessary making some. But it has to take care that the nation's expenditure stays at the right level, that $C + I + G$ stays within the limits set by the factors of production.

This new view has something refreshing about it. It seems simplicity itself. But we shall see that a number of complications have been omitted from it. We shall now consider the first of these. It is the question of the national debt which the government owes its subjects.

4 · THE NATIONAL DEBT

The reproach that Functional Finance causes the national debt to increase immoderately can be parried by pointing out that the budget will not always display a deficit to fulfil its regulatory function. There are times when total expenditure threatens to display a deficit, so that a budgetary deficit must keep the circulation going; but then there are other times in which a budgetary surplus is required to protect the national economy against inflation. In the cyclical fluctuations the public debt varies, but it in no way needs to be constantly increasing. The permanent increase of the debt does not fit into the doctrine of Functional Finance as such, but rather into the stagnation theory, that is to say the view that expenditure in the private sector will constantly be too small for productive capacity. But the stagnation theory has been abandoned; the experience of the post-war years has shown that inflation can be at least as obstinate as deflation.

From the fluctuation of deficits and surpluses on the budget some economists, influenced rather by Keynes, have deduced that the budget does not need so much to be in equilibrium over a period of one year (the normal duration of a budget) as over a whole business cycle. Budgetary equilibrium thus remains the norm, but the period changes. The budget period must really comprise a whole business cycle. In this way an attempt has been made to reconcile Keynesian budget policy with the classical one. Just as happens with such well-meaning compromises, the theory of the anticyclical budget has brought little enlightenment and has confused minds to a not inconsiderable extent. The train of thought seems to be connected with the concept of regularly returning waves in economic life, waves which in length and amplitude display a uniform and thus predictable rhythm. This is the favourite idea of the old-fashioned cyclical theory. In actual fact economic life does fluctuate, but the waves are not nearly so regular and above all not nearly so predictable that a government could base a budget policy on them. Anyone who has been concerned with the practice of an anticyclical policy will shake his head at so theoretical a set-up. And if in addition the idea of a budget covering several years is attached, whereby expenditure must be specified for a number of years ahead, it requires little imagination to hear the bitter laughter of the civil servants and the politicians, who already have trouble enough with the one-year budget. This is quite apart from the difficulty that nobody can estimate where exactly a country is in the business cycle at the moment when this system is introduced.

The proponents of the long-term anticyclical budget have therefore done modern views of financial policy a disservice. They have distracted attention from the fact that Functional Finance directs the Chancellor of the Exchequer to act every year as he thinks fit, to accept fluctuations in the public debt as long as they do not exceed all bounds, and not to worry about the periodicity of what is believed to be a business cycle.

But when does the national debt exceed all bounds?

A very widespread view on this is the following. The national debt imposes on posterity the burden of interest and redemption. It may therefore be contracted only if posterity inherits not only the increased debt, but also the government investments which can cover the extra expenditure with their profit-earning ability.

It is often said that a generation that does not follow this principle robs its children of their future. And in this respect a further distinction can be made between the very strict view that money should be borrowed only if the investments concerned can show a profit from the point of view of business economics – such as an electricity works, a railway line, a swimming bath – and the somewhat more flexible idea that it suffices if the general productivity of the country has increased through the investments – e.g. roads and bridges. Feelings have often run high in debates between the strict and the flexible. At this moment they interest us less; for both groups of debaters are wrong.

The first mistake they make is to think that the national debt as such represents a burden on posterity. An internal debt means that the government must pay interest and redemption to some of its subjects after other subjects have furnished these sums. Money is transferred from the pockets of the one to the pockets of the other. As the state's taxpayers and credits form part of the same national economy and of the same generation, the national economy as a whole does not become any poorer or any richer from the transfer. It may not therefore be said that an increase in the national debt burdens posterity. This cuts away the ground from under the moralistic view of the balanced budget. This view regards the public debt too much on the analogy of a private debt. It confuses macro-economics with micro-economics.*

The misunderstanding regarding the 'burden' is a particularly obstinate one. Many regard the refutation of it as a sophism. Perhaps the following will help. Our heirs will have to live under a burdened government; that is unpleasant for them. But at the same time they inherit the government bonds. This compensates for their distress. In a certain sense the one cancels the other out.

---

* However, in classical theory the idea that the creation of a government debt puts a burden on future generations may be defended as follows: I depends on S. If the government borrows parts of present savings, present investment will suffer and therefore future labour productivity and welfare will suffer also. This is only acceptable if government investments are increased. In other words: in classical theory government should borrow only for investment purposes. This moral prescription collapses if we drop the view that I depends on S. It should also be noted that in this classical view the burden on our children is not caused by the *existence* of a public debt but by its *creation*; an important distinction that is often lost sight of.

Anyone wishing to debate with supporters of the naïve burden theory can use this argument. He can say – jokingly – that the present generation could greatly favour posterity by considerably increasing the public debt. For our children are enriched by securities which provide an income without their having to work for it. But I fear that the opposite party will go home with the feeling that they have been done.

There is a second reason for criticizing the prejudiced view that the government debt will *per se* burden later generations. Even if this debt should cause difficulties in the future – this can very easily be the case, though for other reasons than the naïve burden theory assumes – then it should be borne in mind that a deficit on the government account yields benefits which need not consist in the profit-earning ability of the capital goods purchased by the government. For the theory of Functional Finance teaches us that the extra government spending keeps the circulation going. This means that consumption is higher than it would have been. But it also means that private investments are higher; for, as we have seen, these depend on consumption, and even to a somewhat greater extent (acceleration). Owing to the budgetary deficit not only is national income saved from a decline, but also the expansion of productive capacity can continue. Without a deficit on the budget later generations might perhaps get a smaller stock of capital goods; the productivity of labour and prosperity would be harmed by this. In return for the greater national debt we have not only the inheritance of a bundle of government securities but at the same time something that is much more important: a larger national income in the future. Quite apart from the specific projects which the government financed with the loans! These have nothing to do with the matter; in principle they cannot even be pointed to any longer. There is no connexion between the budgetary deficit and certain detailed items of expenditure; there is only the macro-economic connexion between the deficit on the budget and the too small total expenditure $C + I$, which we want to remedy.

Perhaps the compliant reader has now gradually come to the conclusion that the size of the internal national debt is completely immaterial. After all, he reasons, it merely entails a transfer of money from one pocket to another, which does not make the national economy any richer or any poorer. But once again, things are not as simple as that.

For this transfer has certain consequences. The taxpayer forks out more money to provide his fellow-citizens with interest and redemption, and his reaction to this may perhaps be less enterprise. Too great a transfer of income and capital also causes a decrease in the propensity to save, and thus makes the national economy less proof against a future threatening inflation. Sometimes the new government bonds are difficult to place, and the government must have recourse to short-term debts, which may also entail a tendency towards future inflation. And finally a big national debt is just the thing to create in the minds of its holders the illusion that they are richer than they actually are. The national debt may not make the community poorer, but it certainly does not make it richer. And if the state's creditors are given a false feeling of wealth, there is a chance that the propensity to save will suffer, again with inflationary consequences. (The latter is sometimes called the Lerner effect of the public debt.)

It is therefore evident from this short summary of the drawbacks of too large a national debt that the latter's size is not entirely immaterial. However, it is something quite different if this debt is regarded as a burden because it seems to weigh heavily from a micro-economic point of view, which it does not, or because it can create monetary problems in the future, which it may. The first is a misunderstanding, the second a real difficulty, although the extent of this difficulty must not be exaggerated. All the same, a Chancellor of the Exchequer may not forget this side of the matter. For this reason alone Functional Finance is a less simple matter than is occasionally suggested. There are still other reasons for this; they will be discussed later (Chapter XII, section 2).

5 · THE HAAVELMO EFFECT

Before we leave the government and its part in the circulation for the time being – however important this subject has been ever since Keynes – one more remarkable aspect will be elucidated. This is what is called the Haavelmo effect, which forms a bone of contention for a number of economists.

T. Haavelmo* has investigated what happens if the government increases its expenditure and at the same time increases the tax burden to such an extent that the additional expenditure is covered right from the start by extra government income. This is therefore a tax policy that appeals to many adherents of the classical school, and one that also seems sensible in a period in which the Chancellor of the Exchequer often finds it difficult to resist political pressure for increased expenditure – a situation which many a postwar Minister of Finance knows all about. Even in such a situation it may help sometimes if a Parliament which is in the mood for extra spending on all kinds of fine and useful things is told that it will at the same time have to find the additional revenue. The members then will sometimes shrink back from what at first seemed so attractive. But let us now assume that Parliament is consistent and puts up the necessary funds: t is raised so far that ΔG is compensated by ΔT; not after the multiplier has first done its inflationary work, but right from the start. In economic jargon: ΔT is equal *ex ante* to ΔG. What is the position now?

At first sight it seems clear and obvious. It is tempting to reason as follows: extra government expenditure has been added. This has created extra income with respect to the (let us say) newly engaged civil servants. Now if nothing else happened the money income would have increased by ΔG, plus the multiplier effect of this. But things do not get so far. For the extra incomes are at once taken back again in the form of a tax increase. The budget remains in equilibrium. The total expenditure of income remains the same, and so do total employment and total production. But the nature of the production changes. First a certain amount of consumer and investment goods was produced; this amount has been contracted by the extra tax levied. It has been replaced by the production of an additional government product which does not come on the market but is paid for via the extra taxes.

If I understand Haavelmo's theorem aright, it is particularly useful in uttering a warning against this apparently obvious reasoning. For it is wrong. If you pay close attention to the circulatory effects of taxes and government expenditure, you must

* 'Multiplier Effects of a Balanced Budget', *Econometrica*, 1945.

conclude that national income *has* changed in size and employment too. For just look at the income that gets into the hands of the households. It first had a certain size. To this was added the extra government expenditure; at the same time a corresponding amount was drawn off in the form of extra taxes. This therefore means that after the whole operation the households receive exactly the same sum as before. True, this sum is divided differently among them; the new civil servants have an income that they did not have at first; the taxpayers retain a correspondingly smaller spendable income. But the total income that can be used for consumption (and saving) is the same. It is thus possible, and even probable, that the total consumption expenditure in the private sector will also remain the same. And for the same reason private investments will not need to fall. The production of C and I goods is therefore the same as before, as is employment in private business. But in the government sector employment has increased, as has the production of the collective product. Total employment has thus been increased to the extent of the additional government expenditure. The national product has also increased; for whilst $C + I$ remained the same, a piece of ΔG was added. Although the extra government spending has at once been made up for by higher taxes, economic activity has still increased. This is the Haavelmo effect.

The perceptive reader will note that this reasoning is based on a particular assumption, viz. that the newly engaged civil servants previously had no employment, and that the paper on which they write, the desks at which they sit, and the coconut matting on the official staircase can be produced by productive forces previously unused. If this is not the case, and if the factors of production have to be taken off other assignments, then ΔG no longer leads to ΔY. The one income is then substituted for the other, the total flow of income to the families does not increase, and the increased tax burden takes a bite out of it. The spendable income of the families is then smaller, and so are private consumption and private investments.

Now what is the practical importance of the Haavelmo effect? It means that a depression can be remedied by the government even without a budgetary deficit. Employment can increase even without uncovered expenditure being incurred: if the level of the budget is raised, however balanced it may be. Even if public works are performed and these are covered by taxes, employment increases. Of course it would have increased more if taxes had not been raised or even lowered; but even a balanced budget increase has a reflationary effect.

There is something else that we can learn from the Haavelmo effect. In a depression a government should preferably not reduce its total expenditure. Even if it were to make the tax burden lighter at the same time, the result would still be wrong. This would indeed be spoiling the ship for a ha'porth of tar.

The significance of Haavelmo's discovery can also be defined as follows. It was formerly believed – and is still believed by many today – that the government only increases activity via a budgetary deficit or cuts it back via a budgetary surplus. Now we see that not only deficits and surpluses but also changes in the *level* of the budget are of importance to total expenditure. A considerable change in views, in other words.

6 · IS FUNCTIONAL FINANCE A DANGER?

When I first made the acquaintance of Keynes's theory while I was a student, it made a deep impression on me – an impression which is still to be seen in this book. It was not so much the equality of *I* and *S*, which in those days was regarded as one of the most striking aspects, as the political view of government finance that seemed strange to me. At the time governments all over the world were struggling to get out of the depression. Economy was recommended, a stable financial policy seemed more than ever essential, every penny counted. And suddenly, in a short book written by a friend of Keynes and a fervent admirer of the new theory,* it was being asserted that the best possible way of getting out of the depression was a nice big budgetary deficit! It seemed to be an unprecedented breach of the sacrosanct financial rules, a policy that could only lead to disaster. True, in Germany Schacht was already busy putting such recommendations into practice, but this merely strengthened the impression that the whole affair was extremely suspect.

If I see matters aright, this feeling still governs the thoughts of

* Joan Robinson, *Introduction to the Theory of Unemployment*, 1938.

many. The budgetary deficit seems such an apocryphal means of economic progress that it is not easily accepted, particularly by the world of finance. Whilst Keynes's theory has on the one hand brought economic theory closer to the businessman's problems – sales have always formed a problem for business; they did not form one for economics until Say's Law was abandoned – he has alienated the financier and the banker. And the businessman too has his qualms. The business community wants stability, and as far as the government is concerned this seems to be embodied in the balanced budget, which moreover must be a limited budget. High government expenditure imposes a burden on the nation that the latter cannot bear in bad times especially. And so, keep the budget small and keep it balanced. And now we see Keynes and Lerner recommending the opposite, and Haavelmo adding his bit. Small wonder that Keynesianism has a bad name with many.

And yet these prejudices cannot endure if they are soberly examined. For what does a so-called prudent policy lead to in a depression? To an intensification of the deflationary gap. It is worth while examining this somewhat more closely.

Let us assume that economic life is suffering from a deficiency of demand. Consumption and investments are bringing the entrepreneurs an insufficient return. They cut down on production, whilst the national income was low enough as it was. As a result of this tax revenue falls off. The government sees a deficit come about, so that those who are firm believers in budgetary equilibrium urge that expenditure be cut. This thrift makes the situation worse, especially by the Haavelmo effect. Lower government expenditure means still lower incomes for the households. Moreover, a multiplier comes into action. Since total expenditure shrinks still further, the profit-earning ability of the investments decreases, and there is every danger of these investments decreasing further. Perhaps the accelerator comes into operation. The result is still lower incomes (again propagated by the multiplier), which in turn lead to lower tax revenue. And so we get a renewed insistence on cuts in government expenditure.

This cumulative process of income, expenditure, and tax shrinkage leads to poverty and unemployment. It could have been stopped if the government had deliberately tossed the sham stability overboard and had increased expenditure and reduced taxes. True, the national debt would have grown. A number of financiers who could not get used to the new idea would have become nervous. In their clubs they would have spread the idea that the economic setbacks were now going to culminate in a disastrous government policy. Perhaps this gloomy idea would also have infected a number of entrepreneurs, who for this reason would lose still more of their already limited enthusiasm for making new investments. This is then the only real thing that we have encountered so far in the negative consequences of Keynesian policy; for a drop in investments has a depressive effect on the circulation. But readiness to invest is not only a matter of psychology. The businessmen who left their clubs with much headshaking might perhaps note the first repercussions of the budgetary deficits once they had returned to their offices: higher sales, caused by the higher incomes. Given a correct application of Functional Finance, their profit and loss account will refute the club's gloom. The reality of the accounts department will in the long run probably overcome the unfounded pessimism of the world of finance.

Now we were talking about a depression. The recommendations of Functional Finance at a time of inflation encounter less intellectual resistance, but all the same they are often not fully understood. For in such circumstances a high level of taxes is the means of keeping the swollen demand for goods, services, and the factors of production within bounds. The world of finance has no objection to this in itself, although it is conceivable that some grumbling will be heard here and there about the possibility that the real blame for the inflation lies in the Keynesian theory – the stagnation theory usually being meant. But the high taxes that are necessary in the boom encounter criticism from another quarter: the taxpayer. He feels himself threatened – by whom? By Keynes? No – by the state, which is trying to amass a fortune at the cost of private acquisition of property, which is strangling private enterprise by nationalization, which is accumulating power, in the form of exaggerated public property.

And so political reasoning proceeds to play a part in the battle waged about the level of taxation. And this is of course quite right to the extent that on the one hand the size of government expenditure and on the other hand the distribution of the tax burden among the taxpayers are political matters. But the trouble is that, in the process of budget-making, political views may come to the fore that regard budgetary surpluses as a reason for reducing taxes. This is the characteristic of a failure to understand Keynesian policy. Taxes must be reduced if resources are underemployed, if sales become too small and the economy needs an incentive to expand; and, in the reverse position, they need to be increased.

A correct use of government finance can greatly benefit economic stability. The irrational fears that spring from an outdated financial folklore can only have a harmful and inhibitory effect. But a government that wants to follow a modern policy will have to take these fears into account. It will have to try to win over the wrongly inspired forces – that is a chapter in itself. It is also hampered by other difficulties – Functional Finance is rather more complicated than the above might suggest. Real life does not consist of simple graphs. Public finance has many other aspects besides regulation of national income and outlay. But this does not detract from the fact that the basic principles of Functional Finance are reasonable and must be kept constantly in mind when following a sound budget policy.

CHAPTER VII

Old and New in the Theory of Money

1 · WHAT IS THE THEORY OF MONEY?

I should imagine that there are few economic subjects which the layman finds as mysterious as monetary theory. Money in itself is a rather mysterious affair – we are daily concerned with it, and it plays an important part in our lives, but most of us have only a faint notion of where it comes from, how the monetary system is regulated, what forces act on it. People suspect that bankers have something to do with it, but banks are obscure institutions and it is not easy to get an idea of what goes to make up a banker's daily round. And if, on top of this, theories are developed about these mysteries, some are inclined to surmise an extreme of scholarship far beyond their comprehension. And yet this awe is exaggerated: the essentials of money theory can be grasped without any great effort, although in this field, even more than in other fields of economics, imagination should be tempered with common sense if strange views are to be avoided. Illustrative of this is the fact that many reformers of society who have more nerve than special knowledge set their sights at monetary matters. They want to abolish money as being the source of all economic ills, or they want to saddle us with monetary systems the efficiency of which may, to put it mildly, be doubted. These reformers often suffer from a lively imagination and a lack of critical sense. If they had been a little more hard-headed they would have realized that their plans do not hold water and that in any case money is much less the real *bête noire* of society than they think.

This chapter is an attempt at hardheadedness. It will try to give the problems arising out of money a more modest place than is often done by economists. This will annoy a number of experts. I may warn the reader that this chapter is based on highly subjective opinions which the author happens to hold.

Let us first look at the subjects money theory deals with. If I see matters aright, there are five.

MODERN ECONOMICS

The first problem relates to the 'nature' of money. Formerly quite a lot was written on this more or less philosophical subject, above all by German economists, but the subject is hardly topical nowadays. Of course we have to know what money is; right, then, it is a good – any good whatsoever, irrespective of its physical nature or further properties – which is generally accepted by people in exchange for other goods. You can pay your tailor with coins from the Mint or with banknotes (from the Bank of England); but if you give him a hundred-franc note from France he will look askance and perhaps prefer not to make use of your offer of payment in this form. Consequently, the French franc is not money in Britain; it is not generally accepted. Nor can you pay your tailor with a claim which you have on someone else, unless this 'someone else' happens to be a bank. This is a most important point; claims on banks are accepted as money, at least among businessmen, and therefore *are* money. It is some times asserted (in examinations, for instance) that these special claims are not genuine money, but that view is not to be recommended. Every businessman knows that his bank balance is money, good money, ordinary money (unless it is a savings account – you cannot pay people with that. The savings account is 'near-money').

We do not need to say much more here about the 'nature of money'. To track down this deeper essence, you can go into the historical development of money (beginning with shells and oxen, passing via the Italian goldsmiths and the Maria Theresa thaler to the situation today), but this exercise has little point for our purposes.

Of greater importance is that part of money theory that concerns itself with the functions of money. Money is above all a medium of exchange, i.e. it has the function of facilitating the exchange of goods. If there were no money, the producers of goods would have to search for a partner who needed their product at that very moment – quite a business for the butcher and the baker, let alone for the car manufacturer. In other words, the medium of exchange saves work. But money is also a measure of value. The pound is used in the same way as the gallon and the kilowatt, viz. as a fixed unit in which other quantities are expressed. The value of a house is measured in pounds. The unit of

126

account and medium of exchange usually coincide, but in difficult times they differ; exchange is then performed by means of almost valueless monetary units (e.g. marks), but accounting is done in gold or in dollars, or in cigarettes. This difference is a sure sign of deep monetary disorder and of social disruption.

Money is not only a unit of account and a medium of exchange; it also represents one of the many forms in which a rich man can keep his wealth. It is a 'store of value'. This aspect of the matter will concern us more deeply – for we shall see that this is one of the areas where there is a difference of opinion between 'old' and 'new' theories.

A third subject with which money theory usually concerns itself – and most thoroughly – is the 'monetary system'. In the nineteenth century and the first decades of the twentieth century the discussion centred above all on the relation between money and precious metals. Money was originally metallic currency – gold and silver coins. Later the goldsmiths issued I.O.U.s which could be exchanged for gold, and later still bankers adopted this custom. In this way there came into being the banknote, a piece of paper issued by a large national bank which on demand could be exchanged for gold. This state of affairs, in which all kinds of money in a country, and in particular the banknotes, can be exchanged at the central bank for gold at a fixed price, is called the Gold Standard. The nineteenth century was the heyday of this arrangement. There were also situations in which silver, or even gold and silver side by side, occurred as a basis for the supply of money. A great deal was written about the pros and cons of these standards, and the problem became particularly pressing when the Gold Standard was suspended during the First World War, reinstituted after the war, and then abolished in the 1930s under the pressure of the Depression. The acceptability of paper money is no longer a special problem today; banknotes are accepted, not because they are convertible into gold, but because people know and trust that others will willingly accept them in payment. They are money because everyone regards them as money.

And the same is also the case with the claims on banks. They are money because you can pay others with them. These claims – they are called deposits – can be exchanged at the bank for coins

127

and banknotes, but you don't need to do this before you can use the deposit for making a payment. I should like to give somewhat closer consideration to this point, because it relates to the creation of money.

Most people think that money is made by the state, and that is partly true, too. And through the central banks – in Britain the Bank of England, in the U.S.A. the Federal Reserve System – banknotes are issued. But what many do not know is that about half of the supply of money is manufactured by others than the state and the central banks. This half is the money on deposit or bank money: the claims on the private banks. Such a claim comes into being through the transactions between the bank and its client; the government remains outside it.

The claim on the bank – the deposit, that is to say – can be created in two ways. The first way is by the client taking coins or banknotes to his banker. He thus acquires a claim which he can use to pay others with. In fact the community's supply of money does not change as a result of this. It might be thought that it has changed, because a sum of cash has been transferred from the client to the banker (the quantity of cash is constant), whilst moreover the claim on the bank has been newly created, and thus has been added to the existing quantity of money. True, this view of the transaction is not illogical, but the economists consider another view more suitable. It is their custom not to regard the coins and banknotes which are being kept in the bankers' safes as part of the stock of money. This is just an economist's habit. And therefore the depositing of money in a bank is a substitution of money; cash has disappeared out of circulation and has been replaced by an equal amount of bank money. The total quantity of money has remained the same.

But now note the other way in which a claim on a bank can come into being. A banker can give a businessman credit. The bank then 'opens an account' in the books and gives the businessman the right to 'draw' on this account without his first having put money into it (right of overdraft). In other words, a claim is born out of nothing, and this claim is money, for the businessman can pay his creditors with it. As long as this deposit is outstanding, the community's quantity of money is increased. But this means that the banker and his client, in unison, have managed to make money that did not previously exist. The bank is therefore not only a storehouse and a clearing house for money; it is a money factory.

This truth is not generally known. Even some bankers believe that they only lend the money that they have received from others. They ignore their own creation of money. The economists became aware of this creation of money about a hundred years ago (one of the first to see this possibility was a Scotsman, H. D. Macleod), and it goes without saying that since then the banks have attracted their attention greatly. In manuals and textbooks many pages are devoted to this creation of money, with particular reference to the extent to which the banks, against their liabilities, must have a certain amount of cash in the till. This 'cash ratio' has to exist because some businessmen approach the bank for payment of their claims in banknotes or currency notes.

Many special publications on the operations and the significance of banks have seen the light of day, which is only to be expected, since banking has a long and extensive history. The organization of banking differs in various countries and times. So do the place and the function of the central banks – generally the only banks that issue banknotes. There is a rich field for study here. But for a rough idea of how a national economy works it is not necessary to go into these institutional matters. We shall see later that Neo-Keynesian views attribute a smaller influence to banking than do some older theories. To be able properly to understand what follows it will suffice to remember that the banks, by giving credit, create new money. The reader who finds this surprising should quickly re-read the preceding pages and, if he wants to acquaint himself with the finer details, consult another book.*

The problem of monetary systems embraces considerably more than has been briefly outlined here. The international side of monetary arrangements is also of theoretical and practical importance. Under the gold standard the rates of exchange (i.e. the prices of the various national monetary units expressed in terms of each other) are fixed by the gold contents of the different currencies; it will be clear that this must be so, for every currency is connected to gold via convertibility and, given a free trade in

* For instance A. C. L. Day, *Outline of Monetary Economics*, 1957.

gold, the price of gold is about the same throughout the world. If the Gold Standard is abolished, the rates of exchange cease to be fixed; they can then move freely and are determined by supply and demand. If the governments do not wish to have the fluctuations in the price relationship of the various currencies, they can try to manipulate the rate by buying and selling foreign exchange. They can sign conventions with each other, fixing the rate. The central banks of the countries concerned are then obliged to buy and sell each other's currency at a fixed rate. This is the present situation; by the Bretton Woods Agreement (1944), which set up the International Monetary Fund, the currencies are interlinked by fixed rates of exchange.

The international aspects of finance have meanwhile become very complicated as a result of the payment arrangements which the various countries made with each other during and after the Second World War. The disequilibrium of the balance of payments, which we found in Chapter V was caused by lack of balance between saving and investment (which in turn were a result of the overladen investment programmes which the various countries had to accomplish after the war, despite their still low production), made it necessary to subject payments to a series of rules and to place them under the control of governments and central banks. These systems, which were at first bilateral in set-up, have gradually been made multilateral and have been widened in scope. In Europe the European Payments Union played a role in this; it was a kind of cashier for European money transactions. The International Monetary Fund in Washington, which was set up by the Bretton Woods Agreement, is a most important and interesting institution in the world's monetary affairs, but its functions and problems cannot be dealt with in this small book, which concentrates on the national problems of money.

Let us return to these. We have listed three: the nature of money, its functions, and the monetary system. Our inventory comprises two other subjects: the value of money and the effect that money has on economic events. The latter two are of great importance for our purposes.

The value of money is an old problem, which attracts attention again and again, and about which new views are constantly being formed. The next chapter deals with it.

We shall first try to form an idea about the effect of money on the circulation of income and expenditure. To put it another way: to what extent must we include in our model special relations showing the effect of money on the economic process? We shall see that differences of opinion may arise over this matter, in that some Neo-Keynesians are not prepared to ascribe an important role to the money factor, whilst others regard this precisely as one of the great weaknesses of the Keynesian system. It is to this problem that the rest of this chapter is devoted.

2 · THE INCOME SPHERE AND THE CAPITAL SPHERE

Anyone who wants to acquaint himself with the controversial subjects in modern money theory can best do so – at least so it seems to me – by starting from the distinction between the income sphere and the capital sphere. For instance, cast your mind back to the flow of goods and money as we once saw it. Now in Fig. 7 only the money flows are drawn; the movement of goods and the flow of the factors of production have been left out of consideration. We see the national income Y on its way from the firms to the households, and we see how the government adds an extra little flow of income – salaries of civil servants, rent for buildings, etc. – and we also see how the government drains off part of it in the form of taxes. The households cause this money to flow on in the form of consumption expenditure C, but part of it remains behind in the form of S. Now this flow of money goes to the capital sector. This comprises the stock exchange, where shares, bonds, and similar securities are dealt in, and further the banks, the life assurance companies and finally also those parts of wealth which are kept in the form of money and which are presently to acquire special importance in our story. The rest of the money flow we call the income sphere. This comprises the payment of the productive services, the factors of production, consumption expenditure, and also investment expenditure (i.e. the buying of capital goods).

Now the characteristic difference between the income sphere and the capital sphere is that with the money spent in the income sphere a flow of goods and factors of production is propelled along. Consumption expenditure draws the consumer goods out of the machinery of production, and so keeps up the level of production and employment. The investment expenditure – i.e. the spending of money on capital goods – gives work to the engineering industry, the building trade, the shipbuilding yards. The money that the firms spend on the factors of production creates

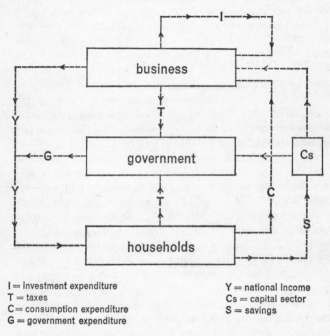

I = investment expenditure
T = taxes
C = consumption expenditure
G = government expenditure

Y = national income
Cs = capital sector
S = savings

Fig. 7: The circulation of money

the national income – it forms the direct counter-entry of the work done by labour, the productive services of capital, of land, and of the entrepreneurs. In this way the creation and the spending of income keep alive the firms' economic activity. Work and prosperity are thus created.

Expenditure in the capital sphere is different. The buying of securities directly creates no other employment than that of the staff of the banks and the stockbrokers. This employment is extremely small compared with the sum spent – only a few tenths of one per cent of it are devoted to factors of production. With the rest the buyer of securities purchases claims. He does not buy consumer goods. This is the Keynesian definition: saving as a negative, deflationary act. The money goes to the capital sphere, where it does not contribute to the sales of goods. This part of the flow of money has lost its pull on production.

But classical theory has different views on this. The classicists also see this part of the flow of money as the creator of employment: namely of employment in the capital goods industry. The buyer of securities makes his money available via the capital market to the investing entrepreneur; the latter puts factors of production to work that produce new machines. Without the prior act of saving this could not have happened. Consequently, in the classical view saving promotes sales just as much as consuming does – it evokes production just as much, but another form of production; not of consumer goods, but of capital goods. This is the familiar argument which we have already met, and which now also proves to be of importance to monetary theory.

For classical theory sees no purpose in making a distinction between the income sphere and the capital sphere. Money is money, and money keeps moving. It moves from the firms to the households, and from them back again to the firms – either via the market for consumer goods or via the capital market. In the first case there is a direct increase of sales and employment; in the second case this increase comes about indirectly. It is immaterial to employment and production how the money moves. It may enter the capital sphere, but it exits again immediately at the other side – it then returns to the income sphere via the purchase of capital goods. In the classical view saving does not have a deflationary effect.

This whole argument is further reinforced by the special view which classical theory has of money as a liquidity. We have seen that money has three functions: medium of exchange, measure of value, store of value. Now classical theory does not believe in the last of these three very much. It attributes this function to money, but without considering it important. Anyone who keeps his capital in the form of money – i.e. who hoards his savings instead of investing them – is losing interest. You don't do that, say the classicists; in olden days perhaps, or in backward regions, or in time of war; but otherwise money in an old sock is an anomaly. Entrepreneurs urgently require new money – hence their willingness to pay interest for it. Hoarding money is doing a shortsighted injury to one's own financial interests. In the classical view it does not occur in a modern world, where people hold as little money as possible. All the more reason to regard the capital sphere as a temporary residence for the money flowing through.

But this 'modern world' of the classicists collapsed in 1929. Since the Depression the capital sphere has proved quite capable of absorbing great pools of money. And Keynesian theory can also explain why.

This explanation is twofold. On the one hand we now know that not every saving leads to a corresponding act of investment. We have seen that the basis of Keynesian theory consists in a reversal of the relation; it is not saving that leads to investment, but vice versa. Saving can even have a negative effect on investment; it reduces consumption – and investments are ultimately made on behalf of sales. We have seen that this does not in itself mean that S must become larger than I; whether this happens proved surprisingly to depend on quite different things, namely on the relation between the sum of government expenditure and exports on the one hand and the sum of taxes and imports on the other hand. But, however this may be, the flow of savings to the businessmen who were eagerly awaiting them does not always prove to go as smoothly as was formerly believed. This is in itself a reason to give a somewhat more generous place in the theory to the distinction between the income and capital spheres than would suit the classicists. But there is another reason as well.

This second reason lies in the 'hoarding' of savings. The term 'hoarding' does indeed create the impression of the old sock, of suspicious rich men in backward countries without a proper capital market, without dependable possibilities of investment. But this is misleading. In modern countries too it may very well be attractive for the investor to keep part of his wealth in the form of money. Keynes pointed this out, although he hardly needed this for his explanation of the phenomenon of unemployment; it is part of his explanation of the rate of interest (via this rate the hoarding influences the acquisition of capital goods and so, indirectly, employment).* To give expression to the fact that he had in mind something quite different from the classicists with their out-of-date hoarding phenomenon, Keynes does not speak of hoarding but of 'liquidity preference'. The word can be more easily associated with rationally acting possessors of wealth than is the case with the old term, which is redolent of stone jars filled to overflowing with gold coins and suchlike romantic conceptions.

The preference for extra liquid funds (i.e. more liquid funds than one needs for one's normal transactions) may have various motives. The most characteristic of these is distrust of the value of securities. If someone keeps his capital in the form of money instead of buying shares or bonds, he loses interest; but, if stock market prices drop, this disadvantage may easily be outweighed by the loss that he would have suffered on the market value of his shares. A general drop in the stock market amounts to an increase in interest and vice versa; we can therefore say that the investor displays a great liquidity preference if he expects an increase in interest. He then exercises an extra 'demand for money'. Keynes called this reason for holding extensive money funds the speculation motive. In the terminology of the stock exchange a man with such a preference is called a 'bear'; a man who expects a rise in the stock market and thus disposes of his investment funds is called a 'bull'; and a man who is neutral is sometimes called a 'sheep'.

Bulls, bears, and sheep occasionally live peaceably side by side. The bears take over the liquidities which the bulls do not wish to possess. The capital sphere is then in equilibrium. But sometimes the bears predominate. Then the quantity of money in the capital sphere increases. However, it would be wrong to assume that this money has been withdrawn by the hoarders from the income flow in a deflationary way, and that the bears are responsible for a depression. If hoarding is to have a deflationary effect, then bears, to satisfy their need for liquidity, have first to save more.

* It is as well to point this out, since some believe that Keynes ascribes deflation to the hoarding of income money – a misconception that clouds insight into Keynesian theory and which was already warned against in section 4 of Chapter III. The misunderstanding is promoted by, among others, F. Benham.

Saving and hoarding then go hand in hand; in this particular case saving is, as it were, provoked by the desire for greater liquidities. The real deflationary factor is then the saving, the absence of consumption. That is what the entrepreneurs notice: they are left with the goods produced. They do not suffer from hoarding as such, but from saving. The hoarding that takes place in the capital sphere is secondary.

An increased need for liquidity, i.e. a victory for the bears, is in itself hardly a factor likely to disturb the circulation of income and expenditure. True, the phenomenon has a disturbing effect, but in quite a different field. It reduces the supply of capital. There are savings enough – the circulation has attended to that – but they are not passed on to the entrepreneurs for investment. Now it is quite possible that the entrepreneurs are not troubled by that fact – namely in so far as they are in no way planning to implement major projects. The bears in that case hoard the money which remains unused anyway.

The latter situation is characteristic of the capital market in a depression. The capital sphere is wallowing in money, in part because there are bears that do not trust the stock market, and in part because the entrepreneurs are not eager to borrow money. This abundance of money accompanies the depression; but it does not cause it. It is saving (or taxation and importing) which has a deflationary effect in the income sphere, not liquidity preference as such. The latter is confined in its effects to the capital market, and has hardly any effect, or at least no direct effect, on the circulation. This is the position of some Keynesians regarding the role of money. (It is not Keynes's own view; in the General Theory the rate of interest forms the link between the two spheres.) The separation between the capital sphere and the income sphere has induced them to construct models in which the money factor no longer explicitly occurs. This is a strange matter which we shall have to examine more closely.

3 · MODELS WITH AND WITHOUT THE EFFECT OF MONEY

To appreciate how surprising the moneyless model is to many economists, we must first realize that at the time when the

General Theory was published there was a school of theoreticians who ascribed the disturbances in economic equilibrium purely and simply to the effect of money. The fluctuations of prices and of production, the continually altering upswing and decline of economic life, in short the trade cycle, were explained on the basis of the expansion and contraction of the amount of money in circulation. Inflation and deflation were identical with an expansion and a reduction in the flow of money, which, in their turn, are explained by changes in the stock of money and its velocity of circulation. This is a very common view even today, and indeed not only among professional economists.

It is somewhat difficult to indicate the place occupied by this monetary school in economic theories as a whole. So far we have spoken only of the classical versus the Keynesian school. This is of course a gross oversimplification. For, although the classical school might in principle have taken Say's Law as its foundation, and although it might have left little room in its system for unemployment, the classicists could not nevertheless shut their eyes entirely to the periodically recurring depressions. However, they had banished investigation of the business cycle to a separate corner of economic theory – the corner reserved for the monetary specialists. Writers on finance and banking were well aware that wave movements occurred which carried production along with them, and which were difficult to reconcile with Say's Law. But these writers were usually too deeply immersed in their field of research to bother very much with the idea that supply always creates its own demand. They believed it, and left it at that. But the banks could create an additional demand not arising out of production. The first to draw the consequences of this was the Swedish economist K. Wicksell (about 1900). He connected the theory of income determination with the theory of money. What does this connexion look like?

Well, the answer is quite simple if we remember that a bank can make money. A bank can give an entrepreneur a claim on itself, and with this claim, born of nothing, the entrepreneur can pay others. The claim is money, money in the form of a deposit.

Now the basic idea of Say's Law is that the demand for goods and services comes from those who have first earned an income in production. But now demand is suddenly exercised by entrepreneurs who have not yet earned their money but who have received it from a bank. They exercise a demand for investment goods, without the purchasing power for that purpose having been created in production. And if presently the investments are made, incomes are admittedly created in the capital goods industry, but these end up in the hands of the factors of production that have helped in the production. And so this money travels further *en route* towards consumption. The original creation of money continues to play a part as an inflationary factor, until the credits have been repaid and the money has returned to the bank – it is then destroyed. In this argument the creation of money by the banks means inflation. And conversely a contraction of the circulation, i.e. a depression, was more or less placed on a par with a contraction of the quantity of money. Here too the banks were particularly envisaged.

In this way the monetary cycle theory came into being, which was defended twenty or thirty years ago with great vigour and skill by such economists as R. G. Hawtrey and F. A. von Hayek. In their opinion the cause of inflation and deflation lies in the increase and the decrease of the quantity of money. The matter rests with the banks. If they are compliant and generous, and if they force interest down below the level at which investments are in equilibrium with savings, then the entrepreneurs turn up in large numbers to borrow money. This stirs up investments. The money accordingly enters into circulation and falls into the hands of consumers who wish to buy consumer goods for it. However, the machinery of production is already hard at work making capital goods for the entrepreneurs. A struggle for the productive capacity breaks out, so to speak. At first this struggle goes in favour of the capital goods, for they have the bankers behind them. But the bankers cannot endlessly continue along the path to inflation. The nature of their business entails that the credits granted must always be covered to a certain extent by coins or banknotes – the customers might demand part of the money on deposit in the form of cash. Expansion is brought to a halt by the absence of these cash reserves. The creation of credit breaks off. The businessmen are left in the lurch by the bankers. They no longer have the financial resources required to complete their projects. And so a crisis occurs, the abrupt end of the boom.

And then comes the depression, which in this argument is the necessary consequence of a preceding boom. The bankers' liberality has disappeared and bank credits are restricted. As a result of this, the quantity of money is reduced. In itself, this already has a deflationary effect. Perhaps the consumers begin to hoard the scanty income that they receive. By so doing they constrict the flow of money still further. Bankers and hoarders together are responsible for the depression.

This reasoning is, as I see it, rather un-Keynesian. And yet it is also difficult to recognize classical theory in it. Personally I am of the opinion that this monetary view of the business cycle, at least in certain variants, is the classical way of thought in disguise. For after all it recognizes Say's Law, but sees bankers and hoarders as wrongheaded offenders against the fundamental law. The Keynesians, on the other hand, do not believe in the law – we rejected it fundamentally in Chapter III. Perhaps the following simile can make matters clearer: as regards Say's Law the monetary school (such as Hayek and Hawtrey) are to be regarded as heretics. They are believers with certain aberrations. The Keynesians are not heretics; they are unbelievers. Considerable confusion has resulted from some heretics (i.e. adherents of the monetary school) having put themselves down as unbelievers (Keynesians), while it also happens that genuine Keynesians cast their views in the form of monetary theories. Here is one of the major sources of obscurity in modern economics.*

But let us keep aloof from this battle of the 'scribes' and consider reality. We have seen that monetary theory points to the bankers as controlling the business cycle. They make and break economic life, by first being generous and then being close with their credits. Now this is not only un-Keynesian, it is also unrealistic. Banking does not wield that much power. The banker can help an entrepreneur to bridge his financial requirements. He can also refuse. In the latter case the buying of new machinery is

* The situation is made considerably more complicated by the fact that, before he wrote the General Theory, Keynes was a supporter of the monetary theory. In his *Treatise on Money* (1930) he stood close to K. Wicksell (*Geldzins und Güterpreise*, 1898), who is Hayek's spiritual father. It is occasionally claimed that the system of the General Theory really does not differ so much from that of the Treatise. . . . In this corner of economics school-forming is involved and subtle.

perhaps somewhat restrained. But in practice a shortage of finance will not form the great check on expansion. In 1929 there were no factories left uncompleted through a lack of capital, but there were factories enough which, although excellently finished and very well equipped with machines, were emptied by a lack of sales. The financial crisis certainly does not get off scot-free for the events in 1929; it gave an enormous shock to business and it curtailed the spending of the disappointed and sometimes ruined people who lost on the stock market. But the decisive factor in the Depression was the damage to total expenditure. And the theory of total expenditure is Keynes's theory.

Whilst the monetary theory gives all the credit and also all the blame to the bankers, they do not appear in the simple Keynesian story. The Keynesian model that we described in Chapters III and IV contains no equation reflecting the monetary factor. The entrepreneurs occupy a strategic place – but it is immaterial to Keynes whether they do their financing with share capital or with new bank credit. The savers are also important. True, they do not determine the size of national savings but they do determine the size of the national income which makes S equal to I (see Chapter III). As savers they certainly play a part in the circulation, but once they have saved and have bought securities their radius of action is confined to the capital sphere. These 'capitalists' can still struggle a little by swapping one security for another, they can influence the stock exchange as bears and bulls, and perhaps force the interest rate up or down; but this has not much to do with the income flow. The money factor is irrelevant, both to the bankers and to the buyers of securities. The Stock Exchange hardly occurs in the whole set-up. At least, that is the situation in the simple Keynesian theory – which we shall presently have to amend so as to come closer to reality. But it is as well, by stating the extreme non-monetary point of view, to show how greatly monetary theory has exaggerated the part played by money, the banks and the Stock Exchange.

In order to explain the latter in another way, an example may be taken from public finance. Up to now we have followed monetary theory in observing the creation of money by the banks. But the government can also create money. If this happens on a large scale it naturally leads to inflation. History contains many an unpleasant example of this: the 'greenbacks' in the United States; the German mark after the First World War and the Hungarian inflation after the Second, which led to a complete destruction of the monetary system. But even if we leave out of consideration these extreme cases of monetary pathology, it seems obvious that the government and the central bank, by an excessive issue of money, can harm economic life, devaluate money, and cause inflation. How, then, can 'moneyless' theory maintain that the money factor is a negligible quantity?

The answer to this question enables me once again to explain the fundamentals of Keynesianism. That is after all the purpose of this chapter, if not of the whole book.

Keynes does not deny that the government can create inflation via public finance; on the contrary, his political conclusion is precisely that a certain reflation of the circulation can and should be effected by the government and not by private households and business. But the Keynesian analysis of the effect that public finance has on the national economy is expressed in other concepts than those of the older monetary theory. Keynes does not consider the injection of money by the government – he considers government expenditure in relation to taxes. If this expenditure increases, income is created which is spent on consumer goods; consequently the multiplier begins to operate, and the national income and employment increase. This may imply a budgetary deficit, and such a budgetary deficit may be covered by the creation of money. In that case the government finances by new banknotes or by selling short-term bonds to the money-creating banks. But the additional money – and here is the catch – is not a prerequisite of the reflationary effect. For it may also be that the government covers the budgetary deficit by borrowing money on the capital market from the savers. In that case no new money is created. And yet G is greater than T, and yet the multiplier is in operation, and yet more is produced, more work is done, more is earned. There is reflation without the injection of money. This is achieved by transferring money from the capital sphere to the income sphere. The government functions as a pump between the two spheres; via borrowing, money is pumped into the income sphere. Keynes does not concern himself with this pumping. It is more or less immaterial to Keynesianism in its orthodox form whether money is created or whether money is pumped across via the process of borrowing and spending. What concerns the Keynesian is that the spending is done. In his way of thought quantities such as C, I, and G occur, expenditure components that is to say; and the stock of money will behave as the spenders of the money wish. From the macro-economic point of view the bankers and the buyers of securities have been dethroned; they have been demoted from the powerful occupants of a key position to the servants of the collective body of entrepreneurs. The government keeps its power, not so much because it can make money, but because it can adjust expenditure and taxes, each of them separately, to the level demanded by the economic system.

This connexion is most clearly evident when the Keynesians go on to consider an injection of money from public finance which for once does not take place in the income sphere. This case occurs when the government repays part of the national debt. Let us assume that at a given moment a long-term part of the national debt falls due, so that the Chancellor of the Exchequer has to find money to meet these obligations. Let us further suppose that the revenue from taxation is not sufficient to cover this additional financial obligation, and that the government does not wish to raise taxes. The Treasury then falls back on the creation of money. New money is made to pay the holders of state bonds. The community's stock of money increases. Now note the difference in approach to this phenomenon by the monetary theory and the Keynesians.

Older monetary theory will be inclined to attribute an inflationary character to this creation of money. The state's creditors have suddenly acquired money. They will want to spend this. Perhaps they will try to buy existing securities with it, but in that case the money passes into the hands of those who sold the securities and who are now perhaps going to buy goods. And otherwise the money soon goes to entrepreneurs, who buy machines and factories with it.

Some Keynesians are inclined to see this differently. They do not deny that in this situation the government creates money, but they consider this, for the moment, rather unimportant. For the money has not been pumped into the income sphere but into the capital sphere. It has not come into the hands of workers, trades-people, and industrialists who spend it on consumer goods or factors of production, but into the hands of passive capitalists. If these are bears, the money will stay where it is. If they are bulls they will spend it, but only on other securities. For why should somebody whose bonds have been redeemed suddenly go out and buy his wife a fur coat? That would be dissaving, and if he feels like doing so he will go right ahead and do it, and not wait until the government redeems its bonds. If the bulls predominate, we have the difficult case of nobody wanting the new money; there is no demand for it. Therefore, we might reason, the interest rate will drop and it will keep on dropping until the capitalists are prepared to retain the money with which the Chancellor of the Exchequer has saddled the capital market. In this way the capital sphere becomes a kind of mousetrap, which the money enters but does not leave. The usual way of describing this is to say that to the orthodox Keynesian the demand for money is elastic.

Now that we have put the matter in this way it has at once become clear where the weakness of this extreme theory lies. It can eliminate the effect of money only by assuming that the capital sphere is a money trap and that financial considerations do not enter into spending decisions. Expenditure depends, in this extreme 'moneyless' view, on income; not at all on the stock of money. But in actual fact liquidity certainly exerts something of an effect on consumption and investment decisions. Neither the tendency to invest nor the propensity to consume is entirely independent of the presence of liquid resources in the capital sphere. The bankers and the Stock Exchange certainly can influence investments, though not to the extent that the older money theoreticians believe.

And in fact this influence of the money factor does come to the fore in the General Theory, namely via the rate of interest. Classical theory regarded the rate of interest as determined by the interaction of S and I; this was impossible in Keynes's theory, for S is made equal to I by Y. In Keynes's view the rate of interest is determined by the quantity of money and liquidity preference. If the quantity of money increases, the rate of interest drops because the capitalists must be compelled to retain that extra money, and they will only be prepared to do so at a lower interest rate. But, in the system of the General Theory, investments are stimulated by the drop in the rate of interest. And so an increase in the supply of money does have an effect, though an indirect one, on the circulation.

At a later stage doubts began to be cast on the effect of interest on investments. We saw – in Chapter IV – that investments are determined above all by total expenditure. If the rate of interest is given only a small regression coefficient in the investment equation, the bond is severed which links the capital sphere to the income sphere. This is precisely the line taken by some Neo-Keynesian economists. In this way the moneyless model comes about.

One of the reasons why this model is not satisfactory is because I, whilst it does lead to S, does not do so immediately – the process takes time. In that interval something has to be done about a tense financing situation. This something is the creation of credit. If the expansion of the nation's plant continues, I keeps its lead on S all the time. In that case the creation of money is a phenomenon attendant on balanced economic growth. To put it another way, growth may stagnate if the supply of money does not run smoothly.

For all these reasons the money factor has to be introduced. Come to that, we have already encountered this point. When we had built a model along the simplest lines of the Keynesian theory in Chapter IV, we saw that in practice this model proved too meagre. Mistakes were made with it; in particular a post-war depression was predicted in the United States which did not eventuate. We saw that this came about because consumption had been regarded as a function of income only. But the propensity to consume proved suddenly to increase, especially in 1946 and 1947. The cause: the households were in possession of money. It proved that people's liquidity affected their propensity to consume. Now this element is not properly incorporated in the simple model. It is up to Neo-Keynesianism to apply a correction on this point. We can also put it this way: the model must be made more realistic.

4 · A SYNTHESIS

I have tried above to give a survey of old and modern points of view on the place of money in the circulation. Both have been formulated in a rather extreme way to show the difference. The old point of view – old in the sense that it predominated in the period between the wars – is that money dominates economic life. The makers of the money, i.e. the money-creating government and the bankers, derive their power from it. They bring about inflation and deflation. The opposite viewpoint is that the quantity of money and the creation of money are not over-important to the circulation. Of course, there has to be money, but it comes along all right. It comes along if the entrepreneurs, the 'managers of government expenditure', the exporters, and the consumers need it for their expenditure. It is not money that is important, but income. If the quantity of money is greater than really matches the national income, bears will be found who hang on to that money. In this way they neutralize the creation of money. And if at a given moment there is not enough money to make all payments required in a certain state of the national income, an appeal is made to the banks to provide the extra liquidities. Otherwise bears will just have to be transformed into bulls; a peculiar biological operation, which is performed with the aid of the rate of interest.

I shall now try to assume a point of view between these two extremes. It seems to me unpractical to return to the monetary theoreticians who are related to classical theory. They are too inclined to stress the wrong things, even if the logic of their reasoning holds good. Moreover, if an attempt at theoretical development, taking their theory as a basis, were made, there would be the danger that the fundamentals of Keynesianism would be lost sight of. Anybody who really wants to improve the theory must in my opinion build on Keynes, and not on his opponents. I am stating this right at the start to make it clear whose side I am on. The moneyless Keynesian model can be amended. This must not be done by introducing a new concept of hoarding; it is my firm conviction that it should take place on a basis of the logical structure of the Keynesian theory as explained in Chapters IV to VI. The factors determining the national income continue to be capital outlay, the propensity to consume, exports, government expenditure, the propensity to import, taxation, and labour productivity. Acting together, they determine how much is earned, how big production will be, and how large employment will be. What we have to do now is to introduce the money factor into this interaction.

Put in this way, the matter is simple. For we have only to check what the theoretical connexion is between the presence of a stock of money on the one hand and the decisions on expenditure on the other, and then try to cast these relations in such a form that they can be included in 'the model'.

The expenditure which we have in mind is consumption expenditure, investments, exports, and government expenditure. As regards the first category, it is clear that the volume of consumption can under certain circumstances be influenced by unusually large cash holdings by households. True, this case is not normal; a recipient of income who is not a buyer of securities will usually have little reason to maintain a large cash holding. He gets his money on the last day of the week or the month, and then gradually spends it. But sometimes the situation is different. In times of an abundance of money and a shortage of goods quite a considerable supply of money can occasionally accumulate in the possession of the ordinary recipients of income. Perhaps this goes so far that the recipient of income almost looks like a bear. But this animal quality is only temporary. One fine day he will want to spend his money. Consequently, an over-liquidity of the joint recipients of income is a factor which tends towards a temporary future increase of the propensity to consume. A lot of money in the hands of the consumer does not in itself mean inflation; but it does mean a possibility of inflation for the future. Since the lot of money is usually the product of a more or less inflationary situation – for instance after a war – this potential inflation often comes on top of an actual one.

Something similar can happen with capital expenditure. Here too the presence of liquid assets among the entrepreneurs or those from whom they borrow money may lead to increased spending. We have seen that the classical view that the size of I is determined by the funds available for financing purposes is one-sided; but it is not entirely devoid of reality. The financing question certainly plays a part, and for some firms (small shopkeepers, for instance) a very considerable one. A high liquidity facilitates investments. A low liquidity position, especially of banking, may have an adverse effect on the volume of investments. In that case there is no money to form a temporary bridge between I and S.

As regards exports, here too a lack of available credit may exert a restraining influence. In the case of larger transactions the exporter often has to finance in advance. Not only must he first make his product before he can supply it; he often has to wait for payment afterwards. In large non-recurrent orders for capital goods it is nearly always required of the exporter that he gives credit to his customer. He must therefore cover a temporary financial requirement, for which liquidities are needed.

For the government the situation is somewhat different. If necessary it can create the money that it cannot borrow. Whilst a permanent financing deficit is hardly conceivable in private expenditure, the government can permit itself greater latitude in this field. It has in reserve the central bank to cover the deficiency between expenditure on the one hand and taxes and long-term loans on the other. But sometimes the central bank is unwilling. In many countries it is formally or factually independent of the government, a position which it may use to lend force to demands for careful financing. Often this warning voice does not help very much, at least as far as the central government is concerned. But in most countries authorities on a lower plane – cities and counties – can run dry. We saw that in the Netherlands in 1966, when municipal investments were checked by liquidity difficulties. And so, in extreme situations, there is a certain tendency for liquid resources to influence government expenditure, too.*

These simple relations can now be introduced into the Keynesian model without the latter's essence being changed. All we have to do is not only to make consumption, investment, exports, and government expenditure dependent on the factors mentioned in earlier chapters, but also to recognize a certain influence of the

---

* There is a curious analogy with international currency such as gold, dollars, and sterling, which may become scarce for certain countries. Now that gold production is falling short of the needs of international payments, some economists predict a liquidity crisis on a world-wide scale. It is clear that such a crisis can always be prevented if an international authority (for instance the International Monetary Fund) could create bank money that was acceptable to all countries, or at least to all central banks. The idea of such a super-central bank has been defended by R. Triffin (*Gold and the Dollar Crisis*, 1960). But as long as this kind of authority does not exist, the problem of international liquidity will remain with us.

quantity of money. Not a predominant influence; a certain influence. The econometrists will tell us the exact extent of this influence amid the other determinants.

Now I realize that the econometrists are being burdened with a difficult piece of work by this attempt at a synthesis between the Keynesian and the monetary theory. It is not so difficult to prescribe that the regression equations of consumption and investment (and perhaps of exports and government expenditure) must contain a variable which represents the liquidity of the buyers of securities, the banks, and the recipients of income; however, it is no easy task to put this idea into practice right away. Firstly, it is not easy to find a suitable variable to represent liquidity. For we are concerned not only with the quantity of money (which can be measured), but also with the demand for money by the investors. If this demand is a large one, money is retained without this leading to additional expenditure. Also, the bears' liquidity preference is a fairly capricious factor; first an investor decides to be a bear, then he wants to be a bull or a sheep. It is extremely difficult to crystallize this disposition in a quantitative relation. And, finally, liquidity is not a factor that is always in operation; between certain limits it has little or no effect on expenditure.

Consequently, it is perhaps best not to include the quantity of money itself as a variable in the I and the C function, but only to consider excess liquidity and too little liquidity. The basic idea here is that there is such a thing as a normal liquidity ratio (relation between liquidity and national income) and that departures from this influence expenditure.

In this way a greater effect of the quantity of money on expenditure might perhaps be found than if the quantity of money were included directly as an explanatory variable. The latter has been done by Klein and Goldberger and by Zellner; they have found only modest values for the influence of money.* This ties in with the above argument, but perhaps it does not do justice to temporary, unusual situations.

We are concerned here with one of the many unsolved problems

* L. R. Klein and A. S. Goldberger, *An Econometric Model of the U.S.*, Amsterdam, 1955. A. Zellner, 'The Short-Run Consumption Function', *Econometrica*, 1957.

of Keynesian theory. Certainly the situation in the capital sphere must make its effect felt to some extent in the Keynesian model if we are to have a realistic theory. If this does not prove successful, we shall have to fall back on pre-Keynesian monetary ideas, which would be a retrograde step in the history of economics.

5 · MONETARY POLICY: ESSENTIAL OR NON-ESSENTIAL?

The expression 'monetary policy' is used by economists in a broad and in a narrow sense. In the broad sense they mean by it all the influence which the government exerts on the flow of money. In that case the government's expenditure policy and its tax policy are the principal instruments; Functional Finance, i.e. the manipulation of the budget, interpreted in that way, is a form of monetary policy. However, a narrower definition is more practical. Monetary policy would then mean the policy of the government and the central bank with regard to the creation of money. That is thus the issue of banknotes by the central bank and of circulating money by the state, but it is also government policy with regard to the money-creating banks. Monetary policy in this narrow sense stands side by side with the manipulation of the budget. Monetary policy and budgetary policy supplement one another. As to their mutual importance, there is a certain difference of opinion connected with the background of monetary theory described above. Some consider monetary policy a dominant part of financial and economic policy; this is to my taste a somewhat old-fashioned idea, and it often happens that those who follow it are adherents of 'old' money theories. Others – the Keynesians – consider monetary policy less important; they prefer to rely on budgetary policy for the maintenance of a balanced circulation. To grasp this difference of opinion it is necessary for us first to check what form monetary policy may assume.

It comprises various elements. The most obvious one concerns the creation of money by the state. However, it is only in exceptional cases that new coins and currency notes are made in large quantities; it is not normal for the government to try to cover its financing requirements in this way. The quantity is rather attuned to the needs of the community for cash.

The situation with the creation of government bills is different. The latter can quite definitely expand and contract accordingly as the state has to finance expenditure for which no tax revenue or long-term loans are available. In that case the state can borrow the money from the central bank and the latter creates the bills if required.

But, even without the state having expenditure to incur, the Chancellor of the Exchequer can influence the quantity of money in circulation, namely by influencing the national debt. He can borrow money from the public, not because he needs it, but because he wants to drain an excess of liquidity from the capital sphere. (This was practised in the Netherlands around 1960.) The government can also change the form in which the national debt is kept. There are four forms possible: long-term debt (bonds), short-term debt (bills) placed with private persons, short-term debt placed with banks, and debt with the central bank. The last two have the creation of money as the counter-entry; by reducing or augmenting the amount of this debt the government can cause the quantity of money to increase or decrease. Even without something changing in government expenditure or in tax revenue the Chancellor of the Exchequer, by converting one form of debt into another, can influence the quantity of money. This part of monetary policy is called 'Debt Management'. One of its variants is the open market policy; the Treasury buys or sells government bonds or bills, and thus increases or decreases the quantity of money. In this way the capital sphere – for it is in this sphere that these operations take place – can be saturated with money or be partially drained of money. In the Depression the monetary authorities hoped that they could revive the economic situation by saturation with money – an often vain hope. By applying the open market policy one merely removes obstacles from the path of financing capital expenditure, but if nobody expects a profit from these investments, this does not help. Perhaps the rate of interest will fall, but we have seen that this is not a vital factor in the buying of capital goods. The change in the composition of the national debt is therefore a powerful means of changing the supply of money, but not necessarily of changing expenditure. The open market policy is more effective if there is an excess of liquidity. In that case it can make a valuable contribution towards the stability of a national economy because – as we have already seen – an over-supply of money does not leave expenditure alone in the long run.

There are still more methods of changing the stock of money. These consist in influencing the creation of money by the banks. The government (and the central bank) can try in four ways to check or to encourage the creation of credit (that is to say the creation of money) by the private banks.

The first way is that of the supply of cash. Bankers need cover for the credit they grant, and this cover consists in the coins, currency notes, and banknotes issued by the Treasury and the central bank. By keeping down the quantity of this kind of money, the banks are ultimately hindered in their creation of bank deposits. The open market operations can therefore be used for this purpose.

The second way is to lay down reserve requirements. This is usually done by the central bank. It tells the banks that they can give as much credit as they like, and to whom they like, but they must take care that at least x per cent of this credit is covered by cash. By manipulating this percentage, the central bank influences the possibility which the banks have of creating money. This is especially practised in the United States, where the Federal Reserve System (the central banks) possesses considerable powers in this respect. Something similar is done in the Netherlands by the Netherlands Bank.

Then there is a third method. The central bank does not prescribe a minimum reserve ratio, but concerns itself with the nature of the credits. It says to the banks that they may grant no credits, or only a limited number, on deposit of securities as collateral – for it suspects that this money will be used for speculation on the stock exchange (buying 'on margin'), and it is anxious to prevent this. Or the banks have to give priority in their credit policy to certain industries, and restrain the others. (This is a modern French practice.) Such methods are called qualitative credit control, as opposed to the quantitative described above.

And finally we have the fourth method which the central bank uses to try and harness the private banks to monetary policy: Bank Rate policy. This is the oldest method. It is again based on the fact that the money-creating banks need cover and that the latter consists in banknotes or, in particular, credits from the central bank. If a bank's liquidity becomes too low, and the bank consequently threatens to lose the freedom of manoeuvre in its credit policy, it borrows from the central bank – or, in the U.K., from the discount market, which in turn borrows from the Bank. The latter asks for interest in return; this is the Bank Rate or Discount Rate. By raising this the central bank tries to frighten off its clients – the discount houses and the private banks. It will do this if the creation of money goes too far. The banks then get expensive credit from the central bank, and will also increase their own rates of interest. It is then hoped that this will restrain the businessman's demand for credit, and so have a moderating effect on the supply of money.

Thus monetary policy possesses a series of devices which in the course of time have been developed into a delicate policy. Much might be said about the technique of this, but we are more concerned with the question whether these instruments, with all their aspects, are particularly effective in controlling the level of activity. It goes without saying that those who use it (and they often think in monetary terms!) may have a favourable opinion of the effectiveness of monetary policy; they are strengthened in this opinion by the 'old' money theory, which was disputed above.

In fact monetary policy is not so powerful that it can be used to dominate the pace of an economy. There are two reasons for this relative impotence. The first is that some of the devices operate on capital values rather than on earnings. This applies in particular to Debt Management. The second reason is that interest does not play as large a part in decisions on investment as was once believed; anyone who is going to build a factory finds sales a much more important factor than the rate of interest. This makes the Bank Rate policy less effective than was formerly thought. Its influence is not dominant either in restraining or in encouraging.* This relative impotence of monetary policy is not

* In the nineteenth century the Bank Rate had a colossal effect on the international movement of capital. When the Bank of England raised its Bank Rate, short-term money wishing to profit from the advantageous interest flowed in from all over the world. This affected the balance of payments on capital account. This relation is quite different from the one we have in mind. It still plays a part in international payments.

assessed by everybody in the same way. Some expect more from monetary policy than others. I am not going to discuss every shade of opinion here, but I shall restrict myself to stating my own opinion in brief. It amounts to the following.

In a depression a generous monetary policy and a low Bank Rate can do something to facilitate revival, but not very much. It is more important that the impetus to activity is set in motion by impulses in the income sphere and thus on spending. Budgetary policy is then much more effective than monetary policy. It is even rather dangerous in a recession to lay too much stress on increasing the supply of money. For then the capital sphere is saturated with money, which might lead to difficulties later: if the economic situation is put back on its feet the prevention of an inflationary disturbance which may follow can be hindered by the presence of extensive liquidity. Consumption and investment can then blossom forth without it being possible to use budgetary policy against them. To put it in another way, too generous a monetary policy in the event of deflation unbalances the economic system. Consequently a government, when practising its budgetary policy, should not be careless regarding the supply of money.

Monetary policy is more effective in curbing an inflationary disturbance than in a depression. Checking is easier than encouraging. The piling up of excess liquidity should surely be prevented, especially by Debt Management. But it is difficult to go much further. It should be remembered that a high Bank Rate is easily eclipsed by the expectation of high profits. This may not hold good for all entrepreneurs – there are, for instance, traders who need large credits for keeping stocks. It was these traders that the old monetary theory had particularly in mind. But more important are the investing entrepreneurs. Someone who has a new factory built needs bank credit, but not to the extent sometimes supposed. The bulk of funds for financing purposes comes from a firm's savings – 80 to 90 per cent of the gross investments. The interest forms only a small part of the total cost sum forming the basis of the investment, particularly when we bear in mind the uncertainties of sales facing the businessman.

Quantitative and qualitative credit controls are perhaps more vigorous means of combating inflationary developments than an increase of the Bank Rate. But they work very crudely. Some entrepreneurs will meet with a rebuff from the bank. Others, who still have reserves, will quietly continue investing. In this way local bottlenecks may occur in economic life for which most central banks hesitate to assume responsibility. If the monetary situation becomes extremely tense, the central bank is often unable to restrict the supply of money too greatly, since then great interests are harmed and the danger of a financial crisis becomes imminent. This limits its restraining influence. In my opinion monetary policy is a supplement to budgetary policy that is not to be despised, but the latter is far and away the more important instrument for controlling the economic situation.

The supporters of the dominant monetary policy do not believe in this relation of the instruments. They see too many objections to manipulation of the budget. We shall return to this when we speak of Keynesianism in practice. We shall then see how some pessimists believe that Functional Finance can never be realized, so that monetary policy is the only hope. This view seems to me defeatist and therefore not without danger. I shall try to refute it in Chapter XII.

CHAPTER VIII

The Value of Money

1 · THE VALUE OF MONEY AND THE PRICE LEVEL

As the reader knows, we are engaged on building a 'model'; that is to say, we are trying to form a picture of the relations governing the economic process. We have inter-related a number of factors: consumption, investments, foreign trade, government expenditure, and taxes, together with the influence of money; but we have not yet spoken of the value (purchasing power) of money. Nevertheless, this variable also plays a considerable part in economic events, and we must now have a look at it.

The value of money can best be understood by remembering that it is measured by what one can buy for a given quantity of money. If the collection of goods that you can buy for one hundred dollars is a large one, money has a high value, and vice versa. Consequently, the purchasing power of money is determined by prices, and we must find out what factors govern the average price level. This part of economic theory is sometimes called the macro-price theory (as opposed to the micro-price theory, which examines the prices of single goods).

For a long time, people have pondered on the purchasing power of money. When money still consisted mainly of gold and silver coins, it was obvious that the value of these metals at the same time represented the value of money. Even when banknotes came into use, and in particular in the nineteenth century, this 'metallistic' theory was adhered to; it was then believed that all money was ultimately convertible into the precious metals, which indeed tallied with the facts under the Gold Standard. But other points of view besides the metallistic theories came to the fore at the end of the nineteenth century. The German G. Knapp believed that the value of money was fixed by the government. This is true to the extent that government determines the relation between the value of the coins and of the banknotes, but this does not fix the purchasing power of the money or, to put it differently, the price level.

More helpful is a much older view – which can already be found in sixteenth-century writers such as J. Bodin and B. Davanzati – associating the value of money with the quantity of money. This view still lives on in public opinion, and with reason too. The more money there is, the less it is worth. Stuff the economic system full of it, and prices will rise. That is where the word 'inflation' comes from; it means blowing up (the quantity of money) and in popular speech is almost synonymous with a rise in prices. The reader knows from the preceding chapters that matters are a little more complicated than that. We have defined inflation as too high expenditure ($C + I + G + X$); and prices did not enter into this expression any more than the quantity of money did at first. The stock of money was not introduced into the model until later (namely in the previous chapter), but this was not done in the simple manner of the theory that puts an increase in the supply of money on a par with inflation.

We shall go further into the relation between the quantity of money and the value of money in section 3 below. The reasoning that establishes this connexion is called the quantity theory, and it occupies a prominent place in macro-economics, although the number of its opponents is growing. But before we come to this it should be stated here that the word 'inflation', which is so often used, apparently has at least two different meanings. To some, inflation means a rise in prices. We shall not use the word in this sense. For a rise in prices is a rise in prices. The expression is clear enough; why must we use another term that may be misunderstood? I know that some do not use the term inflation unless prices do not just rise a little, but soar up; but in that case I speak of a sharp rise in prices, or of a very sharp rise in prices, and I do not need the word inflation to describe that either. If the reader still desires to identify inflation with a rise in prices, I advise the expression price inflation. Then there is no risk of confusion with that other concept of inflation which we have used before: expenditure inflation, in which the total demand for products (on account of consumption, investment, government expenditure, and foreign trade together) is greater than the nation's plant and the available manpower can keep up with.

Price inflation and expenditure inflation are not the same. It is true that one can lead to the other, and how that comes about remains to be seen. We must also take care not to mix up a third concept with the previous two: the increase in the quantity of money. For this, too, we really do not need a separate word; it is clear enough what 'an increase in the stock of money' means.

As mentioned above, the theory that establishes a connexion between an increase in the stock of money and the value of money is called the quantity theory. Many regard it as the most modern money value theory. I do not. There are two other theories, both modern as well, and in a certain sense more practical. These are the encounter theory – I am using this term for want of a better – and the cost theory. These are explained below in separate sections.

These preliminary reflections relate to the question of what determines the value of money or, to put it another way, what determines the average price level. A further question arises: what does the price level mean to the community?

A surprising answer is sometimes given. The nineteenth-century classicists (for instance John Stuart Mill) occasionally said that the value of money did not matter. The general price level was held to be irrelevant. And in fact there is a possible train of thought which leads to this conclusion. If all prices become twice as high; if all incomes rise correspondingly; if everybody then has exactly twice as much money as he had before; and in particular if everybody had paid his debts and therefore had also collected all his debts; in that case a change in the value of money would be an unimportant phenomenon. But in reality things are rather different. If prices rise, they rise unevenly, and other quantities are not immediately adjusted. Often wages lag behind, and some incomes (annuities, pensions) adjust hardly at all. When prices are higher most debts are easier to bear, and anyone who has a claim on another, or a large stock of cash, suffers a loss. The government, which always has a large debt with its subjects, sees its position improve if prices rise; it also automatically levies more tax, since the latter is computed on money incomes and money expenditure (and, furthermore, in part on a progressive scale). A rise in the level of prices therefore entails a series of shifts of wealth. Furthermore, with fixed exchange rates, it weakens the competitive position of a country in respect of foreign suppliers of goods, so that exports may as a result stagnate or even drop.

The reader will be aware that these effects of the drop in the value of money are usually regarded unfavourably. They bring social and economic difficulties in their train. Consequently, a stable value of money seems highly attractive. It is still possible to theorize about whether a slight rise in prices might not perhaps be useful (for instance to give production something of a fillip if profits were previously too low to keep the production process going), and sometimes a certain drop in prices may also be useful, namely if prices have risen too sharply beforehand. Furthermore, it may be advocated that rising productivity, i.e. a gradually falling real cost level, be expressed in lower prices. In all these cases a great deal depends on the situation as it is at any given moment. But as a general rule it does not seem foolish to hope for a stable value of money. And unduly abrupt rises and falls in prices must definitely be avoided. This often leads to a certain government policy which will be discussed at greater length in the last section of this chapter. But first we are going to have a look at the various theories on the value of money.

2 · THE QUANTITY THEORY

The basic idea of the quantity theory is that the value of money is determined by the quantity of money. The more money there is in circulation, the more prices will rise. In some older variants of this theory the two quantities were even assumed to be proportional; the price level rises and falls in proportion to changes in the quantity of money. However, this 'naïve' quantity theory obviously does not give a proper picture of reality. For if the national economy grows, and trade becomes more intensive, more money is needed. This additional money does not lead to higher prices. It may also be that wealth-owners wish to keep more money in cash than before; in that case, too, the quantity of money may increase without anything happening to the prices.

To escape these difficulties a new variant of the quantity theory has been brought to the fore, which is connected in particular with the name of the American Irving Fisher (1867–1947). This proceeds from the idea that it is not so much the stock of money itself that determines the value of money as the flow of money. Money moves. This is expressed by multiplying the quantity of money by the velocity of its circulation. The product of the two factors is the total sum of expenditure during a given period. In this connexion the quantity of money is called M – elsewhere we have used this letter for imports, but this does not really matter; only in this chapter does M mean money – and the velocity of circulation V. The product of M and V is called the effective quantity of money. MV has become a much-used shorthand expression for total demand. It belongs to the vocabulary of the monetary school. (A Keynesian would prefer the shorthand expression $C + I$. However, these two quantities, MV and $C + I$, are not equal. $C + I$ refers to the final sales of consumer and capital goods; MV also embraces all intermediate transactions and is many times greater than $C + I$.)

Fisher confronts this MV with the total flow of the things that are bought for money. He calls the volume of trade T. These turnovers have to be multiplied by the price level P. The product PT is the flow of turnovers in a given period, expressed in money. It will be clear that this PT must be equal to MV, since the total flow of money on the market is equal to the total flow of goods. In this way Fisher arrives at the 'equation of exchange' $PT = MV$, from which P can be solved; $P = \dfrac{MV}{T}$. Prices rise accordingly as the quantity of money and the velocity of circulation of the money increase; prices drop accordingly as the volume of trade rises at a given money flow. This is the modern version of the quantity theory that is to be found in all the textbooks on economics.

The correctness of this equation $P = \dfrac{MV}{T}$ is to the best of my knowledge disputed by nobody. MV must be equal to PT; the flows of money and goods keep each other in equilibrium. If the flow of goods increases, prices drop, at least as long as MV remains the same.

It is not the accuracy of the equation of exchange that is attacked, but the use made of it. The equation suggests that M, V, T, and P are independent of each other. This suggestion is misleading. For if M increases, it may be that the velocity of circulation V decreases; not by chance, but because the extra money has been injected into the capital sphere which, as we have seen in the previous chapter, sometimes tends to function as a kind of money trap. It is also quite possible that an increase in the quantity of money, if it takes place in the income sphere, evokes an increase in production and therefore in the volume of trade T. This can be seen in a depression; an increase of M does not then lead to higher prices, but to a higher total expenditure and greater employment. Only when these quantities begin to approach their ceiling do prices rise. This increase in prices may assume serious proportions as soon as total expenditure on goods and services exceeds productive capacity. The latter in itself suggests that the quantity theory, although based on the right equation, perhaps does not after all cast a clear light on the actual factors determining prices. For it is silent on the production ceiling, on the presence or absence of what we previously called a 'Hayek situation': the struggle between the consumer goods sector and the capital goods sector for the scarce factors of production.

Reasoning further along these lines, we encounter a real objection to Fisher's quantity theory. It may be that the price level rises without the cause for this being in the supply of money or the velocity of circulation, or in the volume of trade. Just suppose that wages rise. The unions have demanded a general wage rise and have got it, for instance because it was thought that prosperity should be distributed in another way. These higher wages lead to higher prices. P rises, and now changes will have to occur in M, or V, or T, or all three; for the equation $PT = MV$ continues to hold good. But it does not explain the level of the prices; anyone who wants to know why the prices rose should not consult Fisher's equation of exchange, but need only glance at wage policy. Here we come across a fundamental one-sidedness of Fisher's theory; it is born of the wish to derive the value of money from the quantity of money. Why is this necessary? The value of money can quite well be governed by other elements of the economic model. More will be said about this in the following sections.

Other criticism of Fisher's theory is also possible. I consider it a difficulty that the price level from the equation $PT = MV$ is so comprehensive. For these prices relate to everything that can be bought for money. If any article should be excluded, it is no longer true to say that the total flow of money must inevitably be equal to the total flow of turnovers. Viewed in this way, however, the turnovers comprise not only the sale of consumer goods and capital goods, but also the turnovers of intermediate products and even of factors of production. Every wage payment is included in the product PT; T therefore also comprises employment and P the wage level. There is still more; the stock market is included in the equation. A rise in the market price of shares is included in the factor P, and larger turnovers in securities increase T.* And, worse still, the flow of payments MV also includes the payment of taxes; it is hardly possible to make a breakdown into a price and a volume component. Both P and T prove to be complicated conglomerates of highly divergent elements, and no splitting-off of limited sectors is possible.

There is another difficulty. The velocity of circulation of money is rather difficult to grasp. If money moves more quickly, there may be various reasons for this. Perhaps the recipients of income are spending their incomes somewhat more quickly. Perhaps businessmen are holding smaller quantities of cash in proportion to their turnovers. Perhaps, too, wealth-owners have decided to transfer the wealth that they have kept in liquid form to the income sphere. Perhaps the government lets the money flowing into the Treasury flow out again somewhat more quickly. The velocity is a complex concept; it does not lend itself easily to a breakdown into different components. The same holds true for its reciprocal, the 'cash balance'; a concept introduced in Cambridge by Pigou and later by D. H. Robertson.

Yet this breakdown has been tried. The concept of cash balance draws attention to the human decisions which influence the demand for money. Since the mid fifties M. Friedman (Chicago) and his school have tried to analyse the factors behind this demand. Quantitative research points in the direction of the rise in prices being an important variable; it explains the behaviour of

* Since this is extremely unsatisfactory, some economists have taken pains to banish stock exchange transactions from the theory. For instance, J. W. Angell supposed, for the sake of discussion, that securities are bought solely with money not used before; an expedient which strikingly illustrates what far-fetched means have to be used to save the quantity theory.

the velocity of circulation in hyperinflations. Friedman's work has led to a revival of the quantity theory. However, the main drawback of this approach remains that money, not income, is the starting point of the reasoning. This seems an unnecessary limitation.

3 · THE 'ENCOUNTER' THEORY

The conclusion from the preceding section is that the explanation of the value of money by the stock of money summons up too many difficulties to be really practical. If we want to get to know the factors determining the price level, we must detach ourselves from the – in itself – obvious idea that the explanation must begin with money. Moreover, we must not start looking for *the* price level at which all goods, factors of production, and securities are heaped together; in some respects it is simpler to draw up a separate price theory for consumer goods, for capital goods, for the factors of production, for securities, and the like. Of course such a disaggregated price theory also has its disadvantages; theoretically it is perhaps less elegant than Fisher's, but it stays closer to reality.

It is not my intention to try out a complete theory of the various price levels in this section. We shall concentrate our attention on the prices of consumer and capital goods. In the next chapter a separate theory concerning the price of labour comes to the fore; this again is of an entirely different nature. The prices of securities that are determined in the capital sphere will not be considered in this book.

Let us first have a look at the price level of consumer goods. On the market an 'encounter' takes place between a flow of goods and a flow of money. The price level proceeds from this encounter. At the moment of exchange the flow of money and the flow of goods are of course equal; exchange is simultaneous. (This is the same observation as that on which Fisher's equation is based.) If, before the encounter, the flow of money is greater than the flow of goods, prices will rise to such an extent that equilibrium is restored. It follows from this that prices are the quotient of the flows of money and goods.

Starting from this, we need only investigate on which factors the two flows are dependent. We have already discussed the flow of consumption expenditure (the consumption function). The money that the households spend on consumer goods depends on their incomes and other factors. Among the latter we have introduced the liquidity ratio, i.e. the cash holdings in the possession of the households, as a separate factor. However, this factor will cause temporary differences in the propensity to consume rather than form a new fundamental determinant.

The supply of consumer goods is of course determined by the decisions of the entrepreneurs. They can easily manufacture more products as long as the firms are not working flat out and there are unemployed. An increase in consumption then leads not so much to a rise in prices as to an expansion of production. If the limit of productive capacity has been temporarily reached, the increased demand will force up prices. Perhaps this will make it attractive to step up capacity; investments then increase. But, to be able to produce the capital goods, means of production are again required. If these are already all occupied, the battle begins between the producers of consumer goods and the capital goods industry for the available factors of production. In that case prices rise sharply.

The price level of capital goods can be approached in similar fashion. It likewise depends on the encounter between two flows: the entrepreneurs' expenditure on investments and the production of investment goods. The first flow depends on the factors determining the tendency to invest. We have said something about these factors in section 3 of Chapter IV. We found that total sales, their expected increase, profits, and sometimes savings as well are concerned. Here too the liquidity ratio should not be omitted, but it probably occupies a modest place. There is a lot that could be said about the exact connexion between these factors and we shall not try to do that here; one thing that is certain, however, is that anyone desirous of explaining the price level of capital goods ends up with these factors. They are more real and more direct than the quantity of money and the velocity of circulation of money. They live in the minds of countless entrepreneurs faced with the question of whether or not to expand their factories.

The flow of money determined by the considerations of the

entrepreneurs and spent on new investments encounters the flow of capital goods. What we said above about consumer goods holds good for this too. The productive capacity of the capital goods industry and, on a longer-term basis, the possibilities of expanding it, determine the size of the flow of goods. The price of capital goods brings the flow of money and the flow of goods on the market into equilibrium with one another.

In this way we can explain the prices of the two kinds of goods – consumer goods and capital goods. I prefer this method to the quantity theory. Money does appear in the reasoning, but not in a dominant fashion. We do speak of a flow of money, but the extent of this expenditure is not made dependent on the community's supply of money. Expenditure depends above all on the incomes of the households and the (gross) income of the firms. The 'encounter theory' fits into the circulation idea (price increases are related to the inflationary gap) and has little connexion with the 'old' theory. It abandons the idea that the value of money must *per se* be explained by money itself. This avoids a number of difficulties connected with the quantity theory.

However, one drawback remains. The 'encounter' theory casts little light on a rise in prices resulting from a rise in costs. It is true that this element is contained in it, since we have seen that the flow of goods depends on productive capacity, so that reaching the production ceiling leads to a rise in prices. Yet this side of the matter does not come clearly to the fore. This is certainly a drawback. It is particularly striking when one considers the relation between the prices of consumer goods and the prices of capital goods in an inflationary situation. If the consumption and the investment sectors begin to fight for the means of production, the prices of the factors of production rise. This may lead to an accentuation of the price increases which proceeds not so much from the encounters of flows of money and goods on the markets as from the increase in costs. Now this 'cost inflation' must be separately elucidated. For this we need a third price theory: the cost theory.

4 · THE COST THEORY

The idea that prices may be explained by the costs of production was the one generally prevalent in the nineteenth century.

However, objections were also always made to it. Paintings are often expensive, without great costs having been involved in their making. The same goes for antique furniture. In these special instances the cost theory does not work, but that does not particularly matter for our case, since we are talking about the price level, and such *curiosa* carry little weight in that. What is more important is that the cost theory cannot explain the complete price; for the price contains not only costs but also a profit margin. We shall therefore have to go more deeply into this matter.

The price level is determined in part by the cost level. This is doubtless a correct proposition. But it is not exact enough. We can make it more accurate by remembering that it is not in the first place the total costs incurred by the firm that are important, but the costs per unit product. For this wages are important, and also depreciation, interest, the costs of raw materials. We must know what portion of wages is included in the unit cost, and what portion of raw material costs. It seems to me that it is easy to realize that these cost factors weigh less heavily according as the productivity of the factors of production concerned is higher. If wages remain the same, and the productivity of labour rises, the wage factor in the cost price becomes proportionately smaller. If wages rise just as much as the productivity of labour, the wage costs per unit product remain the same. This idea may also be applied to the other factors of production. In this way we find the rule that the level of unit costs is equal to the wage level divided by the productivity of labour plus the level of interest and depreciation divided by the 'productivity of capital' plus the rent divided by the productivity of land. When imports play a role, their price and their 'productivity' should also be taken into account. This gives the factors determining the level of cost prices; they are the prices of the means of production and their respective productivities.

As I said earlier, this does not give a complete impression of the price level; for costs are not in themselves prices. The difference between the two is the profit margin. We must draw up a separate reasoning for this.

The profit level depends in general on two things: on the one hand on the degree of competition and on the other hand on the development of sales. If competition is fierce the profit margins are usually less than in monopolistic situations. The latter is particularly evident when we see what happens in the case of a decrease in costs, for instance as a result of the rise in productivity. If there is lively competition between the entrepreneurs, lower costs will be passed on in the price. The consumer profits from it. If competition is overshadowed by price agreements, or if businessmen are scared of what they consider to be cut-throat price decreases, prices remain rigid; falling costs lead to a higher profit margin. The same can happen if the prices of raw materials drop; with inflexible prices this means that the gain is not passed on to the customer, but disappears into the pockets of the suppliers.

The increase of sales is also important for profits. If the total demand is small, the entrepreneur must be satisfied with a small profit total. If sales increase, so does this total. And this happens in particular if excess demand develops. An increase in demand which exceeds the production potential of a country may lead to higher profits. In this situation profits swell, not only through the increase in sales ('in breadth') but probably also via larger profit margins ('in depth').

The theory that accounts for the price level by costs must be supplemented by observations, in the spirit of the above paragraphs, concerning the profit margin. This brings us back to the 'encounter theory'; for the sales that influence profits are precisely the flow of money that encounters the flow of goods. Cost theory and encounter theory supplement one another. Together they offer a practical approach to the problem of prices which is more concrete and simpler than the quantity theory.

It is consequently not surprising that this form of reasoning is particularly applied by the practical man. If a businessman wonders how the price level will behave, he studies the markets within his range of vision; he asks himself whether wage increases are in the air, and he makes an estimate of how demand will develop. If he thinks that demand will remain at a reasonable level, he assumes that wage increases and other established or expected increases in costs can be passed on to the consumers, with constant profit margins. If he expects a drop in the market, or increased competition, he will suspect a lower profit margin, and vice versa.

The same method, but in a somewhat more elaborate form, is followed by the econometrists who are building a quantitative model for a whole national economy. They need a 'price equation' which can help them to explain – and forecast – prices. This price equation usually has roughly the form as given above. This therefore means in practice that the model-builders, who must make an assumption in their reasoning regarding the price level in the following year, first investigate how wages, import prices, and such 'large' cost categories will probably develop. They then have a look at demand; they estimate the extent to which the market will allow the shifting of the rise in cost to the buyers. They must of course take into account the degree of competition and government policy (to which we shall return). The government sometimes puts a stop to the passing-on of cost increases; this was repeatedly tried in the Netherlands also, and more recently in Britain.

The fact that practicians and econometrists follow the cost theory – somewhat supplemented by elements of the encounter theory – naturally does not automatically imply that this theory is a first-rate one. It may very well be that other theories lead to a deeper insight into hidden relations. But this much is certain, that the cost theory and the encounter theory together form a sufficient aid for a simple and practical approach to the problem of the value of money. In my opinion their combination is to be preferred to the quantity theory, which, whilst well thought out and capable of inspiring scholarly observations, encounters a series of practical objections and is also too closely connected with the typical monetary approach.

The cost theory has a further advantage. It reminds us that the prices that the consumers pay find their way in the form of returns to the entrepreneurs, who spend them again on the factors of production. Someone who forgets this may reason as follows: if prices rise, people can buy less, and in that case the real national income drops. This would be true if the money income of the factors of production remained the same, in spite of the rising prices. But that is illogical. Higher prices lead to higher incomes. Primarily these may be higher profits. However, they may also be higher wages, or higher rents. This is a matter of distribution, which will be discussed in the next chapter. It is therefore not correct to think that 'higher prices' are identical with 'lower real incomes' and less prosperity. Somewhere somebody's income must increase as a result of the price increase.

Another *raison d'être* of the cost theory lies in the fact that the price of some factors of production comes about in a special manner, outside the normal supply and demand mechanism. These prices are more or less detached from the interaction of spending and production, and they cannot be explained by a quantity theory or the encounter theory. This is the case with the wage level. Wages are determined by negotiation between unions and employers and laid down in collective labour agreements. Many economists therefore regard the wage level as given. The same applies even more strongly to the prices of imported raw materials. In the open countries these form a considerable portion of the cost price – in the Netherlands even about one third – and these prices have little if anything to do with domestic events. Wages and prices of raw materials are data inaccessible to any quantity theory. It is realistic to start from this truth. Here is one of the reasons why the monetary theory of the value of money, in contrast with the cost theory, often appears so abstract and so academic.

This way of thinking teaches us that the costs of production can exert an independent influence – a 'push' – on prices. This influence, if it works in an upward direction, is sometimes called cost inflation. Cost inflation is then subdivided into wage inflation, inflation caused by import prices, etc. Profit inflation is a related phenomenon. We have already pointed out above that these concepts are really rather confusing; inflation can mean so many things. But if the words are nevertheless to be used, it is as well to keep three things separate: expenditure inflation (in Fig. 3 the presence of an inflationary gap); price inflation, i.e. a pronounced rise in prices, caused by the encounter between a money flow and a goods flow (price inflation may therefore be the result of expenditure inflation; this is the 'demand pull' theory of rising prices); and cost inflation, i.e. the independent cost increases. All three forms of inflation are interrelated. Usually the inflation process begins with expenditure, as a result of which prices rise; if this continues so far that a marked scarcity of factors of production occurs, cost inflation begins to rear its ugly head. This can in turn aggravate price inflation. This is the 'leapfrog' process of wages, prices, and expenditure, a process that can be properly understood by using the cost theory and the encounter theory together.

The idea that higher prices and excessive spending may stimulate each other has recently been contested. It does not fit into the classical theory, which sees prices as a stabilizer: a higher price level should mean less spending, not more. This stabilizing influence has been pointed out by D. Patinkin, who reasons that the value of people's real cash balances will go down as prices go up. Because of this the holders of cash will try to restore the old level of the real balances, which means a lower velocity of circulation, i.e. less spending. This stabilizing mechanism is called the Pigou effect. According to Patinkin it also works the other way round: in a depression prices go down, the real value of cash balances increases, people release money, the circulation expands. The price level acts as a stabilizing force on spending, production, and employment: a typical anti-Keynesian relation.

I do not believe this. The Pigou effect is a new and sophisticated addition to the old theory of money. It stresses a relation that may exist, but normally as a very minor factor. The impact of a greater liquidity preference is usually counteracted by a greater supply of funds by the banks, and overshadowed by the waves of spending generated by higher money incomes that are, in their turn, the result of higher prices. It is only in a liquidity crisis, when the banks have reached the limit of their lending capacity, that the Pigou effect really works. But then it acts as a destabilizer, not as a stabilizer.

5 · THE GOVERNMENT'S PRICE POLICY

As the reader will be aware, the governments of the various countries of Western Europe and the United States now and again try to influence prices. They do so above all in the case of an inflationary gap, which might lead to the leapfrog process outlined above: cumulative price and cost inflation. This is a harmful process; it favours the debtor, forces people with fixed incomes to join the ranks of the underprivileged, harms a country's competitive position on foreign markets and undermines confidence in money. Needless to say, the government counters this by aiming at price stabilization.

Price policy follows two lines of approach. The first is that of the government subsidy to the entrepreneur or to the consumer. This can be an excellent method if the aim is to keep a certain good cheap so that everyone, irrespective of his income, can buy it. However, this has nothing to do with combating inflation. On the contrary, the subsidy increases the real value of purchasing power, stirs up the circulation, and encourages overspending. A government that tries to combat rising prices with steadily increasing subsidies is heading inevitably for an inflationary gap.

The second method of price stabilization is to influence the decisions of the entrepreneurs who fix their prices. This influence may assume the severe form of a price freeze – in which every price increase is forbidden – or the less strict form regulating the costing procedure to be followed or forbidding entrepreneurs to pass on certain cost increases. In a weaker form the government can try to persuade entrepreneurs not to increase their prices. Sometimes this 'psychological' line of behaviour is supplemented and backed up by the possibility of special price regulations in strategic sectors as a silent threat. Also attempts are often made to promote competition, to counter monopolies and price-fixing agreements, and thus to increase price flexibility. This policy of encouraging competition is therefore indirectly aimed at price determination. The exact form chosen – the severe, the psychological, or the indirect – differs from country to country and sometimes from industry to industry.

The potentialities of such a policy are regarded differently, depending on the macro-price theory to which one adheres. A proponent of the quantity theory will be easily inclined to underrate the success of such attempts. For to his way of thinking the price level is determined by the quantity of money (which in turn is determined by the creation of money by the banks) and the velocity of circulation of money. Viewed in this way, rising prices are a symptom of a fundamental disequilibrium. Keeping prices down is 'artificial'; it does not help, for the money will find a way out. The government can save itself the trouble.

The cost theory, combined with the encounter theory, views this differently. Prices are determined by the level of money costs and by the profit margin. If expenditure rises, prices threaten to rise more strongly than costs: the profit margin increases. If this happens the entrepreneurs acquire an extra possibility of profit. The additional profits will be passed on in the form of larger incomes. Higher profits invite wage claims, and so a cost inflation may develop. But costs are at the same time incomes. If the incomes of enterprises and households increase, investments and consumption will rise. A price increase – i.e. an increase in the money flow – can exert a stimulus in the interaction of prices, costs, and expenditure. This process is not necessarily checked by higher prices; it may even be incited by them. And then there is some point in price policy; it pours oil on troubled waters.

Of course the importance of such a price policy should not be exaggerated. There is no question of driving out an inflationary process starting with excess demand by keeping prices stable. An inflationary gap forms a basic factor which must be combated by a government policy, for instance in the form of Functional Finance. Price and wage policy fails to bring about this fundamental adjustment. But it is true that a policy which is directed towards balanced expenditure can be aided by a stabilization of prices. And furthermore a government that wishes to combat inflation by means of budgetary and monetary policies can suffer a severe setback from rising prices and wage claims. Price increases can cut across the balancing efforts. Price stabilization is then the prerequisite of a more fundamentally directed policy.

This important matter (important because it recurs regularly in practical politics) can also be illustrated from another angle. The quantity theory, and more generally older monetary theory, is too inclined to regard prices as more or less mechanically determined quantities. The price level is, as it were, fixed by the economic laws of the market. It goes its own way, and no government can do anything about it. However, this view overlooks the fact that prices are often not so much 'formed' by the market as 'made' by men, in this case entrepreneurs. They are 'administered' by big firms. Of course, in their price policy, the suppliers cannot detach themselves from the market. Sales possibilities set limits to what they can ask for their product. But these sales possibilities do not form fixed data. In turn they are connected with the price level; for if prices are high and the incomes which are paid to the factors of production from these prices flow on briskly to the households, sales will not need to suffer any adverse effects from a price increase. From the point of view of the equation of exchange we may say that the quantity of money or the velocity of circulation will tend within certain limits to adjust to the inter-play of wages and prices. The influence goes not only in the direction of M and V to P, but also conversely.

If this is true, and prices and wages possess a certain degree of independence of monetary and market data, determined as they are by influential entrepreneurs, why should the government not try to have its own say in this matter? If excess spending causes increased prices and increased prices provoke cost inflation, and cost inflation in its turn brings about increased expenditure, why should the government have to submit in advance to this price determination and have to confine its influence to the budgetary and monetary fields? This is not evident *a priori*. Of course, it may prove that the government's price policy is in certain circum-stances less opportune, less practical, less effective on account of its political and psychological consequences; but this does not affect the principle. Theoretically, price policy is a supplementary means of governing the economic process which should pre-ferably not be missing from the arsenal of economic policy. And especially not in countries that believe in private enterprise, because private enterprise only functions well in a balanced economy.

CHAPTER IX

The Wage Level in the Model

1 · WAGE PROBLEMS

Keynes's theory has led to new insights in various fields of economics. We have already been able to note this with regard to the relation between saving and investment, with regard to the determination of the national income, with regard to the balance of payments, and above all with regard to government finance. We have also seen that the theory of money and prices has developed in a new direction under Keynes's influence. However, the significance of Keynesian theory for wages seems to me to be even more important. To be able to define this significance somewhat more accurately, a survey will first be given below of the various wage problems which confront the economist.

The first problem, which has been attracting attention for centuries now, is what determines the level of wages. This is of course a major problem of economic and social welfare. The wretched condition of workers in Europe during the nineteenth century gave rise to numerous pessimistic views and forecasts. In 1803 Malthus saw no other prospects for the workers than famine, disease, and misery, as the inevitable consequences of over-vigorous multiplication and of the shortage of food. His contemporary Ricardo, together with Adam Smith the founder of the classical school, did not have a much more favourable view of the situation. Continuous overpopulation would permanently keep wages down to the subsistence minimum; the wage level would be just sufficient to keep people from dying. A temporary rise above this level would soon lead to such an increase in the surplus population that the old level of poverty would be restored. In the middle of the nineteenth century Marx based his sombre view of the future of capitalism on a similar wage theory, which Lassalle called the 'iron law of wages'.

These gloomy views, which seemed to be confirmed by actual events of those days, were not without their opponents, however.

Adam Smith himself had offered more pleasant prospects in 1776. Increasing production would lead to more prosperity, probably for the workers as well. The Frenchman J. B. Say, known to us for his fundamental law of markets ('supply creates its own demand'), already pointed out in Malthus's day that wages are determined by the productivity of labour; the employer will be compelled by competition to pay the worker a wage reflecting what he has produced. Rising productivity leads in the long run to rising wages.

However, this productivity theory could not get a firm footing as long as economics was not in a position to solve the problem of how output, proceeding from the cooperation of a number of factors of production (labour, capital, land, entrepreneurship), had been 'created' by each of these factors of production. As long as this problem had not been solved, the economic contribution of each separate factor of production was an open question. This point became urgent around 1870, when a new doctrine of value developed in Austria and elsewhere. Economists began to realize that the value of everything that is produced is based in the final analysis on the satisfaction of the consumer's wants. The value and the price of the factors of production are determined in turn by the value of the final product. But how is this value to be imputed to each of the factors of production? How is the value of a table to be broken down into the value of the cabinet-maker's work and the wood?

The 'imputation problem' was solved at the end of the nineteenth century by a number of economists, including J. B. Clark. They investigated what happens to the volume of production if one unit of labour is added to the labour already employed. The increase in production thus created is called the marginal product of labour. Now the basic idea is that with every addition of labour to an existing production process an increase in the quantity produced can be achieved, but that this accretion becomes increasingly smaller with successive additions of labour. The marginal product decreases as the quantity of labour increases, assuming that all the other factors of production – machines, land, and enterprise – remain the same. As long as the marginal product of labour is greater than the wage, it is profitable for the employer to hire more workers. He therefore keeps on demanding extra labour until the wage and the marginal product of labour are equal. In the state of equilibrium, therefore, equality of wage and marginal product prevails. This wage level theory is called the marginal productivity theory. It is applied not only to work, but to every means of production, and thus forms a starting-point for a general theory of the distribution of the national income.

This marginal productivity theory has been the subject of considerable controversy since its discovery about seventy-five years ago. It has repeatedly been attacked, touched up, changed, reformulated. Up to the present day it has had its critics and its proponents. Most economists are more or less in agreement with the idea that wage and marginal product of labour are equal. But they ask themselves whether it is true that the marginal product determines the wage. It might also be that wages are not so much the result of competition between employers as of collective agreements between employers and unions; and in that case the employers adjust to this wage level the quantity of labour which they can profitably employ. The marginal productivity might then be the guide to the level of employment, since in this situation it is not marginal productivity that determines wages, but wages that determine marginal productivity. This sequence of reasoning stresses the power factor, and in this case the concept of marginal productivity has less importance than in the view held by J. B. Clark, who says that productivity determines wages. Yet it may be said that roughly speaking a certain correspondence exists between wages and productivity. If productivity rises, so do wages. We shall return to this relation later, for it is of great importance to practical wage policy. However, we shall see that this correspondence is in fact based less on marginal productivity than on the power and the aims of the unions.

We have outlined the marginal productivity theory here because it forms a well-known tenet in economics manuals. Many writers confine themselves to this side of the matter; they discuss marginal productivity and suggest that therewith the problems of wages have been solved for the greater part. That is a pity, for the aspects of the wage problem which are important nowadays no longer lie there. You have to know something about the marginal productivity theory to understand why it is of less practical importance than was formerly assumed. The really pressing problems are to be found in the consequences of Keynesian theory. Now Keynes neither attacked the marginal productivity theory nor warmly defended it. He took it as given and directed his attention elsewhere as far as wages were concerned. We shall also do that. Nevertheless, it is as well to discuss in greater detail the question of what factors determine the level of wages; for, as we have seen, wages help to determine prices and thus the value of money. The explanation of the wage level brings us to the unions; they will be dealt with further in section 3 of this chapter.

The genuine Keynesian wage problem is a different one. It is not: What determines wages? It is instead: What effect will the level of wages have on the economic system and in particular on employment? If wages are forced up, will the result be unemployment, as classical theory believes? Is it true that insufficient production, unemployment, and depressions must be ascribed to too high a wage level? Or does the cause of these disturbances lie elsewhere? As we already know, the essence of Keynesian theory is that disturbances are caused by a deficient or an excess demand, and not – or hardly – by an incorrect wage or price level. We have now touched upon one of the most incisive problems of modern economics. Let us further consider it.

2 · THE EFFECT OF WAGES ON EMPLOYMENT

It is, in particular, with reference to the effect of the wage level on total employment that the Keynesian and classical theories part company. The difference between the two trains of thought perhaps comes more sharply to the fore here than in the matter of the influence of government expenditure and revenue on employment. The older theory of the relation between wages and employment has been abandoned by practically every economist, but it still governs the more popular views. No wonder: the classical theory regarding the relation between wages and employment is of an attractive simplicity and an apparently convincing logic.

This apparently correct reasoning is as follows. If wages, the price of labour, rise, it becomes more expensive for the entrepreneur to keep workers in employment. He will have to ask more for his product. A more expensive product is more difficult to sell.

Higher wages may therefore mean lower sales; lower sales mean lower production and less employment. Labour, therefore, is subject to the same rule as all other things: the higher the price, the smaller the quantity sold. Unemployment is a sure sign that wages are too high. The depression is mainly the fault of the unions. Wages must be reduced; sales and employment will then increase again. By reducing wages sufficiently, unemployment can be eliminated completely.

That there is something wrong with this reasoning is already apparent from the fact that the converse argument can also be defended. Whilst the classical school was at its heights, opposite views were occasionally heard. At the end of the last century J. A. Hobson asserted that unemployment was the result of a lack of purchasing power among the mass of consumers. The rich have purchasing power, Hobson said, but they use it insufficiently for the purchase of consumer goods; the poor would like to do so, but they do not have the money. As a result, consumption stagnates. Sales and employment could be stimulated by a more uniform distribution of the national income; increase wages, and employment increases too. The reader, having followed Keynes's theory in the preceding pages, will recognize in Hobson a forerunner of Keynes, and the General Theory does in fact mention this stagnation theory in approving terms.

The view that higher wages lead to greater purchasing power and thus to larger sales keeps on popping up. In the 1920s it was the German union leaders who brought it to the fore – the theory is of course a godsend to the unions. But to others as well. Henry Ford defended a similar argument, and definitely not on abstract grounds only. 'I give my workers higher wages than other employers,' he said, 'and that makes them feel happier and work better. With their greater purchasing power they buy my cars. This makes these cars saleable in large quantities, and they can be produced cheaply. Despite the high wages, the costs of production go down and profits go up. But the most important thing is that a large market is opened up. High wages promote mass consumption and are therefore a prerequisite of a developing national economy.'

The theories of Hobson and Ford spotlight a weak side of the classical theory, but neither of them is itself complete. Classical economics wrongly proceeded on the assumption that the national income and therefore the total demand for goods remained constant despite the change in wages. This ties in with the main classical idea: national income is given by productive capacity, and by Say's Law. Classical theory stresses the cost aspect of the wage, but neglects the purchasing power aspect, so that incorrect conclusions are drawn, or conclusions which hold good for a single industry or a single firm, but which cannot hold water on the macro-economic plane. On the other hand, the purchasing power theory is macro-economic in set-up, but, like classical theory, it is one-sided. In some variants it confuses wages with national income. National income does not necessarily have to rise just because wages do; it may be that profits, or interest, decline, so that the total purchasing power does not so much increase as shift from one recipient of income to the other. A very weak spot is the confusion of the wage level and the wage bill; if one goes up, the other may remain constant because of a decline in employment; the wage bill may even go down. And Ford's view is highly coloured by the fortunes of the young automobile industry in Detroit. Ford was right regarding his own industry in those years, but it is dangerous to apply these experiences to a whole national economy.

In the 1930s, when unemployment formed a burning problem, the two one-sided theories coexisted. The economists of the day insisted that wage cuts would be beneficial. Great economists such as L. Robbins and L. von Mises attributed unemployment to too high wages. Less official views claimed the opposite. It was difficult to say which of these theories was more correct.

Meanwhile some had already attempted a synthesis. The Dutchman J. Goudriaan had already expressed the opinion at the beginning of the 1930s that the cost aspect and the purchasing power aspect of a wage increase cancelled each other out, so that ultimately employment would be changed neither by a wage increase nor by a wage cut. This was more or less proved in the mid 1930s, when M. Kalecki investigated events in France.* It does not often happen in the social sciences that a combination of circumstances is such that one can almost speak of a theoretical

* M. Kalecki, 'The Lesson of the Blum Experiment', in: *Economic Journal*, 1938.

experiment. This was by way of exception the case when, under the Blum Government, the French wage level was increased in a short span of time by a large percentage. Prices went up, but employment did not decrease. It did not increase either. The considerable unemployment continued, barely affected by the marked movement of wages.

This seemed to indicate that the truth lay somewhere between the classical and the purchasing power theory. However, a theoretical foundation for this was still lacking. It was supplied by Keynesian theory. In Keynes's view employment is determined by national income, and the latter by total expenditure. Total expenditure consists in expenditure on consumer and investment goods. The first depends on the national income and the propensity to consume, the second on the estimate that the entrepreneurs make of future sales and future profits. In this list of factors determining employment the wage level does not explicitly occur. If wages exert an influence, they must do so via the propensity to consume or via investments. Now in the case of a wage increase the propensity to consume may occasionally increase to some extent. If the wage bill rises at the expense of total profits, the distribution of income is levelled out more, and often less of a levelled-out income is saved – Hobson was already aware of that. In that case employment increases a little via the propensity to consume. But perhaps the opposite reaction occurs via investments. For the entrepreneurs who have to pay the higher wages probably think that this will reduce their possibilities of profit. Even if they are not entirely correct in this supposition from the macro-economic point of view – for wages come back to business in the form of greater returns – the effect on investments can still be negative, so that the flow of goods shrinks a little and employment decreases after a multiplier process. Keynes concluded from the two opposite reactions that the wage level would probably have a negligible effect on employment.

This conclusion was not sufficiently supported by his own theory. For the causal reactions which Keynes introduces are present in principle, but nothing is certain beforehand about their intensity. It might very well be that the reaction via investments is stronger than that via consumption, and that the ultimate result of a wage cut is greater employment. It is also possible that higher wage rates lead to a lower wage bill because employment contracts, and in that case the propensity to consume does not rise at all. Keynesian theory does not express itself on this quantitative side of the matter. Here we have a typical example of a case where the quantitative method has to be called in to assist. If there ever was a problem in which the econometrists' aid was indispensable, this is it.

The first investigation that took place on the basis of an elaborated model was made by J. Tinbergen.* It more or less confirmed the Keynesian idea that employment is fairly insensitive to wage changes, at least on a short-term basis. Further computations made by H. J. Witteveen and others point in the same direction.† However, all this is not yet entirely decisive. For in the long run a high wage can make it profitable to introduce machines that replace labour, so that for this reason a somewhat more limited growth of employment occurs. It also depends on the economic condition of the community that we have in mind. If business is expanding well, wage increases may be an element in the pattern of growth, whilst the same wage increases would fit less well into a stagnating national economy. Finally, it is also important that the insensitivity of employment applies macro-economically only; some industries may get into considerable difficulties through high wages, whereas others may profit from them. A special case of this is formed by the export industry: wage increases here merely raise costs, and not sales as well, for sales depend not on the domestic purchasing power but on the foreign one. Consequently, wage increases in the export industry may have a definitely adverse effect on the demand for labour.

And so numerous actual circumstances may occur which determine the effect of wages on employment. However, one thing that is certain is that the classical theory, with its general proposition that wage cuts dispose of unemployment, is on the wrong track. The flow theory demonstrates this immediately: wages are both costs and income. Wage increases and wage cuts influence the price level in particular – that is evident from the last chapter. And therefore wage policy is very important, but not to the extent

---

* *An Econometric Approach to Business Cycle Problems*, 1937.
† H. J. Witteveen, *Loonshoogte en werkgelegenheid*, 1947.

that total production or total employment depends on it to a great extent.

Now if it is true that, roughly speaking, employment does not depend in a strategic way on wages but on other things, this fact is of great importance to the social process. For if wages can rise and rise without unemployment occurring, it may be asked where the end of this wage rise is. When it was still believed that wage increases, if pursued too vigorously, would evoke unemployment, this belief contained a natural restraint on the endeavours of the unions. If this restraint is not present – what about the social balance of power then? Before we go further into this, we should first briefly consider the question which we discussed very provisionally in the previous section: What really determines the wage level?

3 · WHAT DETERMINES THE WAGE LEVEL?

We have seen above that the marginal productivity theory of wages is still adhered to by the economists, but that they do not believe that marginal productivity is the factor determining the level of money wages. The attitude adopted today is rather that the money wage is formed under the influence of the unions. The latter negotiate with the employers, and the result is a collective labour agreement – an agreement in which minimum wages are fixed. The contents of these collective labour agreements determine the wage level in broad outline.

To find out how these collective wage negotiations are conducted, we must in the first place know what the unions are really aiming at. Sometimes that is quite clear. The small and primitive union wanted one thing only: a higher wage. It took what was going. There were two restraining factors: the reaction of the employers, who exerted counterpressure, and, in the background, the danger that higher wages would lead to unemployment, something which could easily occur in a small industry, to which the macro-economic theory does not apply.

But this pursuit of an ever-larger wage is not always character-istic of a large union. This is a good thing. For if the union becomes so large that it begins to play a macro-economic part (in other words, if the wage that it commands represents so large a sum that it influences national income) the restraint that higher wages lead to less employment no longer applies. In that case a quite different restraint appears on the scene: higher wages lead to higher prices. The union that is large enough proceeds to bear a certain joint responsibility for the occurrence of a cost inflation. A union of this size is quite different from a monopolist seeking his own shortsighted advantage, with whom it is sometimes compared. It is a political body that must learn to think macroeconomically. Its wage policy must make allowance for the public interest – naturally a public interest seen through the eyes of the union leaders, and not at the expense of the union's own interests. But it is remarkable how the unions in some countries – and the Netherlands practically leads the world in this respect – have managed to give expression to both the public interest and their own interest in a balanced policy. The analysis of wage determination is the analysis of a struggle for power in collective bargaining. But the theories which have concerned themselves with this struggle are difficult to grasp. They are complicated thought processes which are too much even for many an insider, and which do not contribute a very great deal to an understanding of the practical matters which we have in mind here. This applies in particular to the theory of games of J. von Neumann and O. Morgenstern, which has borne few if any fruits for the problem of wages.*

It is more practical to observe the content of the wage policy jointly followed by employers and employees. In order to avoid prolixity, we shall consider below the case of a wage increase. If I see matters aright, the problem of wage increases hinges on three strategic points. These are prices, unemployment, and productivity. These three factors determine the general level of money wages.†

Price movement is obviously a factor determining the wage level. If prices rise the leaders of a self-respecting union are practically obliged to ask for wage increases. If they do not do so, the members will probably become discontented, and a gulf may

---

* *The Theory of Games of Economic Behaviour*, 1944. My own theory of bargaining (*The Wage Rate under Collective Bargaining*, 1959) is also special and difficult reading, and moreover not very useful.

† See J. Pen, *Wage Determination Revisited*, Kyklos, 1958.

even be created between the leaders and the members, which is something a union leader does not like at all. Furthermore, if prices rise the employers will often be in a position to pay higher wages; in any case this is true if the price increase is the result of an increased demand.

Nor is it difficult to see that employment conditions play a part in wage determination. Accordingly as unemployment is greater, it becomes more difficult for the union to wield its power. If there is full employment, the supply and demand position in itself exerts forces which gradually push up wages. The profit of business is generally good. A strike would harm profits. Employers will not resist wage claims, because they feel that part of the burden can be shifted to the buyers of the product. If labour becomes definitely scarce, and if a real tension occurs on the labour market, then the union hardly needs to exert additional power; wages rise automatically. The unions will try to increase those parts of the wage structure that lag behind.

Whilst the effect of prices and employment on wages is easy to understand, the effect of productivity is somewhat more difficult to grasp. It might be thought that an increase in productivity must lead to higher wages on account of the marginal productivity theory. Perhaps there is some truth in this. But the relation between wages and productivity that I have in mind is a different one. We are concerned here with a topical point in wage policy occurring in various countries, and to which I should like to draw the reader's particular attention.

For the wage policy of a large, responsible federation of trade unions is keyed to a lesser or greater extent to the idea that the distribution of the national income must satisfy certain requirements. Wage policy is used as a means of influencing this distribution. For the distribution of income there are various criteria; the criterion to which the union usually adheres is the share of labour in the national income. This quantity is expressed by a fraction, for instance $\frac{1}{2}$ (in the Netherlands) or 70 per cent (in the U.S.A.). This figure can be measured statistically. If it becomes smaller, the union considers the distribution of prosperity to be in danger, and then attempts will often be made to correct labour's share by a wage increase.

To realize what exactly is happening here, we must know what factors determine the share of labour. Various economists have given a good deal of thought to this (among others M. Kalecki, who was mentioned above in another context), but their theories are too complicated for our purposes. Fortunately an extremely simple reasoning is also possible. The share of labour in the national income is by definition equal to the total wage bill divided by the national income. The total wage bill is the product of the wage level and employment. The national income may be written as the product of prices and production. Therefore:

$$\text{labour's share} = \frac{\text{wage level} \times \text{employment.}}{\text{prices} \times \text{production}}$$

The left-hand side of this fraction – the relation between wages and prices – is called the real wage rate. The right-hand side is an old acquaintance. If we invert the relation between employment and production we find the productivity of labour. Consequently, the share of labour is equal to the relation between the real wage rate and the average productivity of labour. A simpler formula for the share of labour is hardly conceivable.* It is even tautological, but still it casts light on the importance of productivity to wage policy.

For we see that the share of labour remains constant if the real wage rises to the same extent as the productivity of labour. The gradual rise in the productivity of labour which is the consequence of advances in technology and the steadily growing stock of capital goods must be reflected in the real wage. This can be done in two ways: by reducing prices and by increasing the money wage. If prices are sticky, so that the increased productivity benefits the profit margins, labour's share decreases. The unions will then ask for a wage increase if they are aiming at a constant share for labour. We here encounter a relation between the productivity of labour and wages which is quite different from what the marginal productivity theory suggests. It is a relation arising from union policy.

In this reasoning two of the three strategic factors therefore occur which we have indicated as determining wage policy: prices

* If you think about it, the matter proves to be somewhat more complicated. For the prices which we have introduced are not *per se* equal to the cost of living. A correction can be applied for this, but then the formula loses something of its attractive simplicity.

and productivity. The wage level rises if prices rise, and also if productivity rises. We can put this still more precisely: it emerges from the equation that, in the event of labour having a constant share in the national income, wages are determined by the product of prices and labour productivity. And then unemployment is the third factor of importance. This is a relation which should be borne in mind when we presently assemble our complete model.

4 · THE GOVERNMENT'S WAGE POLICY

If we join together the various elements of the wage theory explained above, we find that the wage level is no more determined by mechanical factors than the price level is. Whereas classical theory thought that the wage level was determined by marginal productivity, and considered a wage increase that exceeded the marginal productivity improbable, and whilst at the same time the wage was believed to have a marked effect on employment, so that a union would blunder if it forced up wages, the modern theory sees this relation differently. The money wage level can rise without employment being seriously harmed. A rise in wage costs leads to a rise in prices, and a rise in prices may in turn lead to a rise in wages. A rise in wages can easily lead to cost inflation, especially if employment is already at a high level and profits are relatively large. This cost inflation is incidentally provoked by a price inflation, and this is illustrated with particular clarity when we remember that a rise in productivity that is not passed on in the form of lower prices influences the distribution of the national income, which the unions then try to rectify by demanding higher wages.

The whole picture points to inherent instability. Processes can easily occur that stir each other up. And moreover two further factors which can intensify the situation must be taken into account.

The first is that it has become evident from econometric investigations, in particular the one by Witteveen, that a wage increase need not lead to reduced profits. On the contrary, Witteveen found that even in the depression of the 1930s in the United States there was a good chance of higher wages leading, on the macro-economic plane, to higher profits. There is reason to suspect that this relation will occur more strongly in a favourable economic situation. If that is so, the relation between employers and employees presents itself in a remarkable light. Previously it was assumed that entrepreneurs and workers had opposite interests where the wage level was concerned. The unions want more wages, and the entrepreneurs resist this. Ultimately a certain equilibrium is arrived at in this way. It can be left to the free market to determine where this equilibrium comes; the parties will have to see to it that they reach agreement among themselves. This view, associated with the 'laissez-faire' idea, is weakened as soon as it is realized that from the macro-economic point of view wages and profits are not opposed to each other, but can move in parallel. The two parties to wage negotiations are then opposed to one another to a much smaller extent. Perhaps, without knowing it, they have a joint interest in a gradually rising wage level. But this rising wage level, which is passed on in the prices, is not in accordance with the interests of the whole national economy. Its victims are those living on pensions and other small fixed incomes, the international competitive position (and therefore employment in the export sector too), the value of money, and the general equilibrium of incomes. The negotiators are sometimes aware of this; they will perhaps allow themselves to be influenced by it, but the degree to which they are prepared to do so is not certain beforehand. Much depends on the nature of the union, on the political situation, on the tensions in the distribution of income, on the willingness of the entrepreneurs to engage in frank and reasonable consultations, and above all on government policy as well. If relations between employers and employees are difficult, if the union has no confidence in the general government policy (or in its tax policy!), if the union members are dissatisfied with the distribution of income, if rival unions are forcing the pace with militant slogans, then wages rise. In that case the employers come round and try to cover themselves by raising prices. Perhaps they will try more than before to secure the benefit of increases in productivity, so that the wage problem is accentuated. Even if all concerned display considerable good will, a stable wage level is not ensured. The equilibrium is unstable. The national economy is then continually threatened with a disturbed equilibrium from the wage sector, and in that case the government cannot continue to stand by idly.

And there is something else, too. Since the possibilities of a Keynesian policy have been recognized, many governments have promised Parliament that they will try to prevent unemployment. This can form an invitation for the unions to use their position of power to improve the incomes of their members. If the union is a responsible one, this endeavour remains within the bounds of what the national economy can bear. But, as stated, it is not certain beforehand that every union can achieve this, especially when the entrepreneurs use the favourable position of the economy to increase their profits. Consequently, within the framework of a policy of full employment a certain responsibility on the part of the government for the general wage level is essential.

It is against this macro-economic background that the government's wage policy must be viewed. It can be pursued in different ways as regards form and content. For our present purpose – understanding macro-economic relations – it is not of much importance whether the government's concern with wages manifests itself in the form of regular consultations, free from obligation, with those concerned, or in the form of compulsory arbitration in the event of wage disputes, or in the strict form that the parties' agreements are subject to government approval. In the Netherlands a complicated machinery has been built up since the war to guide wage bargaining along the right path as much as possible. In the Foundation of Labour the national employers' and employees' organizations meet. They discuss the proposals which have come from the various branches of industry. Without this body's approval no collective labour agreement is valid, and differing wages are forbidden by law. Also *higher* wages are illegal, which is an unusual thing in perceptive Europe. In special cases, viz. in general wage measures (wage rounds), the government itself acts, after having consulted the Social and Economic Council, the top body of the public corporations. This is quite a business. The aim is to promote three-party consultation between employers, employees, and the government aimed at a balanced wage level, a harmonious wage structure, and peaceful employer-employee relations. In other countries such as the U.K. the government's policy is much more restricted. Foreigners are usually most surprised when the technique of Dutch wage control is explained to them. Come to that, such a system is possible only in a small country, where everybody knows everybody else. Elsewhere somewhat difficult conditions still often prevail in wage consultations, but everywhere the government accepts a certain responsibility for what happens on the labour market, although in practice it often has no idea what to do with that responsibility. Let us leave this problem to the politicians, but only after stressing once more the main point of this chapter: the wage level comes about as part of the social and economic situation. 'Wage inflation' may be the result of tensions and conflicts in various fields, such as tax policy, income distribution, price policy, and so on. If a government wants a balanced wage level, it will have to convince the unions that it sincerely aims at harmonious social relations in general.

CHAPTER X

Economic Growth

1 · THE TOPICALITY OF GROWTH THEORY

As long as economics has been in existence it has displayed interest in economic growth – that is to say in the increase of the real national income per head. But the intensity and the focal point of interest have kept on changing. The mercantilists wanted to develop industry and trade to make the state strong and rich, and they regarded restrictions on imports as one of the most suitable ways of doing this. Adam Smith believed that a free development of the productive forces would best serve progress. The accumulation of capital, technological progress, and the increasing division of labour would gradually cause the production per head to grow. Ricardo had a much gloomier view of this: an increasing population would lead to low wages, to a shortage of land, and thus to high rents; profits would suffer from this and growth would, as a result, stagnate. Such pessimism continues to ring through the nineteenth century, and gave economics its name of the dismal science. In Marx's theory, too, 'development' means decline, at least under capitalism; his macro-economics rather resembles that of Ricardo, but has a dramatic conclusion: the collapse of the capitalistic system.

Adam Smith's optimistic view, which has proved much more realistic, also keeps on turning up, for instance in John Stuart Mill and later in J. Schumpeter, who pushed forward the entrepreneur as the man who, by 'new combinations', keeps growth on the go. But the neo-classical theory of the twentieth century begins to display a certain interest in the Stationary State: an economic movement which keeps on turning in the same circle and in which all quantities are at rest. There are no savings, no investments. Economic life has entered its final stage. A. C. Pigou, for instance, elaborated on this strange idea, and the problem of growth disappeared from view as a result.

Moreover, in the 1930s the old pessimism returns in a new form:

189

that of stagnation and the perpetual depression. In the Keynesian world of ideas economic growth remains in the background at first. The conquering of unemployment and deflation was too urgent an aim to allow of an intensive study of a development of income over longer periods. Although reflections on the distant future are by no means absent from the General Theory, as a rule Keynes takes productive capacity and the state of technology as given. He observes the income effect of investments, and not the capacity effect. This is an obvious one-sidedness, in fact exactly the opposite of the one-sidedness which we encountered among the classicists in section 3 of Chapter II.

After the war new interest was aroused in growth, which since then has assumed unprecedented proportions. There are various reasons for this new interest. In the first place the economic renaissance of Europe, and more particularly the increased growth rate, encouraged a study of the phenomenon that was being enacted under the noses of the investigators. Whilst the percentages by which the national income per head in Europe rose over long periods – for instance a century – were about one or two, and really only displayed higher figures – three to four – in the 1920s, the growth percentage in the 1950s proved to increase to four or five, whilst a number of countries (e.g. Western Germany and France) managed to reach still higher annual figures. Other countries, specifically the United Kingdom and Belgium, had to be satisfied with more modest percentages (two or three), and the question therefore arose as to how these differences had to be explained. The rather slow growth rate of the economy of the United States in the fifties also yielded material for new discussions.

But there were more reasons. The rise in incomes made words like prosperity and even affluence much-used terms, and as a result many now realize that their personal prosperity is not all that it should be. Many unfulfilled desires are sharply felt, in both the personal and the collective sphere. Large groups have been left behind. It has come to be vividly realized that these shortages can be eliminated only by an increase in the national income. More social provisions, better education, proper town planning, wider facilities for recreation; scope for wage increases and tax cuts, which render possible more extensive purchases of durable consumer goods and happier holidays; and more free time, which can be pleasantly spent only if it is accompanied by a higher income. All of these are aspirations which have greatly increased since the war and which make requirements of the rate of growth.*

To this must be added the challenge of the communist countries. Their growth figures are higher than ours, although they are not as high as they are presented to us by communist statisticians. But about eight per cent may be a realistic figure for the Soviet Union, and that is more than the free world did achieve. If the figures remain as they are now, the Soviet Union will have caught up the Western world in less than twenty years. Although a greater national income of our neighbours may benefit us, the cold war incites fear and a new interest in growth rates.

However, the problem of growth derives its greatest urgency from the realization that the grinding poverty in three-quarters of the world is intolerable. Much of the growth theory therefore concentrates on the problems of underdeveloped countries. These problems are tremendous and demand a rather different approach – a more sociological one – from the one which we have in mind in this book. The reader will forgive me if I pass over this side of the matter.

All this has made the problem of growth the most important in economics. The limited scope of this book does not allow us to do even imperfect justice to the present state of the theory, which displays very different variants. A fleeting impression must suffice, and in giving this impression we shall adhere to the theme of this book: the difference between classical and Neo-Keynesian approaches. Both are now topical, as we shall see.

2 · A VERY SMALL GROWTH EQUATION

Investments increase both the nation's productive capacity and the national money income. If there is to be balanced growth,

* J. K. Galbraith, who in his celebrated and brilliant *The Affluent Society* (1958) occasionally presents himself as a critic of growth, should not, in my opinion, be classified as such. He wishes above all a better allocation of productive factors, i.e. a bigger public sector, more education, better cities, better design; but this is also a form of growth, for these matters can be more easily realized if there is a greater national surplus.

both effects must be in accordance with each other. This is the basis of a synthesis between classical and Keynesian theory made by R. F. Harrod and E. D. Domar,* which throws a strange light on the rate and the stability of the growth process. The reasoning can be drawn up most simply. It is necessary for this purpose to introduce a new quantity, viz. the relation between a certain addition to the national product (or the national income at constant prices) and the necessary addition to the stock of capital goods. This relation is called the (marginal) capital-output ratio. It is not as new in our reasoning as it perhaps appears; in fact it is the reciprocal of the (marginal) productivity of capital which we encountered in Chapter II. This quantity is represented by g. Depending on the stage of development of the country, it may assume very different values; as a rough guide, it will lie between three and eight. For special industries it may be lower or higher. In Western Europe national figures of four to six have been found. The lower the capital-output ratio is, the better; less investment is then required to arrive at a given percentage of growth.

By definition $g = I/\Delta Y$ (capacity effect; ΔY is the increase of Y). So as not to complicate matters, let us ignore X, M, G, and T. In that case the national income will adjust to that level at which $I = S = s . Y$ (the multiplier of the income effect†). Therefore: $g = s . Y/\Delta Y$. By a small conversion: $\Delta Y/Y = s/g$. This is the growth equation, which has become very popular.

Its popularity is not surprising. For if we examine the equation we see that it establishes a relation between the growth rate of the national income and two simple quantities: the propensity to save and t   capital-output ratio. If production increases at this rate, the new product is sold and the new capital goods remain in use. In this sense growth is balanced. If the actual growth rate differs from this quotient, disturbances occur which have been the subject of most alarming reflections. It has been concluded that the growth must be extremely unstable. We shall come back to this in the next section. Reference may now be made to an-

* R. F. Harrod, 'An Essay in Dynamic Theory', *Economic Journal*, 1939, and: *Towards a Dynamic Economics*, 1948. E. D. Domar, 'Expansion and Employment', *American Economic Review*, 1947.

† Assuming that the marginal and average propensities to save are equal.

other useful employment which can be made of this small equation, and which explains part of its popularity.

For it can give a quantitative impression of the degree of expansion which a national economy will display. Let us assume that the (average and marginal) propensity to save is 20 per cent, a figure that for a country in the West is neither extremely high nor very low. Let us then assume that the capital-output ratio is 5. The growth percentage that follows from our equation is 4. This is a reasonable figure for a Western country. However, a higher percentage is possible; this is evident from recent experience. Both the propensity to save and the capital-output ratio may be more favourable; for instance 25 per cent and 3; this implies a growth percentage of 8. Such simple arithmetic has something very attractive about it, and it has the advantage of drawing attention to strategic factors in development. It therefore goes without saying that the capital-output ratio has met with great interest and that considerable empirical research has been done into this figure. It has been found that the underdeveloped countries are faced with a high capital-output ratio. In combination with a low propensity to save caused by poverty, this gives an unfortunate result. Put s at 10 per cent and g at 7. The growth figure is then $1\frac{1}{2}$ per cent. Not much for a country aiming at accelerated development. Definitely too little if the population increases annually by 1 per cent. And so small as to be catastrophic if the population increases by 2 per cent. We have here one of the many variants of the low income trap: the income per head remains stuck at a low level. It may even decline. Part of the tragedy of the underdeveloped countries is already clearly manifest here.

Population growth naturally contributes to national income, but it is extremely dubious whether this is also the case as regards the income per head. Old classical writers – specifically Ricardo and Malthus – saw a negative connexion between population growth and prosperity, and empirical research work in the twentieth century (P. H. Douglas) points in the same direction: an increase in the working population of 1 per cent would lead to an increase in production of only $\frac{3}{4}$ per cent. But some adherents of the stagnation theory expect from a vigorous population growth an impulse to consumption which would cause *per capita* income to increase. However, it seems better for prosperity to give this impulse by means of a Keynesian policy, for instance by Functional Finance or by adding to the nation's capital stock. In that case a marked population growth is not necessary for growth – in fact it is harmful to it. For with a capital-output ratio of, for instance, 5 and a population growth of 1 per cent, 5 per cent of Y must be invested every year to give employment to the newcomers and to keep up the level of income per head. This is called 'widening capital'. This 5 per cent could otherwise have been used to increase the productivity of labour by 'deepening capital'. In developed countries, population growth is therefore probably a negative factor in growth. And in underdeveloped countries no doubt is possible: overpopulation there is literally fatal.

However, the utility of this small equation must not cause us to forget that the complex growth problem has been reduced to particularly simplistic proportions. That is the work of the capital-output ratio, which compresses a mass of phenomena into one figure. This is not so bad in itself, as long as we are aware of it and as long as this quantity is in fact a constant. However, criticism of the latter supposition is possible. We shall come back to this in the next section.

3 · STABILITY AND THE GROWTH PARADOX

The tenor of the previous section was that s/g is the percentage of growth of national income at which the capital goods are fully used. We shall now see that investment must therefore also increase by the same percentage every year. If this does not happen – if for instance they stay at the same level for a time! – disturbances of a paradoxical nature occur.

For just see what happens if in a given year investments fall short of s/g; for instance because the entrepreneurs have a rather pessimistic view of things. They maintain an investment volume which is high enough in their opinion, and which, at first sight, leads to a possibly modest, but still not unsatisfactory, growth rate. But this rate is smaller than s/g, and this means that a depressive effect on the national money income occurs, as a result of which the capital goods are not fully utilized. Too low investments lead to unutilized capacity or, to put it differently, a slower growth than s/g leads to overproduction! This is the growth paradox.

It requires little imagination to see how serious this can be. Unused machines have an extremely discouraging effect on investing. Consequently, in the following period the level of investment will fall still further below the required level; and this will lead to a further overcapacity. According as less is invested, and growth proceeds more slowly, the forces hampering investment become stronger. To put it another way, a small downwards deviation of the growth rate s/g leads to a cumulative disturbance and in fact to stagnation and depression.

The equation also creates the impression that growth is extremely unstable in an upward direction. If a little more is invested than corresponds to s/g (for instance because autonomous investments increase), more extra income is created than corresponds to the growth of productive capacity. Despite the high investments the machines cannot keep up the pace of demand, so that still higher investments are encouraged. Too rapid growth leads to underproduction – it seems incredible, but it is strictly logical.

Anyone who gives some thought to these processes cannot but come to the conclusion that balanced growth is practically impossible. The smallest departure from the narrow path of balanced growth leads to cumulative disturbances of equilibrium. The original Keynesian theory, which we have developed in the preceding chapters, was not as pessimistic as that. It showed that inflationary and deflationary gaps are possible, that the true equilibrium is a special case, but not that this case is practically impossible to realize. The reasoning of Harrod and Domar is much more disquieting.

And in another respect, too, it is not very encouraging. Growth proves to depend on the degree of utilization of the capital stock; employment does not figure in the story! Even if the growth rate s/g should be achieved, full employment is still not ensured. You could therefore make up an extremely sombre story about a community in which full capacity growth and full employment growth differ.

But at the same time all this evokes criticism. For actual

economic life is not as unstable as all that. The reasoning is reminiscent of the story of the centipede that had always been able to walk well until somebody proved that this was really impossible with all those legs. The story goes that from then on the creature kept on stumbling; but it should instead have decided that there was something wrong with the theory.

Indeed, this criticism has been directed against the pessimistic growth theories. The critics concentrate on the constancy of the capital-output ratio. A fixed relation between investment and additional production implies that additions of labour to a given stock of capital do not summon forth any greater production. (In technical terms, the marginal productivity of labour is zero.) But relations in production are not that rigid. To see this we may set against the theory of Harrod and Domar the classical growth theory, which is based precisely on flexible relations between the factors of production.

When we were discussing the classical system we saw that prices occupied a central position in it. Prices control sales, and they also control the proportions in which the means of production will be applied. For it is possible to make a product in various ways: with a lot of labour and little capital or with less labour and more capital. These two inputs can replace one another, and the extent to which the substitution is profitable for the entrepreneur is determined by the relation between the prices of capital and labour. The classical growth theory deduces from this that balanced growth and full employment have a good chance of being realized. For if at a given moment too little should be invested to satisfy the demand for final products, the demand for labour increases. Wages go up and this stimulates investments because the entrepreneur prefers to avoid this expensive labour. This process is less unstable than the process of Harrod and Domar described above. Conversely, unemployment will lead to falling wages, which makes it profitable for the entrepreneurs to replace capital by labour. Growth then means that the stock of capital goods increases only slowly, whilst the additional product is produced above all by additional labour. The capital-output ratio then falls. In this classical train of thought a flexible capital-output ratio adjusts to the requirements of the situation instead of repeatedly throwing the economy out of balance.

This classical growth theory, which has been interestingly described by R. M. Solow and J. E. Meade,* cannot be denied a certain realism. The 'input mix' is definitely not as rigid as the constant capital-output ratio suggests. The price system plays a part in directing the growth process. But on the other hand we may not rely on so great a flexibility that growth will always be balanced. The interplay of Harrod–Domar effects on the one hand and input substitutions on the other makes the razor's edge of growth less difficult to tread than the pessimists think on a basis of the small equation; but the possibility of cumulative disturbances, or at least of accelerations and retardations of growth, is definitely there. This is clear from the variations which growth figures have displayed in the Western world in the course of the years; and it is also a fact that this instability makes stringent requirements of government policy. It makes the task of Functional Finance, and of the other instruments of economic policy, more difficult. However, it is not easy to state to what extent the classical or the Harrod–Domar mechanism has worked in a given period – say the 1950s – the more so since other quite different strategic factors operate in the process of growth which have not yet been dealt with. The time has come to say a few words about them.

4 · GROWTH AND STRUCTURAL CHANGES

Model-making is based on the fact that certain relations, expressed by the regression coefficients, are constant. These constants indicate the structure of the model. But now the difficulty arises that in growth this structure sometimes changes. This entails serious complications, for which the theory has by no means found all the answers yet.

The first point concerns the consumption function. Consumption habits change in the course of time. People get accustomed to a certain consumption, and shift their aspirations as prosperity increases. A consequence of this is for instance that a temporary drop in income or even a disappointing growth rate is more likely

* R. M. Solow, 'A Contribution to the Theory of Economic Growth', *Quarterly Journal of Economics*, 1956. J. E. Meade, *A Neo-Classical Theory of Economic Growth*, 1960.

to be absorbed by a reduced propensity to save than by reduced consumption (F. Modigliani and J. S. Duesenberry). This operates as a built-in stabilizer. The required rate of growth s/g becomes lower according as a lower growth rate occurs, as a result of which the danger of a cumulative disturbance lessens.

However, the shift from non-durable consumer goods to durables operates in the opposite direction. In growing prosperity the latter begin to occupy a larger place in the pattern of consumption. It is easy to postpone buying or replacing them, This makes the consumption equation uncertain, so much so, in fact, that some have lost all confidence in this equation and thus in the Neo-Keynesian model (e.g. G. Katona, in his *The Powerful Consumer*, 1960). One possible answer to this is to split the consumption function into different components: one for non-durable consumer goods and one for durable consumer goods. The first equation is more reliable than the second; the weakness of the regression coefficients is not avoided, but concentrated in one equation. The division also makes it possible to include a separate equation for the sale of cars, since this plays a special part in growth. For the car is one of the pacemakers of mass consumption, which is regarded by W. W. Rostow as a new growth phase,* and the automobile industry may exercise a strategic influence on the psychological conditions of economic growth.

A further point is the change of structure within production. In olden days in Europe, and in underdeveloped countries, the agricultural sector is the main one. According to some, economic development is therefore practically identical with industrialization, with various industries in the van. At an early stage of European growth these were iron and steel, railways, textiles; in following stages they were cars, chemicals, and electronics. It is of vital importance to growth that the various key branches of industry succeed each other smoothly. This makes tremendous requirements of flexibility and timing. Take as an example television. When this appeared on the scene the electronics industry was faced with the task of providing the public with sets in a short time. The expansion of the industry in those years was fantastic. In a number of years the market was more or less full, and then the growth rate of this branch fell back to a 'normal'

* *The Stages of Economic Growth*, 1960.

figure. If, therefore, no other product is ready to set the pace for growth, stagnation is to be expected. But the appearance of new products is a rather incidental thing, and that makes growth unstable. These phenomena cannot easily be incorporated in a Keynesian model, unless one is prepared to apply a further breakdown of equations (disaggregation), so that every sector is assigned its own equations.

In this connexion it is also significant that industry is declining as a percentage of national activity. The present stage of the Western world is characterized by an increasing importance of the services sector (called by Colin Clark the tertiary sector). We see the beginnings of a relative decline of industry, which is thus suffering the same fate as agriculture. There are indications that practically half of an advanced economy such as that of the United States is dominated by this tertiary sector, and that development is continuing further in this direction. However, it is doubtful whether this process is smooth enough. If it goes too slowly, growth may be checked. Perhaps this phenomenon occurred in the United States in the 1950s; it may have contributed to unemployment.

The shift to the tertiary sector also has its effect on the investment equation. It might very well be that the quantity of capital per unit product in the third sector will be less than that in industry; this therefore means a drop in the national capital-output ratio. But furthermore the nature of these investments is changing: they are being made more in men and less in machines. For this reason, too, education is becoming an increasingly strategic factor in economic development. The effect which this has on a long-term model is still uncertain.

This brings us to another point: the part played by the government sector in growth. It is a well-known phenomenon that the relative size of the public sector increases with the national income. This was already predicted about 1870 by A. Wagner, and consequently one speaks of Wagner's Law. In those days the G/Y fraction was usually not more than 5 to 10 per cent; now it is about 25 per cent and it will perhaps rise still higher. Infra-structure, education, and government-backed research are becoming increasingly important stimuli in the growth process. Where these lag behind not only a disequilibrium but in fact a retardation in growth is to be feared. Also, a large and independently growing government sector can be expected to provide a growth stabilization which makes the economy less sensitive to depressive shocks. Whereas the purchasing power effects of the government sector can still be traced, this applies much less strongly to the effects on productive capacity. The ins and outs of this are not known, and of course this makes the model less reliable. One consolation for economic theory is that the government's influence on productivity works slowly, and this reduces the danger to the constancy of the regression coefficients; but in the long run they may change in an unpredictable way.

A final topical question: what is the effect on growth of the increasing size of business concerns and of the replacement of the nineteenth-century capitalist by the modern manager?

The institutions of big business were impressively described by G. Means and A. A. Berle in their book *The Modern Corporation and Private Property* (1932). What worried these authors was not so much the growth problem as the influence of the concentrations of power and wealth.* The decline in the position of the old-fashioned entrepreneur, who founded great enterprises on his own personal responsibility and his own capital, has led others to suspect that the community's resilience will suffer from this. In particular J. Schumpeter, in his *Capitalism, Socialism and Democracy* (1943), voiced the suspicion that the modern concerns, run by managers with a certain tendency towards a humane but bureaucratic company policy, would radically change society. Dynamics disappear with the old-style entrepreneur. This might, in Schumpeter's view, even form one of the causes of the downfall of capitalism!

Now this kind of pessimism seems to me to be wrong, for various reasons. In the first place the change in structure which created the modern manager has not proceeded so far that the old entrepreneur has disappeared. He is still with us and is continuing to make his contribution to growth. In the second place, the big concerns do not hamper economic development. On the contrary, they have institutionalized growth, and offer capitalism

* The latter question will not be dealt with here; it is discussed in my *Harmony and Conflict in Modern Society*, New York, Toronto, and London, 1966.

new chances of a social nature. The industrial giants are spending huge sums on research (so that the progress of technology is no longer the work of individuals, but of teams); if necessary they take enormous risks, and are able to plan long-term investments. They are also capable of a progressive policy towards their workers. Moreover, they have seen their way to infusing every section of their concerns with the ideology of expansion and productivity. W. J. Baumol in particular has drawn attention to this latter point. In his opinion expansion is given greater priority by the concerns than profits.* If that is true, the structural change in industry leading to larger industrial units and a less personal management is making a positive contribution to growth.

In fact the figures bear out the optimists. As remarked above, the growth percentages of the national product for the 1950s were at a higher level than ever before. Figures of about 5 per cent were quite usual in Western Europe; some countries have even achieved 7 per cent. The fact that the growth rate in the United States in the same period was rather on the low side (less than half of the European figures) is definitely not due to bureaucratization of the concerns, but to a combination of restraints: both Harrod–Domar effects (accentuated by an overtly 'classical' budget ideology of the Eisenhower Administration) and disequilibria between sectors. But, since 1960, there has been a remarkable transformation connected with the automation of processes in American industry; wage costs per unit of output have been falling and the rate of growth, now over 4 per cent a year, has speeded up. The last word has not yet been said about an exact diagnosis of this matter. Growth still poses many unsolved questions.

* *Business Behavior, Value and Growth*, 1959.

CHAPTER XI

Fitting the Jigsaw Together

1 · TEN EQUATIONS

Up to now our reasoning has run as follows. We were looking for the factors that determine the national income and which at the same time give the size of other important macro-economic quantities, such as consumption, investments, taxes, prices, wages, imports, and exports. To trace the new and the old theories on these relations we first outlined classical theory: national income depends on the productivity of labour, and price relationships attend to the general equilibrium. Then we dealt with Keynesian theory: national income depends on total expenditure. Macro-economic equilibrium is established by the 'multiplier', i.e. by a change in the national income itself. We illustrated this approach by a model which contained only three equations (the consumption function, the investment function, and the income equation $Y = C + I$). We found that both Keynesian and classical theory could be illustrated by this model. We then put it in graphical form, and from this graph not only the national income but also employment emerged (after a further factor, the productivity of labour, had been added).

But this model was too simple. Though it contains the key features of macro-economics, it is insufficiently realistic. We then discussed international trade, public finance, prices, and wages separately. A chapter was also devoted to the part played by money – a subtle and rather controversial topic. Finally it was the turn of economic growth. We have thus separately considered a number of problems by means of the Neo-Keynesian doctrine, but in fact these things are closely inter-related. It is now time to fit these parts into a whole. We shall do this by means of a model of the same kind as the one described in Chapter IV; the only difference is that it is more extensive. It is more or less true that every chapter of this book so far yields one or more equations.

The equations are given below in words, not in symbols. The

advantage is obvious: the model does not look as frightening. The disadvantage is that a somewhat larger area of paper is covered and also that it cannot be immediately seen whether one quantity influences another quantity positively or negatively. In mathematical notation this is apparent from the sign of the regression coefficient. To rectify this, the sign is given in brackets behind every quantity. Plus means that an increase in the variable leads to an increase in the dependent variable; minus means the opposite. The exact relationship between quantities (e.g. proportionality) is left open, except in a few special cases where we are obviously concerned with addition, division, etc. Here are the equations, ten in all.

1. *The national money income is the sum of consumption, investments, exports, and government expenditure minus imports.* This is the fundamental income equation. It corresponds to a point on the 45° line in the graph of Chapter IV.

2. *The real national income depends on the stock of capital goods and the amount of labour employed.* This is the production function, which links inputs to outputs. Classical theory reads the equation from right to left (full employment is given and, together with capital, determines total output); Keynesian theory reads it from left to right; real national income is given from the quotient of national income and prices; employment follows from this but of course has a maximum value. Given the production function and the level of production, labour productivity is fixed.

3. *Consumption depends on the national income* (+), *the distribution of income* (+), *the quantity of money in the hands of the households* (+), *and (personal) taxes* (−). This is a consumption function. The form which we have given it indicates that we regard the quantity of money as a factor causing temporary aberrations of the propensity to consume. Another form, which would probably be more highly appreciated by the proponents of the old money theory, is this: Consumption depends on the quantity of money (+). This seems to imply that there is no such thing as a 'normal' propensity to consume; it readily conforms to the quantity of money in circulation. This goes too far for me; I consider it too un-Keynesian. But anyone who wants to can interpret matters in this way. Many other variables might be

introduced; for instance the growth of the national income (as distinguished from its level), demographic factors, and so on.

4. *Investments depend on the stock of capital goods* (−), *the growth of the national income* (+), *profits* (+), *the quantity of liquid assets in the hands of the entrepreneurs* (+), *and (business) taxes* (−). This, then, is a kind of flexible accelerator supplemented by elements of profit theory and of monetary theory. Allowance has also been made for the influence of taxes, an influence which still causes many a problem. Furthermore, savings could also be included as separate variables, as a further concession to classical theory. The rate of interest, too, might be included. We discussed this complicated and as yet uncertain matter in section 3 of Chapter IV. It may be that we have included too many variables in a well-intentioned attempt to reconcile with each other all the different theories on the entrepreneurs' investment policy. A most simple equation: *I depends on the inflationary gap* (+). It must be left to the econometrists to verify what plays a part in practice and what does not.

5. *Exports depend on foreign demand* (+), *the price level in relation to that of the competing countries* (+), *and the rate of exchange* (+). In the export equation the significance of the price level comes to the fore as a determinant of the competitive position on foreign markets. We shall therefore have to explain this quantity as well presently.

6. *Imports depend on the national income* (+) *and the inflationary gap* (+). It might be thought that the propensity to import also depends on the price relationships between home and abroad. Anyone who wants to may confidently include this price relation (and also the rate of exchange) in the import equation. Often it will not mean much in the whole interplay of factors, but you never know.

7. *Tax revenue depends on the national income* (+) *and on the tax rate fixed by the politicians* (+). This equation is just as primitive as No. 6. As we have introduced personal and business taxes in Nos. 2 and 3, the tax equation should be split into these two parts. It can be further subdivided in accordance with the kinds of tax: turnover taxes, import duties, income taxes. We shall not do so here; for our purposes these complications are not necessary. However, in the econometrists' practical models a

further subdivision is often made, the more so as good figures are available on this subject.

8. *Increases in the price level depend on wage increases* (+), *increases in labour productivity* (−), *the import price level* (+) *and the degree of competition* (−) *and the inflationary gap* (+). This price equation is a summary of the chapter on price theory. It will without a doubt incur the displeasure of the econometrists, since the degree of competition which appears in it is extremely difficult to measure. Well then, they will just have to leave this out. The equation lends itself easily to being split.

9. *Wage increases depend on the inflationary gap* (+), *increases in labour productivity* (+), *and price increases* (+).

10. *The inflationary gap depends on the actual national money income* (+) *and the national money income which corresponds to full employment* (−). The latter can be read off from equation no. 2. The gap may be positive or negative. This variable is important, not only for its own sake, but also because it appears in other equations (6, 8, 9, and perhaps 4).

2 · A NUMBER OF THE MODEL'S PROPERTIES

The above ten equations give the framework of the macro-economic theory developed in this book. If you take the trouble to count the variables you will probably see that there are twenty-seven. Of these, ten are determined by the system and seventeen are given. The choice of these numbers is arbitrary. We might have written down eleven equations on the basis of exactly the same reasoning, for instance by writing down a fairly obvious equation like: unemployment equals the difference between the potential and the actual working population, or by adding a complicated growth equation. The preceding chapters might easily lead to twenty-five equations. But ten is a round figure.

It has already been pointed out that the division of the variables into 'given' and 'to be found' determines the logical form of the theory. It is therefore useful to investigate which properties and characteristics of economic life we have assumed as given, and which we have 'explained' by the model.

For this purpose we divide the given properties and char-acteristics into five groups. The first group relates to the working population, the stock of capital goods, and the natural resources of the country in question. These quantities pop up at various places in the model, explicitly or implicitly. The stock of capital goods influences production, the productive capacity, in conjunction with the movement of sales, determines the profit margin;* the working population, in conjunction with employment, determines unemployment. But, above all, these quantities together determine one of the strategic factors of the model: the productivity of labour. No separate equation has been included for this quantity. One could have been, for productivity depends among other things on the development of production. But that would have got us into awkward complications, which should be avoided in a book aiming at simplicity. However, the productivity of labour has been included as a variable determining another quantity – prices. And finally it must not be forgotten that the productivity of labour is the fundamental factor in the overall productive capacity per head of the population. One final equation ought really to be drawn up in the model: welfare depends on the productivity of labour (+) and unemployment (−), since these two variables determine the real income per head. But again this equation brings with it a whole string of difficulties. For welfare depends on still more things: on the distribution of income for instance, and on the nature of the goods produced, on the length of the working day, on working conditions in the firms, and so on. The literature on this 'welfare function' is extremely extensive and neither unanimous nor encouraging. It has a much more philosophical nature than would fit in with the set-up of this matter-of-fact book.

The second group of given quantities from which our model proceeds concerns the relations between the national economy and other countries. They are the foreign demand for goods produced by the national economy, the foreign competitors' price level, the import price level (and also the rate of exchange, but this belongs in group No. 5). A country is unable to influence these quantities; only the rate of exchange is subject to its own government's policy. These data influence exports (and thus employment, the creation of income, consumption, and in-

* This model contains no separate equations for the level of profits or for the distribution of income – an unsatisfactory state of affairs.

vestment at home). Import prices have been introduced because they help to determine the price level of a country. For some countries these external data are of vital importance.

The third group of data has a monetary character: the quantity of money in the hands of the consumers and the quantity of money in the hands of the entrepreneurs. We shall leave open the possibility of these monetary factors influencing consumption and investment, although this certainly does not mean that we are returning to the view that these quantities of money are really strategic factors in economic life. For the earned income which people have available is more important than the supply of money. The cash holdings present are more incidental factors, which in an unstable situation make their effect felt, but which normally play no other role than the oil which makes a machine run without too much friction.

The fourth group of given quantities is formed by the degree of competition and the profits resulting from this. These factors are important to the development of prices and to the distribution of income. Via these two elements they also influence the general wage level, as we saw in the chapter on wages.

The fifth group of given variables has a political character: the level of government expenditure, the tax rate, and the rate of exchange. These are typical 'instrument variables' (see below).

By means of these five groups of quantities and the ten equations the system is determined. The model ensures that the national income (and the growth thereof), employment, consumption, investments, taxes, imports, and exports, and also the wage and price level, are all represented. These ten quantities are linked together by regression coefficients. How? That is something which cannot be explained in a few words. The reader must re-read the preceding chapters: the best way is to have another look at the graph which depicts the heart of the Keynesian theory, and then to remember that this graph has to be supplemented by the Keynesian theory of the balance of payments and the government budget. In each instance the national income ensures that an equilibrium occurs between inflationary and deflationary components, and that savings, imports, and taxes together keep investments, exports, and government expenditure in balance. In this interplay the determination of prices and wages can also be incorporated. One of these regression coefficients deserves special mention, because it is the most typical Keynesian one: the marginal propensity to consume (equation No. 3). But there are many more.

It has already emerged from the preceding observations that the macro-economic theory defended here is by no means regarded as a perfect system that must be considered the ultimate in economic science and that can only be admired. Numerous relations have merely been touched upon. We have slurred over important problems. On various points a certain course has been adopted, whilst another course might just as well have been followed. This theory is still in full development, and the view given of the present state of affairs is subjective and open to many kinds of criticism. It may be useful to examine a few aspects of these different alternatives somewhat more closely.

Ideas may differ on the most desirable way of detailing the system. We started with three equations and have now advanced to ten. That is still a rather small number; we are therefore working with a simple theory as yet. On many points further specification is possible, as a result of which the number of equations increases. Reference has already been made to the possibility of stating more precisely the factors determining tax revenue by treating the different kinds of taxes separately. But the influence of taxes on C and I can also be more closely analysed. A first step in this direction is to write consumption not as a function of Y but as a function of $Y - T_c$, where T_c represents the amount of direct taxes contributed by the households.

A further possibility of making the model fuller and therefore more realistic is offered by the influence which the distribution of income has on the propensity to consume. A more uniform distribution of income (levelling out) leads to a higher relation between consumption and national income – Hobson was already aware of this fifty years ago (see Chapter IX). Some kind of measurable index for this was included in the consumption function. But it is also possible to draw up separate relations which describe the distribution of income. For instance, total wage income may be specified (whereby the effect of social insurance and incomes paid over in a special manner, such as old age pensions, can be brought into the model). The level of profits can be explained, too. All of this is illuminating also when considered by itself; apart from its effect on consumption the distribution of the national income is an interesting and sometimes hotly debated matter, which plays a very considerable role in political differences of opinion.

In other ways, too, the number of equations can be enormously increased. Consumption goods can be divided into durables and non-durables; sales of the former depend especially on the rise in incomes and the (expected) rise in prices. Investments can be divided into investments which depend greatly on sales and others which are less dependent (autonomous investments). Investment in stocks of goods (final goods or materials) may also be introduced. The price equation can be divided into a number of equations for separate price levels: consumer goods, investment goods, export goods. Government expenditure is susceptible to further analysis: investments, other material expenditure, salaries, transfer expenditure. These components have different effects on the macro-economic situation. Imports can also be subdivided: imports for direct consumption, for investment, for stockpiling. In that case we do not have one propensity to import, but a number of partial propensities. Further, separate equations can be inserted for special sectors of the national economy, such as agriculture or the automobile industry, which occupy a special position.

If the latter method is followed, and separate sectors are represented by separate equations, the number of possibilities of further specification of the model becomes enormous. For in principle it is possible to examine every branch of industry separately. At the same time the relations between the various branches of industry are then spotlighted. The chemical industry supplies agriculture, and the engineering industry supplies the chemical industry. Shipbuilding buys products from the electrical sector, and the coal mines supply just about everybody. This network of relations can be depicted only by highly complicated models. W. Leontief was the great pioneer in this field.* Now a school of highly trained econometrists tackles these problems. This 'input–

* *The Structure of the American Economy*, 1943.

output analysis' can with something of an effort be regarded as a detailing of a Neo-Keynesian model, but in actual fact it is something quite different. The strategic relations which we have in mind are swallowed up in the interaction of the branches of industry. Input–output analysis greatly enhances our insight into inter-industrial flows of goods, but it obscures our understanding of the typically Keynesian relations which form the subject of this book.

Somewhere between the extremes of oversimplification and overdetailing lies a usable model. Ours has 10 equations; the one used by the Netherlands Central Planning Bureau – we shall come back to this – has about 50. No mean number, but much larger systems have been devised. A lot depends on what the model-builder is aiming at. A few comments on this follow.

3 · WHAT DO WE DO WITH THE MODEL?

There may be various reasons for drawing up a model. The most obvious objective is to summarize economic relations. The quantities which influence each other are assembled in a convenient manner, and moreover in a manner which in principle expresses the quantitative nature of these relations. Even if no further efforts are made to look for really statistical relations, there has been a gain: the theory has been made concrete. One can easily see on which points one disagrees with the author. Weak links in the reasoning stick out like a sore thumb. In the above model, income distribution (the level of profits) has been treated scantily. This can be seen within five minutes. The rate of interest is missing. And so on.

A model can serve other purposes. For instance, it can be used to describe a process. Changes in one quantity evoke changes in other variables in a following period. This propagation can be examined by means of the model, even if the intensity of the relations is not known exactly. We have to introduce certain 'lags and leads' between the variables. In this way we can get an impression of the stability of the system. It is, however, true that definitive results cannot be arrived at like this. For the movements of economic quantities depend above all on the intensity of the reactions. We saw this quite clearly when we examined the effect of wage changes on employment. It applies in all cases where various effects clash.

An important step in model-building is quantification. This means determining the regression coefficients which represent the degree of influence. This is characteristically the work of the econometrist. He will start from the statistical material couched in the form of time series. To this he applies the correlation calculation, which establishes the equations. A particular difficulty which occurs in this technique is caused by the time-lag in the reactions. Consumption does not react to today's income, but to yesterday's. Investments need time to adjust. Taxes are deducted from the income of a given year, but they may already have influenced the decisions of an earlier year. Changes in prices are passed on after a delay. Wage adjustments take time. All this means that the time series cannot be simply 'placed on top of each other'; they must be shifted a little in time before the corresponding quantities fit in with each other. The problem of 'lags and leads' has already been discussed many times in theory – one speaks of dynamic and static theories, depending on whether the lags and leads have been incorporated in the model or not – and it has often simplified the description of events in time,* but it causes difficulties for the econometrist, since he must establish the time-lags between the time series *in concreto* before he can arrive at significant results.

The correlation calculation gives a double insight. On the one hand the econometrist can tell us whether the theory was sound – whether the model gave a proper 'explanation' or whether certain equations prove not to have had a realistic view of the

---

* In a static theory, in which today and yesterday are eliminated and a state of equilibrium is analysed, causality is a more difficult concept than in a dynamic theory. In the past economics concerned itself intensively with statics, until it was found that dynamics is really clearer. Our explanations of the Keynesian theories are meant to be dynamic: first this happens, then that follows, and after that comes something else again. I am mentioning this because insiders may perhaps think that they detect traces of the orthodox Keynesian statics in me.

actual relation. To the extent that the econometrist encounters such difficulties, the theory must try and supply him with better equations. A model that is suitable for writing on a blackboard for instructive and pedagogic purposes can make an econometrist despair – it is not inconceivable that some of our equations possess this disagreeable property.

On the other hand, the econometrist lets us have the regression coefficients. This is a great step forward on the road to knowledge. For these quantities tell us which factors are important and which are unimportant; they give the model its exact structure. You can look at it this way: the unquantified model makes a more or less orderly whole out of the chaos of possible economic relations. And yet this order is still far from definitive. It does not become so until the value of the regression coefficients is fixed. Some important regression coefficients of our model are the propensity to consume, the propensity to import, and the tax rate; the effect of wages on prices, and of prices on exports; the effect of unemployment, prices, and the productivity of labour on wages. And then there is the difficult question of the regression coefficients of the investment equation.

With a quantitative model available the theoretician is in a strong position if he wants to explain the workings of the national economy. But explaining is only a modest aim. More ambitious are those who also want to forecast the course of events.

We are now skating on thin ice. Whilst models were not invented to form the basis of a forecast, they are very closely associated with this in the minds of many econometrists. That is logical, too. If the regression coefficients are fixed, and therefore the degree of influence is given, we can investigate exactly what the variables will do if changes occur in the situation 'from outside', for instance through economic policy, or through foreign markets. This means that we can derive the value which the variables will assume if the autonomous quantities, which are determined outside the model, change.

A typical example of an autonomous quantity is that of government expenditure. It is determined politically. True, part of this expenditure is connected with the variables of the model – if the unemployed are supported by public funds, this item of expenditure will automatically increase if unemployment increases – but to a considerable extent they are genuinely exogenous. This does not mean that the economist does not have to concern himself with them – it merely means that the macro-economic model is incapable of explaining this quantity, and inserts it as given. Now if the model offers an exact picture of reality, it can be used for forecasting in the sense that the impact of a given change in government expenditure is correctly reproduced by it.

Viewed in this way, forecasting is based on two things: the autonomous variables must be filled in correctly (they must therefore be separately predicted outside the model) and the regression coefficients, which have been calculated from data from the past, must hold good. The latter does not always happen; it is the nightmare of every forecaster. At the same time it is the jumping-off point for the more clinical critics of this method. (The emotional criticism is a separate chapter – we shall discuss this on page 223.)

It is understandable that some model-builders, impressed as they were by the new technique, overrated the constancy of the regression coefficients. Perhaps it is also true that the discrepancies in these figures, considered in themselves, stay within fairly narrow bounds. Nevertheless they are often large enough to cause the precalculated results of the model to differ so much from reality that economic policy can hardly make progress with it. This is a pity, but it is not a reason for abandoning the method. For there is no better one. A forecaster can operate extempore, or by means of primitive methods of calculation; he can also use a model. If the model has been put together at all expertly, it works better than the rough calculation methods of the average practician – although it is definitely inferior to the intuition of a truly great economist, in whose brain a model of much greater refinement is at work. But the existence of a handful of geniuses may not induce us to stop making forecasting models. On the contrary, we must try to improve them.

It makes a difference to the nature of the model whether the forecaster is thinking of a long term or a short term. Usually he aims at a period of one year, but sometimes his ambitions extend further, and he tries to look ahead ten or twenty years (as for instance the Australian Colin Clark, a prophet who has never been afraid of making risky extrapolations). In a short-term model some of the equations can be omitted. For instance, the Dutch Central Planning Bureau does not use a wage equation; the expected wage rate is an exogenous factor which is estimated separately by means of the knowledge which the Bureau has of current wage negotiations.

A special form of the forecasting model is the decision model. The idea which lies behind this, and which is the brain-child of R. Frisch and J. Tinbergen, is as follows. In the explanatory model the basis is formed by certain data, and the model operates in the direction of the variables to be explained: the size of the national income, employment, and the like. However, the econometrist can also reverse this procedure. He can choose certain variables for which we want to assume a certain value for policy reasons. For instance, a government wants an unemployment equal to 0 (apart from seasonal and frictional unemployment). Or it wants a balance of payments in equilibrium ($X - M = 0$). Or it has set its heart on a stable price level. Or better still, it wants all three at the same time. Starting from the targets, the econometrist works backwards by means of the model. He operates in the direction of the variables which the government has under its control, such as the tax rate, government expenditure, the rate of exchange; and to a lesser extent wages and prices in some sectors of the economy. The values of these quantities which match the objectives of economic policy are calculated. Once these figures have been found, the econometrist advises the government to arrange its policy in accordance with them. So a distinction is made between target variables (e.g. employment, the equilibrium of the balance of payments, and price variations) and instrument variables: the exchange rate and the other quantities which can be influenced politically. The desired size of the instrument variables is the objective of the calculating technique. If the model is used in this way, it may form the basis for the government's decisions. Such a model is called a decision model.

It goes without saying that model-building has acquired herewith a fine task. It is, however, a task which makes stringent requirements of the forecasting power, i.e. of the constancy of the regression coefficients. The experience gained with this way of working is still too limited to allow of an opinion on this technique at the present stage. In principle it is splendid; in practice it is definitely still immature. But the method has just been discovered. Let us hope that it has a great future before it.

4 · PLANNING

The various objectives of model-building – summarizing, explaining, quantifying, forecasting, preparing decisions – merge into planning. It is worth while examining this activity, on which so many economists are at present engaged and which plays an important part in the economic policy of various countries.

The word planning has an ominous ring to many, even worse than Keynesianism, to which it is incidentally closely related. This aversion is understandable. The proponents of large-scale and detailed government intervention have too often used this term to describe their endeavours. To many, planning is synonymous with physical control of production, imports, consumption, and investment imposed from above. They associate the concept with a wartime economy, which cannot dispense with detailed control, with the state socialist view of society, with interference for its own sake, and with the political systems on the other side of the Iron Curtain. Planning seems to be contrary to freedom of production, to freedom of consumption, the choice of profession, or perhaps even to democracy.

However this may be, the reader will do well to detach himself from these mental associations if he wishes to understand what Western countries mean by planning. Planning might be described as macro-economic management. Certainly it involves government intervention – but not necessarily detailed interference with the decisions of entrepreneurs and consumers; the intervention may be indirect, almost unnoticeable, viz. via the circulation of incomes and expenditure. It is performed on a basis of macro-economic insight and it has macro-economic objectives: a free, balanced society, in which full employment, stable prices, a satisfactory relation between imports and exports, and a reasonable growth rate lead to the greatest possible prosperity. Other aims can also be pursued, too. An equitable distribution of income can be fostered simultaneously with a balanced economy by fiscal policy, wage and price policy. Social insurance also has both a distributive and a demand aspect. Equilibrium and growth are also interrelated; for a well-balanced demand forms the best foundation for investment, and investment (in capital goods and in labour) forms the main road to economic progress. The (unsolved) problem of the 1950s was how to combine growth with stable prices.

All these objectives together are served by planning, although in practice it would be better to avoid the word. Let us briefly examine its technique.

The starting-point is formed by the demand situation of the preceding year. The data on the national income and its components are collected, together with the necessary information on prices and wages. The relations are examined by means of the model. It is investigated whether the macro-economic situation satisfies the requirements made by economic policy. This part of the technique of planning should be regarded as writing history; it could also be done without econometric method. Nor is the model indispensable; it is useful for marshalling one's thoughts and stating relations precisely, but it could be done without. The situation changes if one leaves the safe refuge of the past and casts a glance into the future. Then the model – i.e. the constancy of the relations between the quantities – has to come to one's aid. And so the planner forecasts the economic situation that will in all probability occur in the coming year. In making this forecast he takes as his basis a given government policy. He deliberately leaves out of consideration those changes of policy which could be directed towards intentional influencing of economic activity. In this way the planner, on the strength of his calculations, arrives at a forecast of the coming year. This forecast is then critically examined in the light of the government's objectives. Perhaps it reveals undesirable things: unemployment, or a rise in prices, or a deficit on the balance of payments, or insufficient investment to guarantee reasonable growth. Alongside this forecast a picture is laid which does not display these undesirable traits. This is the plan. If it is a good one, it is characterized by the realization of a number of objectives which democracy sets for economic life. The planner now has two possible situations side by side: the forecast and the plan. The discrepancies between the two must if possible be eliminated by economic policy. On the basis of this the planner draws up a number of policy proposals, usually in the form of alternatives, which are then submitted to the government. In this sense he is the government's adviser. It is as well to realize that in Western countries he does not have any independent powers, and is in no way able to lay the law down to business.

To make this procedure clearer, let us fall back on a characteristic example of the planner's work. In Chapter IV we saw how $C + I$ can assume an equilibrium value – the False Equilibrium – at which this quantity fails to create a sufficiently large national income to produce full employment. Let us suppose that the forecast displays this False Equilibrium. Then it is at once clear what has to be done: the expected discrepancy between $C + I$ and the full employment position must be made to disappear. We have labelled this discrepancy a deflationary gap. The policy measures that the planning bureau puts forward for the government's consideration are then aimed at eliminating this gap; they entail an expansion of expenditure. The alternatives are a tax cut, an increase in government expenditure, in brief Functional Finance, supported by measures in the field of monetary policy, prices, and wages. In the opposite situation restriction of expenditure, in whatsoever form, is the underlying theme of the recommendation.

Now this example is taken from too simple a model. Underexpenditure is not so much a deficiency in $C + I$ as one in $C + I + X + G - M$. As a result of this, the alternative policies become much more complicated. Besides the manipulation of public finance, measures for promoting X are put forward: price policy, possibly devaluation. Special measures for increasing I may be considered: government support for large-scale projects which demand teamwork from business and government or investment incentives in the depressed regions. Housing can also play a part in these alternatives. Consumption can be expanded by pure suggestion: 'Buy', said President Eisenhower in 1958. Special sectors may be stimulated by special facilities (the French system). The effects of all these measures can be verified. For this purpose the decision model is called in. In more highly developed planning, therefore, all the techniques of modern macro-economics have full play.

Making a well-thought-out plan has a further function, which deserves separate mention. The planner gets most of the objectives of economic policy presented to him on a platter by the government. It tells him just how much unemployment it can tolerate; it explains that it would like to see a certain increase in foreign exchange holdings, so that a surplus of X over M is desirable; it informs him that it intends to expand social insurance by provisions for widows and orphans, for instance; it states a certain growth figure (e.g. 4 per cent). The planner takes due note of all this, but he does not remain entirely passive towards these wishes. He also evaluates them. Some policy proposals seem fine until they are examined more closely. This is particularly the case when they overestimate economic possibilities. Nobody can see that as well as the planner, for his model shows it. It is then his task to warn the government against the overstrained situation which it is in danger of summoning up.

A special warning is called for when objectives are listed which are incompatible with one another. The politician is sometimes inclined to do this. We have had very clear examples of this in the Netherlands. In the years after the Liberation one political party used the attractive slogan: higher wages, lower prices. This is possible. If the government is prepared to subsidize production and levies high taxes to make up for this expenditure, the two objectives can be reconciled with each other for a short time. But the high taxes that are the result would encounter difficulties. That means increasing expenditure, which leads to a rise in prices. In the long run, therefore, 'higher wages, lower prices' would have been a certain path to inflation. The two objectives would have proved incompatible over a longer period. A more recent example is the frequently heard wish for tax cuts, combined with better salaries for various groups of workers and civil servants, more money for road-building, a real attempt to solve the housing problem, slum clearance, education. In themselves both objectives – an increase in G and a reduction of t – can if necessary be reconciled with each other. But in an already slightly inflationary situation this does not fit in with a stable price level, a balance of payments in equilibrium, a peaceful labour market, a healthy economy. In the framework of economic policy as a whole, they are inconsistent objectives, which can be put forward only by an irresponsible opposition, not by a government. A very special task of the planner is to consider the compatibility of desiderata. The model can help him very much indeed in this. The planner and his model therefore form the government's economic conscience. Is the voice of conscience heard among the political hubbub? This is a question for Chapter XII.

The technique of planning has been generally adopted in most western countries. Especially in the Scandinavian countries, the Netherlands, Britain, and the United States, much work is being done along these lines. There are differences in scientific set-up, in technique, in detail work, and above all in official and political organization. In the Netherlands the official planning body is the Central Planning Bureau, which was instituted by law after the Second World War. It is a public office which publishes every year a Central Economic Plan drawn up along the lines mentioned above. The work is very much under the influence of the man who was the Bureau's director for the first ten years: Jan Tinbergen, one of the inventors of modern model-building, whose pioneering ideas have already been referred to repeatedly above. As is only to be expected, planning had at first an experimental character, but gradually it has been possible to note a certain consolidation.

In the United States planning is the work of the Council of Economic Advisers, a body of three men who advise the President on economic policy. The aims of this group are in no sense arbitrary; the set-up is regulated by the Employment Act of 1946, in which 'maximum employment, production, and purchasing power' were defined as the main aims of economic policy. Besides this official body a number of non-official bureaux work in the United States, of which the Cowles Commission for Research in Economics must be mentioned – a group of highly sophisticated thinkers who concern themselves with the theoretical side of research. In Britain the official planners are an anonymous part of the Civil Service, and in particular of the Treasury. They make less use of a formal model than we do in the Netherlands, although, with the setting up of the National Economic Development Council, this is beginning to change.

And so, throughout the free world, an increase may be noted in the influence of economic theory on economic policy. This can only be to the benefit of economic steersmanship: it operates in the direction of a growing rationalization of thought, as a supplement to, and prop of, statesmanship, which should always remain the principal factor in policy. Unfortunately, we are still far away from an ideal situation. The opposition and the checks, the prejudices and the misconceptions are still widespread. This will be further discussed on page 237.

5 · QUANTIFICATION

In contrast with purely theoretical economics, which often makes up its numerical examples, econometrics has to fall back on measurements. Statistics form the indispensable basis for model-building. Data must be collected on the expenditure components, on prices, volumes of production, employment, the balance of payments. Quite a job with the ever-present danger that the observed data will leave something to be desired in completeness or in accuracy. Many statistics lack the exactness which is a pre-requisite of proper quantification of a model.

There is, however, one consolation. As the statistician takes on more and more – and therefore has a more difficult time of it – he encounters an unexpected advantage. He discovers that his data often allow him to approach one and the same quantity from different angles. Think of employment, in itself a complex and somewhat intangible quantity. It is susceptible to direct though usually incomplete observation, for instance by making inquiries among business firms. This method is therefore sometimes followed. But, with the advent of social insurance, figures are also known on the number of insured workers. And then the statistician has available the figure for the total proceeds of wage taxes. Moreover, the unemployed are registered with the appropriate bodies, whilst the working population, i.e. the sum of employment and unemployment, is approximately known from censuses. All these data can be compared with each other. The inaccuracies of the one approach are compensated by those of the other.

The same check can be applied to a large number of macro-economic phenomena. This is the result of the quantities' inter-dependence. As regards production, technical data are known from the firms and sales figures from the trade and tax data (purchase tax). Employment figures also shed light on the volume of production. As far as investment is concerned, we have at our disposal figures on the volume of building, production data from the engineering industry, import data on imported capital goods, and moreover separate inquiries on investment plans can be made as is done by the Board of Trade. Consumption can be calculated from production, from certain import figures, and again from the proceeds of a turnover tax. For a long time now imports and exports have been registered with fair accuracy. All these quantities are finally combined in the calculation of the national income of a country. This calculation is performed in two ways, corresponding to the two sides of the circulation: output, or real income (the right-hand side of the circulation); and the money income (the left-hand side). Tax revenue, wage figures (known from the collective labour contracts), profit estimates (on a basis of annual reports and calculations of prices and costs), and data on leases and rents complete the picture.

The pursuit of a coherent whole of macro-economic data has resulted in a balanced system of statistical registration, known by the name of National Bookkeeping. The components of national income and national expenditure are neatly listed side by side, in the same way as is done in double-entry bookkeeping. Each item occurs twice, debit and credit. There are separate accounts for the households, the firms, the government, and the outside world; these are precisely those parts of the circulation that we have discussed. A separate account is also kept for the capital market (e.g. for banks, insurance companies, pension funds). A number of other subdivisions are also possible. There is a cross-check between the various items.

This double-entry bookkeeping may be illustrated as follows. In the Government account an item 'salaries' occurs on the left-hand side. The same amount may also be found on the right-hand side of the Households account, for that is where the income has ended up. Exports are listed in the Foreign Transactions account, but at the same time (and then the other way round) in the Firms account, for that is where the goods have been produced. The Households account states the quantities Y, C, and S. The Foreign Transactions account shows X and M, and in the Government account we see G and T. In each case the difference between the quantities can be read off.

The system of national accounts was developed in the 1930s, by, among others, R. Stone (Britain) and J. B. D. Derksen (the Netherlands), in conjunction with the statistical study of the national income (in which field the American S. Kuznets has been one of the great pioneers). These statistical surveys supply the material for modern macro-economics. From the very start they stress the transactions between the sectors of the national economy, which is then elucidated by Keynesianism. Planning, too, relies on the national accounts. In some countries, for instance Britain, planning gives more prominence to the book-keeping method than to the actual model-building. In the Netherlands both techniques are neatly balanced. The National Accounts are kept by the Central Statistical Office, a gigantic storehouse for all kinds of statistics; econometric work is also done there, but the planning proper – and model-making, too – is performed by the Central Planning Bureau, as I explained above. The division of work between the two official bodies is based in part on the idea that the Central Statistical Office mainly considers the historical side of the matter, i.e. the objective figures realized, while the estimates and the forecasts are chiefly the responsibility of the Central Planning Bureau. In general the latter body is more 'daring' than the former. What an econometrist of the Central Planning Bureau does not know he calculates. He has to. An employee of the Central Statistical Office is more inclined to say that he does not know something. This tallies very well with the place of the two organizations in the official structure.

The actual econometric quantification concentrates, as we have seen, on determining the correct form of the equations, i.e. on the regression coefficients. There is little point in going more deeply here into the difficult technical problems which occur in this work, such as the question whether the relations can best be described by a straight line or a curve. (In fact linear equations are often used in short-term models, which means that only small fluctuations in respect of the initial situation can be analysed.) Nor is it my intention to give a survey here of the different values of the various coefficients which were found. Some of the most important of them have already been discussed: the effect of changes in the wage level on employment, which proved to be extremely small (either positively or negatively), and the value of the multiplier, which in open countries like the Netherlands works out at less (say 1·5) than it should according to popular views of the strange propensities of the movement of money.

Rather than catalogue the various values of the regression coefficients found, I should like to go into the importance of the quantitative method again. My particular reason for doing this is to refute an ill-founded criticism which keeps on turning up, from economic circles as well; a form of criticism which has a certain emotional appeal. The theme, which is sung in many a variation, is: what about the human element? Man is much too spiritual a being to be comprehended by dry figures. Economics as a science of human activity is denatured by the quantitative method; it is too mechanistic, too coldly scientific, etc., etc. This is an argument which is lapped up by a certain group of anti-Keynesians, and above all by those who unconsciously fear that the new techniques are too difficult and will undermine their position, with its foundation of wordcraft. One of the champions of these critics is W. Röpke, a great economist but one who has also done harm to the science of economics. A characteristic pronouncement by Röpke is that the factors determining economic activity are just as unmathematical as a love letter or Christmas; their sphere is the moral and the intellectual, and they are incalculable and unpredictable.* Such a phrase sounds deep and good, and disagreement with it would seem to be due to materialistic shortsightedness and a preference for the superficial. Nevertheless, this form of pseudo-spirituality is nonsense.

Man is a free being, moved by spiritual forces; but stand on the platform of an underground station in London or a subway station in New York at nine o'clock in the morning, and you will see these spiritual beings, free will and all, crowding their way in and out of the trains. The density of the crowds can be determined. It is highly dependent on certain times of the day and the week.

* W. Röpke, 'The Place of Economics among the Sciences', in: *On Freedom and Free Enterprise, Essays in Honor of L. von Mises*, 1956, pp. 122–3.

On Sundays, for instance, many a station in the City of London or the business district of New York is practically deserted, but then the crowds may be observed elsewhere. It can all be very well verified, determined, even forecast. You can make a model of it, containing the topographical distribution of the suburbs and the business districts, the hours of work of the large offices, the timing of public holidays. And all this can be done in spite of man's spiritual character, in spite of his freedom of will and the moral and intellectual motivation of his behaviour.

Do not misunderstand me. Nobody, including theoretical economists, is forbidden to study the acts and decisions of the individual, who is moved by faith and doubt, passion and cold calculation, knowledge and ignorance, noble and base motives. Such studies are performed within the framework of economics, which has many compartments and methods (some more along the lines of the natural sciences, others more along the lines of sociology, psychology, history). However, it is by no means obvious that by analysing individual decisions we shall acquire much new understanding of macro-economic relations, of the interplay of the great flows of money and goods, and of the working of the national economy. Anyone who analyses the creation of the national income does not do the essence of man an injustice; he fully acknowledges the significance of human freedom (whatever that means), but believes that the result of a whole series of free decisions, taken by numerous independent individuals, is subject to certain regularities, which originate in part in the fact that all these spiritual beings in certain respects do resemble each other a great deal, and especially in the compulsion of the clock, the wallet, the tax collector, production techniques, and other mundane matters. Regularity is an indisputable fact, whatever Röpke, Von Mises, and others may claim on this account.

The true criticism of the quantitative method lies elsewhere. If the theory described in this book is to have any point, the relation between the quantities examined must display a certain stability. The constancy of the regression coefficients has already been discussed several times as a possible weak spot in the whole set-up. The variation in human institutions, sudden collective shifts in the behaviour pattern, the possibility of mass reactions not provided for in the model, all these restrict quantitative economics to a cautious and approximate method, which does not claim to lead to absolutely certain results. The relations which the econometrist finds are not certainties, but probabilities; however, they are the most probable that present-day economics is capable of providing. It is not for nothing that the correlation calculation, the econometrist's comfort and stay, is interpreted in mathematics as an extension of probability calculus. The calculation method which looks for probable relations on a statistical basis is known as stochastics. This stochastic nature, which is inherent in modern economics, constantly warns the insider to be modest and to be on his guard. It prevents bombast and overweening pride, but at the same time it ought to keep the investigator's feet firmly on the ground, which cannot be said of some 'spiritual' theorists.

In the course of the various chapters it has already come to the fore that a number of links in the Neo-Keynesian reasoning are, in fact, not particularly strong from a quantitative point of view. The investment equation in particular is so far a weak spot in every model. As a result, there is a strategic uncertainty present in the model. This makes understanding difficult and forecasting awkward. But there is no reason in this to bid modern macro-economics farewell. For there is no better technique. The flippant critics are not able to provide anything better than broad sociological observations of a charming but often hazy nature and incorrect economic theories based on implicit and therefore unverifiable models. Usually the opponents produce nothing at all, and get no further than grumbling.

And it is as well to remember that the young science of stochastic economics, although it has so far made a number of striking and instructive mistakes (the forecasting of the post-war depression in the United States), has also achieved some encouraging results. This becomes quite evident if the forecasts of various planning bureaux are assessed. And added to this is the fact that forecasting is the most advanced but by no means the sole aim of model-making. Even if the reliability of the regression coefficients is relatively low, the model may serve as a basis for explaining macro-economic movements. It shows how the economist has tackled his subject, it makes the theoretical framework honest and clear. It encourages better thinking. The only conclusion is therefore that the work that started a few decades ago must be continued. Well, there is no lack of such continuation. The new trade is flourishing.*

* Three milestones: L. R. Klein and A. Goldberger, *An Econometric Model of the United States 1929–1952*, Amsterdam, 1955. L. R. Klein, R. J. Ball, A. Hazlewood, and P. Vandome, *An Econometric Model of the United Kingdom*, Oxford, 1961. J. S. Duesenberry, G. Fromm, L. R. Klein, and E. Kuh, *The Brookings–SSRC Quarterly Econometric Model of the United States Economy*, Amsterdam and Chicago, 1965. The latter publication with its forbidding title tries to weld the theories and empirical findings of a large number of scattered research workers. The reader will notice that L. R. Klein has contributed to all three models; the Americans call him 'our domestic Tinbergen'.

CHAPTER XII

Economic Steersmanship

1 · THE COMBINATION OF POLICY INSTRUMENTS

It may have struck the reader whilst going through this book that each sector of the economy discussed – consumption, investment, international trade, the government economy, money, prices, and wages – may in its own field be susceptible to government policy. These various approaches to each sector were briefly discussed. In the previous chapter we investigated how macro-economics, by means of planning, can form a basis for the rationalization of a coherent policy. The question now is to what problems practical economic policy, which is directed towards the equilibrium of the national economy, gives rise. In this section one more theoretical problem will be brought up, which is the direct product of Neo-Keynesianism, viz. how must the policy instruments be combined into one balanced whole? Then the stumbling blocks and pitfalls of such a policy will be discussed in separate sections, above all to bring down to earth the optimistic reader who thinks that now everything is crystal-clear and to confirm the pessimistic reader in his belief that life is more difficult than you think.

For Keynes's original theory the choice of the policy instruments was no great problem. The General Theory itself pointed specifically in the direction of varying government expenditure as a means of regulating the level of activity, and furthermore had public works particularly in mind. Indeed, Keynes had a certain predilection for unproductive works, since then saturation does not occur. We must agree with him that building pyramids is better than having unemployment; but right up to the present day Keynes's opponents make it seem as if Keynesianism is identical with ridiculous projects or with state control of all investments. This is unfair. Urgent projects are always awaiting implementation. Education and housing have too high a priority for us to have to seek useless outlets such as pyramids. But it is true that the General Theory stresses an increase in government expenditure.

With the development of Neo-Keynesianism, this has changed. Besides government expenditure, taxes have entered the field of vision; Functional Finance aims at harmonious manipulation of both of these. It has increasingly come to be realized that the point at issue is not so much *the* government expenditure and *the* burden of taxation as specific items on the budget, and the tax structure. Old forms of policy were incorporated in the analytical way of thought. This created a host of new possibilities for Keynesian influencing of consumption and investment, but also new problems. Furthermore, monetary policy (Bank Rate and open market policy, quantitative and qualitative credit control) proved to be useful as a supplement to budgetary policy; we discussed this in Chapter VII. And, moreover, the opinion emerged that, although the Keynesian view relied much less than the classical one on the regulating effect of the price system, price policy could nevertheless be a welcome aid in maintaining equilibrium. Regulation of the rate of exchange and wage policy come to the fore as special forms of price policy in this respect. Finally, it has been found that the measures directed towards a better distribution of the national income, including the whole system of social insurance, produce effects on activity, so that this increasingly important aspect of policy should also be included in the equilibrium idea.

So rich an arsenal offers if anything too much to choose from. The complicated nature of the policy problem is aggravated by the fact that the objectives are not certain beforehand. Among the early Keynesians the combating of unemployment was so urgent an aim that their advice was almost exclusively directed towards this purpose. Later the combating of inflation was added. However, it proved that after the war the equilibrium of the balance of payments demanded special care. The distribution of income demanded attention, and with it the stability of the price level. And finally, partly under the influence of the Cold War, the need for an adequate expansion came to the fore. The problems of growth were accentuated by the fact that the underdeveloped state of many countries is no longer considered justifiable – in other words, a multiplicity of objectives, each with its own nuances, and a range of instruments, each with its own effects and side-effects. Sort it out for yourself is the obvious comment.

And rightly, too. Compared with the primitive explanations in this book, macro-economic research can be greatly refined. It can try to grasp the whole of objectives and instruments, and a decision model may be a useful aid in this. But the ultimate apportionment of the means must be left to the statesman. The economist is only his adviser (although there is nothing against – and in my opinion even everything in favour of – statesman and economist being combined in one and the same person). The finer aspects of economic policy lie outside the competence of macro-economics; it sees the waves rather than the ripples.

The less delicate variants of the problem of apportioning the means can be approached by Neo-Keynesianism. Instead of abstract reasoning on this subject, which would soon lead us into the dense forest of mathematics, just one of the main problems will be touched upon here. For instance, there is the question whether a combination of policy measures is capable of achieving a group of three objectives: full employment, equilibrium of the balance of payments, and a stable price level. There is reason to ask this question, since it is often denied that economic policy is capable of this *tour de force*. It is often asserted that full employment must lead to inflation, to a deficit on the balance of payments, to rising wages, and that the only method of preventing these ills is to have a certain reserve of labour – in other words unemployment. It is a sombre theory, in which gloomy individuals (who apparently are not very afraid that they will be among the unemployed) sometimes seem to delight.

Since the flow of income and expenditure is, as the word circulation implies, round, you can start anywhere you like. Let us begin with the balance of payments in equilibrium: $X = M$. In that case $I + G = S + T$. However, this equilibrium can come about at too low a level of income, production, and employment; viz. if s, m, and t are so high that too small an expenditure remains. This underexpenditure can be rectified by the government by decreasing t and increasing G, in which monetary policy can assist. $C + I + G$ increase in such a way that income increases and full employment is achieved. But a result of this is an increase in M, which after all is linked to the national income by the propensity to import. In that case M is larger than X, and there is a deficit on the balance of payments.

To remedy this, exports must be encouraged, which can be done by wage and price policy, promoting productivity, and, if these do not help, by devaluation. The exports increased in this way are possible only if factors of production are released at home. Domestic expenditure $C + I + G$ must therefore decrease, compared with the previous situation. This is again a question of Functional Finance and monetary policy. For instance, if there is a sufficient foreign demand, it is possible to find an equilibrium somewhere at which the balance of payments in equilibrium is reconciled with full employment. In practice a considerable amount of trial and error will have to be applied, and the limited mobility of the factors of production will delay and hamper the establishment of equilibrium. But in principle the two objectives can be achieved simultaneously, though on the condition – and this is of vital importance to the future of any small national economy – that foreign demand continues to develop well. If this does not happen, and if exports tail off because chronic under-expenditure prevails abroad, there is not a single national anti-cyclical policy that can save us. For in that case an increase in domestic expenditure is frustrated by a lack of foreign exchange. An open country, more than any other, has an interest in prosperity abroad. Accordingly as European integration is accomplished the significance of correct regulation of the economic activity at an international level will become increasingly great.

But let us suppose that foreign demand maintains its level and that domestic equilibrium is achieved. This equilibrium is matched by a certain price level. It is determined by the price of imports (which depends in part on the rate of exchange), on the wage rate, and on profit margins. The rate of exchange and the wage rate are not free to vary in respect of each other, since they must jointly lead to an export price level that matches the desired growth of exports. Price and wage increases exceeding this level must be avoided; for otherwise, to keep up the level of exports and employment, new devaluations are required, which again force up prices. This is then inflation – not in the sense of expenditure inflation, but in the sense of irresponsible price increases. In the open national economies, which have to earn a good deal of their national income in exports, the equilibrium level of activity therefore proves to be dependent not only on the foreign market but also, and very much so, on the price level – a strange, classical-appearing conclusion, but a conclusion arrived at quite differently from the way followed by classical theory. The question whether macro-economic equilibrium in the sense meant here can be realized thus proves, as far as open countries are concerned, to boil down to the question whether foreign countries offer a large enough market for goods that national business can produce at balanced prices.

Now the pessimists are inclined to answer this question in the negative. They generally have wages in mind; full employment is considered to form a standing invitation for the unions to force up the wage level. I believe that this view is an exaggerated one. The uneven distribution of incomes forms a greater incentive to push up wages than full employment does. True, the absence of unemployment strengthens the position of the unions, but it will depend on the other policy measures whether the unions take advantage of their strong position or not. In this sense a policy aimed at even distribution of incomes can make a positive contribution to wage stabilization, and an unfair distribution of the goods of this world forms a constant threat to the stability of the economy, with all its attendant consequences.

Anyone who wishes to assess wage policy in this connexion may not leave price policy out of consideration. Too high prices, i.e. too high or inflexible profit margins, which threaten to absorb the drop in costs resulting from the increase in productivity, monopolistic grouping, price-fixing agreements, and other forms of price inflexibility, may easily lead to a disturbance in the flow of incomes, in part in the sense that they provoke wage increases. For this reason competitive relations are of vital importance to equilibrium, and a policy directed towards healthy competition should be regarded as an aid to Keynesian policy, quite apart from the other merits that may be ascribed to flexible competition.

This does not mean that the resultant of wage and price relations will always be such that a consistent combination of instruments for achieving equilibrium can be found. It is not Keynesian policy that has then failed, but the pressure groups that try to exploit the situation to their own advantage. The inflationary process that develops from this is a struggle for the distribution of the national income. But I refuse to accept that this struggle must *per se* be fought out with such means that economic equilibrium has to suffer. It is possible that this will happen; but it is not necessary. It is not unrealistic to believe that the presence of pressure groups can be reconciled with a reasonable equilibrium. France under the Fourth Republic and in the years 1963 and 1964 was an example of how things ought not to be, but this need surprise nobody who knew the social and political situation in that country, however slightly. There are no signs that the triple aim of economic policy being discussed here (full employment, equilibrium of the balance of payments, and the prevention of strong price inflation) could never be realized.

We may conclude that economic management is faced with the task of compromising between various objectives, but that the varied nature of the instruments available often, in principle, allows of the simultaneous realization of these objectives. If this realization fails – which is quite feasible – it is not always policy that is responsible, but often a more fundamental state of affairs. A national economy that has lost its balance socially and politically cannot have that balance restored by a purely economic Neo-Keynesian policy. More radical measures are needed. But an otherwise sound community in which enterprising employers and responsible employees are reasonably accommodating towards each other can avoid inflationary and deflationary disturbances if a rational policy is directed towards this.

2 · EQUILIBRIUM POLICY AND POLITICS

In the preceding section it was mentioned *en passant* that, in a community, forces may be active which can frustrate economic policy. It is worth while to apply this idea to the various elements of Neo-Keynesian policy. It is as well to realize that this policy must be conducted in a complex force field, which deserves closer study. It is not my intention to elaborate this theory, in which elements of sociology and political science are combined, but a few remarks may serve to show what is involved. The clearest examples are in the field of public finance.

Some adherents of modern budget manipulation have made it appear too much as if government expenditure and taxes could be adjusted without more ado to the level set by the needs of the income flow. This tends to ignore the fact that the original function of government expenditure is quite different from that ascribed to it by the Keynesians; primarily, the items of expenditure on the budget have appeared on the scene to serve a specific purpose: the issue of passports, the arresting and trying of burglars, the education of young people. The structure of government expenditure is built up politically. There are voters and newspapers with a lively interest in these specific objectives; there are also separate pressure groups at work, advocating specific expenditure. All these views and preferences are considered to find expression via parliamentary procedure. The budget of a Western country is a law or a collection of laws enacted by the legislature. The political realization forms a game with very special rules, in which public opinion, the interested parties, Members of Parliament, ministers, civil servants, scientists, the press, and anybody else who wants to, take part. All these groups exert a certain force.

Now in this force field the macro-economic objectives must be brought to bear. This is in itself no mean task – it implies a constant rowing against the tide. Moreover, the statesman comes up against customs, procedures, theories which go back for centuries and which came into being with intentions quite different from those of Functional Finance. The historical origin of these rules of play lies in the wish to protect the people against the arbitrary power of a spendthrift or warlike ruler. The protection of the citizen against a domineering government demands a different technique of budget manipulation from the rapid and flexible adjustment of budget items desired by modern macro-economics. Constant difficulties arise out of this misalignment between the traditional procedure and traditional objective on the one hand and the desiderata of anti-cyclical policy on the other hand. There is a wide field for study here which has as yet been insufficiently developed. It is worth while supplementing the theory of public finance in such a way that this field, which is still left too much to scientific amateurs, such as journalists, politicians, and civil servants, is covered by scientific discipline. Such a change requires that the theory of public finance frees itself from the narrow-minded fear of exceeding its economic bounds and, realizing the good cause to be served (but nevertheless with the caution befitting science), enters the territory of sociology, administrative and constitutional law, and political science. Only in this way can the gulf which still exists between Neo-Keynesian theory and practical policy be bridged.*

In this way the group of objectives relating to anti-cyclical policy can be made to penetrate the budget. Anyone who thinks that the problems are solved once the economists have drawn their curves is wrong. They are just beginning. Only then can it become evident what forces are operating most strongly in the community, those of the cumulative disturbance of equilibrium or those of the rational endeavours. The result is not certain beforehand. A government, too, can become infected by a general cyclical movement. If it does not take care, the forces for which it should have compensated will sweep it before them, and it will strengthen the departure from equilibrium instead of countering it.

This danger is most evident when there is a boom on. Suppose that total expenditure threatens to develop beyond what national productive capacity allows. There is inflationary tension owing to the fact that $s + t$ is too small. Perhaps the primary cause lies in an (in itself) gladdening growth of exports or of investment. As a result of liberal expenditure, business is encouraged to make high investments, a shortage occurs on the labour market, incomes are large. Tax revenue is also above expectations. Everybody feels happy, even the Chancellor of the Exchequer. The high tax revenue contains a temptation for the government to increase expenditure – wrongly, as we know, for the government economy should act as a brake to reduce the flow of income and to counter inflation. But there are further forces urging increased expenditure. Many budget items relate to provisions complementary to those of business and households. In a boom there are lots of cars on the roads; perhaps the roads are not designed to carry this heavy traffic. A corresponding budget item is increased. Long queues form at crossroads; fly-over junctions are required; pressure groups do their best to get contracts for these large-scale projects. Business requires more energy; the govern-

---

* Work in this spirit is being done, in particular, by the American A. Smithies. G. Schmölders of Cologne also advocates a synthetic way of thought, but he arrives at negativistic and highly disputable conclusions on the policy to be followed.

ment is obliged to make investments on behalf of power supplies.

There is still more, much more. Thus, as the households earn more, a larger number of their children will study. Educational capacity may then prove too small within a short time; and so school buildings have to be constructed, teachers appointed, laboratories fitted out, libraries extended. People visit the theatre and the concert hall more often, since their incomes, swollen by the boom, allow them to do so; and every encouragement of cultural activity costs the government money. Ultimately the stage is reached in which everything seems possible. Members of Parliament advocate new provisions on the strength of the fact that additional expenditure in other sectors has already been permitted by the Chancellor of the Exchequer. 'If that expenditure was justified, this certainly is.' Parliament is then no longer the watchdog of the level of expenditure; it pushes up government expenditure. The fact that the larger parliamentary parties have their specialists in agriculture, transport, education, public health, etc., contributes to this forcing up of expenditure, for the specialists argue in favour of their own sector and may often be regarded as extensions of pressure groups.* The financial specialists of the parliamentary parties then come and tell the government afterwards that total government expenditure and taxation are too high. In a boom in particular this makes correct management difficult. In government finance cumulation occurs, without compensation.

In this political force field one can often observe as an additional complication the division of government bodies into national and local, such as Federal, state, and county. The local authorities often are not very conscious of anti-cyclical policy, to put it mildly. Nor is this implicit in their function. But they play a prominent part in a general encouragement of expenditure. They cannot help this; their expenditure is certainly justified in the sense that it relates to fine and useful things. But through this division of responsibility, little sometimes comes of anti-cyclical policy.

It is this inflationary infection of the government that has

* Attention has been drawn to this in particular by W. Drees Jr, *On the Level of Government Expenditures in the Netherlands after the War*, 1955.

caused some to despair of the possibilities of a Keynesian policy. Never, they say, will parliaments be found ready to cultivate surpluses solely because, for instance, the export industry is doing such good business. Out of defeatism some economists are then inclined to return to the old-fashioned standard of the balanced budget, thus abandoning the results of an intellectual development that can benefit prosperity.

What we in fact need is the opposite of such defeatism. Perseverance is essential if the viewpoint of anti-cyclical policy is to be victorious in budgetary policy. But even then the government is faced with formidable problems. For to remain the master of the opposed forces, it must itself summon up strong forces. For that purpose it must in its publicity paint a black picture of relatively minor departures from equilibrium, in order to mobilize sufficient support for the policy. To enforce a slight restriction of expenditure in 1956 and 1957 in the Netherlands a sombre forecast was circulated which grew into a kind of disaster in the papers. This arouses the danger of panic among people, which does the rationality of steersmanship no good.

A further difficulty pops up. Owing to the fact that the compensatory measures are almost always taken after a certain delay – in spite of planning – the fact that strong counterforces have to be overcome easily leads to too violent counterthrusts. In the case of small fluctuations of short duration this may lead to the opposite of what is desired. The compensatory impulse then comes, because of time-lags, at a moment when the small disturbance has righted itself. And therefore, in the present state of economic science and politics, it is out of the question that perfect equilibrium can be achieved. It remains to be seen whether this can change very much in the long run, even in the most favourable of circumstances. A certain rhythm in economic activity is unavoidable, and in particular a fluctuating growth rate cannot be avoided. However, the government has to guard against inflationary and deflationary disturbances exceeding the bounds of the permissible. Perfectionism cannot but lead to disappointment, and in the young history of Keynesianism this has already appeared several times, and in harmful fashion. I should now like to say a few words about the intellectual counterforces conjured up partly as a result of this.

3 · THE WRONGHEADED OPPOSITION

Perhaps the reader of this book has here and there taken exception to my tendency to polemize. Indeed, I have disputed a series of views, partly because this helps to make the reasoning clearer – the reader can then see on what points he has to form an opinion, an opinion which of course may differ from the author's – but also partly because I regard the views which I have contested as so many obstacles in the way of rationalization of economic policy. For a government which has to operate in a difficult environment anyway, where forces have to be overcome by counterforces, where the future is uncertain and the human mind is unable to see quickly and clearly what has to happen – for such a government it is extremely hampering and sometimes rather irritating that a large number of people remain unaware of the elementary principles of modern economic thought. The irritation can be alleviated by remembering that propositions such as 'the multiplier equals the reciprocal of the sum of the leaks' (see page 95) are not immediately grasped by everybody. However, it is not on this technical plane that this lack of understanding is so much of a hindrance. It is much rather a series of vague misunderstandings, old prejudices, half-truths, misunderstood conclusions, book-learning wrongly applied, political malice, and prejudiced arguments disguised as objectivity which hamper better understanding and more rational action. By way of summary I shall once again give a few samples of such incorrect opinions, which may be fatal to proper economic steersmanship. For a more detailed refutation see the relevant chapters.

1. *Economic life finds its own equilibrium, at which the productive forces, which are after all scarce, are all utilized.* An optimistic survival of the old economics; it fails to appreciate the working of the saving–investing mechanism.

2. *Departures from equilibrium are always temporary.* A misconception. Inflation and deflation can keep on for years. In those periods a relative decline in prosperity results, which is just what modern economics tries to prevent.

3. *A depression must be left to run its course.* A dangerous fallacy. 'Running its course' can be another way of saying that investments be allowed to die away; and if economic policy is

not directed towards stopping this, it is playing with fire. Before you know where you are, a cumulative disturbance of equilibrium develops which has nothing to do with 'running its course' but with a steady decline and unnecessary misery for a lot of people.

4. *General unemployment is caused by too high a wage level.* A logical error, caused by confusing micro- with macro-economics.

5. *The balance of payments is kept in equilibrium by the rate of exchange.* A half-truth. The rate of exchange influences exports, but imports depend on expenditure (or on the national income). Inflation leads to an adverse balance of payments, which within practical limits may not be rectified by tolerable variations in the rate of exchange. Free rates of exchange are therefore wrong as long as there are serious economic disturbances in the world.

6. *The government budget must be in equilibrium.* A familiar prejudice regarding 'sound government finance'. Correct only if activity displays a satisfactory macro-economic equilibrium. If not, this kind of sound finance makes things worse.

7. *The government may only borrow to finance investments; the rest of government expenditure must be covered by taxes.* A variant of 6, and just as wrong.

8. *The Neo-Keynesian budget policy is in essence anti-cyclical policy, so that a balanced budget covering several years is to be recommended.* A well-intentioned argument used by some Keynesians, but awkward and confusing in practice. In any case it has been associated too much with the 'old' anti-cyclical policy.

9. *Taxes may serve only to help fill the Exchequer; other objectives are reprehensible.* Fetishism. One major purpose of taxes is to keep the economy in equilibrium. 'Filling the Exchequer' is, on second thoughts, scarcely an independent objective.

10. *High taxes mean exploitation of citizens by the state.* No. In fact income is transferred from one citizen to another. Only when taxes are so high that they promote a depression or harm productivity is there a real burden. In such a case one can definitely speak of overtaxation.

11. *An increase in the national debt means burdening later generations.* Widespread fallacy; based on confusion between micro- and macro-economics. It is only true if the future tax rate becomes oppressive, so that the national income suffers.

12. *Functional Finance leads to inflation.* A misunderstanding. If the right policy, i.e. one which really satisfies the principles of Functional Finance, is followed, it leads sometimes to reflation, and at other moments to disinflation. It always seeks the optimum.

13. *Keynes's theory leads to a continuous increase in government expenditure.* A misconception. Neo-Keynesianism only says something about the relation between government expenditure and the tax rate. The absolute level is not directly involved. The forces that push up the level of expenditure lie elsewhere.

14. *Just let the price level find its own equilibrium; matters will solve themselves.* This is unrealistic. It fails to appreciate the indeterminate nature of the wage and price levels.

15. *Price inflation is a question of too high wages.* A half-truth. The high wages in turn are the result in various ways of too high or too inflexible prices.

16. *The quantitative method ignores the spiritual character of man and denatures economics.* A snobbish prejudice based on a series of fallacies.

17. *The quantitative method overestimates the definiteness of social phenomena; it tries to give concrete form to the intangible.* A wrong view of the modern stochastic technique, the result of insufficient knowledge regarding the probabilistic nature of econometrics.

18. *Forecasting is impossible: the economic process is constantly changing.* Well, there is something to be said for this. But not as much as the pessimists think. Some pretty good results have been achieved, and model-making is as yet young.

19. *Monetary policy is a more reliable instrument than budgetary policy.* Defeatism. Walking is safer than flying. Budgetary policy is unreliable only if the government either sees matters entirely wrongly or has to operate in an insuperably irrational milieu. It is precisely such defeatism that makes a marked contribution to this impotence.

20. *Wage and price policy can be used to suppress an inflation.* This form of overrating is to be found in particular among French politicians. In fact wage and price policy can be only a supplement, but a useful one, to the combating of inflation. The primary method is influencing the community's total expenditure.

21. *Full employment leads to inflation.* A false representation

of affairs. This happens only in a community that displays tensions (for instance in the distribution of income). It is these tensions that are responsible, not full employment.

22. *The Keynesian revolution is the magic key to prosperity.* A dangerous overestimation; dangerous because it leads to disappointment and so to wrongheadedness. In fact Neo-Keynesianism is not a revolution but an analytical approach to macro-economic problems, which may lead to a technique for rationalizing economic policy. It must certainly not be expected to perform miracles, but let us hope that it will help to prevent blunders.

23. *Keynesianism, planning, and all related forms of thought and action lead to excessive government interference.* A gross misunderstanding. A balanced flow of goods and money means a balanced community, precisely the sort of community in which a good deal of intervention is no longer required. Free enterprise can only flourish when total expenditure matches a nation's total productive resources. Government control of investment is not a necessary element of Keynesian policy. It may be advocated on other (e.g. socialist) grounds. Some Keynesians happen to be socialists (Mrs J. Robinson). Others are more on the conservatives' side (R. F. Harrod). Some conservatives are anti-Keynesians (J. Rueff, L. von Mises) and so are some socialists (R. Mossé).*

24. *The Keynesians want to dissipate the capital accumulated by previous generations.* Wrong, of course. They want to keep economic growth on an even keel. This means the creation of favourable conditions for investment and saving. Keynesians are not against saving; they are against underconsumption that causes a depression. Nothing is as bad for the nation's capital as a depression!

25. *Planning leads to slavery.* A serious misconception, which sometimes is based solely on an incorrect association of ideas – people have in mind state socialist or communist planned economies, which have nothing to do with the rationalization technique which we mean by 'planning' – but which in its more malicious forms consists of a blend of the majority of fallacies, misunder-

* See: P. Lambert, *L'œuvre de John Maynard Keynes*, Tome 1er, The Hague, 1963.

standings, prejudices, and disastrous wrongheadedness catalogued above. This unpleasant combination is sometimes intermingled with political resentment, which I fortunately may leave undiscussed here. For instance, every failure of economic policy, of bureaucracy, of communism and fascism is ascribed to Keynes's theory. The false ideas born of this are too grotesque to be briefly dissected here as regards their origin and mental background. They may be historically explained by the extremely bad experiences which some economists had with the Nazi régime; by the nostalgia of some for the 'good old days' which exist mainly in the thought processes of the classical theory; and by the ignorance of a number of politicians regarding the actual content of Keynesianism. This of course does not pardon the confused thinking that fosters these misapprehensions as a whole.

Now it fortunately happens that the most extreme fallacies are adduced by a small group only, of which Mr H. Hazlitt seems to be the proud leader.* But in a more moderate form the above arguments turn up again and again, now here, now there, and with countless variants. Taken together they form a mental morass in which it is difficult to work. Here is one of the most annoying obstacles in the path of a sensible economic policy; for in a democracy the views of the citizens count, even if in fact they are not tenable. A policy which has in any case to cope with real difficulties, such as a future which is difficult to predict, a number of unwieldy and inaccurate instruments, a force field of opposed endeavours, and the cumulative tendencies in the economic process itself, is additionally hampered in a vexatious fashion by unnecessary fallacies. It is for this reason that I lose my temper when, for instance, I read how an economist such as G. Schmölders, who is most competent in his analyses, continuously does harm to the cause of economic policy by his destructive and far-fetched criticism of the modern views. Instead of drawing attention to real difficulties and trying to improve matters, his arguments are constantly directed towards dis-

* Cf. his *The Failure of the 'New Economics'*, 1959, and the collection *The Critics of Keynesian Economics*, 1960. He is also responsible for the following elegant formulation: 'The Keynesian cult is one of the great intellectual scandals of our age' (Introduction to the above-mentioned collection, p.10).

carding Neo-Keynesian policy.* Nor would it be so bad if he had something to offer in its place! Instead of this negativism I consider a critical but at the same time constructive attitude the most fruitful. Economics still has an ample series of tasks in analysing the total force field of the obstacles and in making recommendations on how to remove these obstacles as much as is possible within the framework of a free democratic society. One of these tasks is to spread elementary knowledge on the new theories. The above reflections are meant in this spirit.

* *Finanzpolitik* (1955) and the paperback Rororo edition, *Konjunkturen und Krisen* (1955), which is aimed at a large public and is therefore all the more harmful.

EPILOGUE

What do we know about economic life? The answer 'not much' would be unfair to all the work that has been done by generations of investigators. And yet the opposite attitude, i.e. intellectual self-satisfaction, is even worse. If something should have become evident from the above, it is that our knowledge of essential economic relations still displays large gaps and uncertainties. Model-making has not eliminated this ignorance as if by the wave of a magic wand, and no economist believes that the present state of the theory forms in dazzling perfection the ultimate in economic science.

On the contrary, the model always remains a weak and un-certain reflection of reality. It must always be supplemented by institutional, sociological, and political observations. Micro-economics finds a place side by side with macro-economic theory. Moreover the equations themselves are never the last word, since they are always susceptible to improvement and refinement. Every relation should form the subject of further research, which may, among other things, lead to the splitting-up of the equations (disaggregation). The Neo-Keynesian way of thought has the great merit of provoking this research work. In my opinion this is where its greatest strength lies: it points to the weak spots in our knowledge, keeps on posing new problems and encouraging the progress of economics.

Viewed in this way, the Keynesian 'revolution' was no revolu-tion in thought but a stimulus to thought. In the 1930s macro-economics had become too complacent. Intellectual stagnation was the result: research into details, however deserving it might be, could not be fitted into a satisfactory model. Things have now changed. The impulses which were given twenty-five years ago are still far from spent; the multiplier process goes on. Economics has plenty of go in it; it certainly has a future.

A Short Glossary

BALANCE OF PAYMENTS: a list of all transactions which a country has engaged in with other countries in the course of a year.

BEARS: investors who do not trust share prices and therefore prefer to stay liquid.

BUDGET: a list of government income and expenditure.

BULLS: the opposite of bears; see the latter.

CIRCULATION: the movement of money and goods between firms, households, the government, and foreign countries; that is, the creation and spending of income.

CONSUMPTION FUNCTION: the relation between consumption and national income.

COST INFLATION: a rise in money costs.

DECISION MODEL: a model used for calculating what values of the instrument variables match the desired values of the target variables. See model, target variable, variable.

DEFICIENCY OF DEMAND: see deflationary gap.

DEFLATION: presence of a deflationary gap; see the latter.

DEFLATIONARY GAP: the difference between expenditure that leads to full employment and actual expenditure.

DEVALUATION: increase in the price of foreign currencies; not to be confused with deflation.

DISINFLATION: reduction of the inflationary gap; see the latter.

EXPENDITURE: what consumers, investors, and the government spend on goods and services.

FUNCTIONAL FINANCE: Keynesian budget policy aimed at banishing inflation and deflation.

HAYEK SITUATION: strained national economy, scarcity of factors of production on the market, a struggle for the means of production.

HOARDING: holding back money, increasing cash holdings.

INFLATION: presence of an inflationary gap; see the latter.

INFLATIONARY GAP: the difference between actual expenditure and the expenditure that leads exactly to full employment.

INVESTMENT: expanding the machinery of production; also the buying of securities.

LABOUR PRODUCTIVITY: volume of production divided by employment.

LEAK: reduction in total expenditure as a result of saving, importing, or paying taxes.

MODEL: depiction of reality (in our case the money and goods flow) by means of a system of connexions (equations) between measurable quantities (variables).

MULTIPLIER: relation between the extra national income proceeding from extra expenditure and that extra expenditure itself.

NATIONAL BOOKKEEPING: statistical registration of incomes and expenditure.

NATIONAL INCOME: the sum of all wages, profits, rents, and interest.

NATIONAL PRODUCT: the total flow of goods produced by a national economy; also known as the real national income.

PLANNING: method of calculation using models, aimed at rationalization of economic policy.

PRICE INFLATION: general rise in prices.

PRODUCTION FUNCTION: the way in which the level of output depends upon the inputs of productive factors.

PRODUCTIVITY: the volume of production divided by the quantity of factors of production (output divided by the total of all inputs).

PROPENSITY TO CONSUME: consumption divided by national income.

PROPENSITY TO IMPORT: imports divided by national income.

PROPENSITY TO SAVE: that part of income that is saved; savings divided by national income.

QUANTITY THEORY: theory of the value of money, starting from the quantity of money.

RATE OF EXCHANGE: price of foreign currency in terms of the currency of one's own country.

REFLATION: reducing the deflationary gap; see the latter.

REGRESSION COEFFICIENT: number expressing the extent to which a variable influences the dependent variable.

REGRESSION EQUATION: connexion between a quantity (the dependent variable) and a number of others influencing it (independent variables).

REVALUATION: reducing the price of foreign currency; not to be confused with reflation.

SHEEP: investors who are neither bulls nor bears, and who therefore believe that shares will remain at their current prices.

TARGET VARIABLE: the quantity in a model which the government aims at giving a certain value by influencing another variable (the instrument variable).

TAX BURDEN: tax revenue divided by national income. It is not a real burden, however strange this may seem.

TOTAL EXPENDITURE FUNCTION: the connexion between total expenditure and national income.

VARIABLE: quantity which changes, i.e. national income, prices, consumption.

VELOCITY OF CIRCULATION OF MONEY: the number of times money changes hands per unit of time.

Note on Further Reading

All general economic textbooks contain chapters on macro-economics. The best general book I know is P. A. Samuelson's *Economics, An Introductory Analysis* (1st impr., 1948, 6th impr., 1964), but there are at least fifty others. The original Keynesian system is explained by D. Dillard, *The Economics of John Maynard Keynes* (1st impr., 1948, many reprints). *The Keynesian Revolution* by L. R. Klein (1950) is also concerned with the work of Keynes and less with later developments. A simpler and stimulating treatise is A. P. Lerner's *Economics of Employment* (1951). Advanced textbooks on contemporary macro-economics are J. S. Henderson's *National Income, Statics and Dynamics* (1961) and G. Ackley's *Macroeconomic Theory* (1961), the most modern and complete work on the subject I have ever come across, but it is by no means easy.

Classical theory is becoming quite modern again, especially in the field of growth. See J. E. Meade's fascinating *A Neo-Classical Theory of Economic Growth*, 2nd ed., 1964.

Of the anti-Keynesians, H. Hazlitt's painstaking criticism of the *General Theory* should be mentioned: *The Failure of the New Economics* (1959). Mr Hazlitt is also the editor of a collection of essays: *The Critics of Keynesian Economics* (1960), with contributions by J. Viner, L. von Mises, and others.

For a biography of Keynes, written by one of his friends who contributed to the genesis of the *General Theory*, see R. F. Harrod, *The Life of John Maynard Keynes* (1951).

If the reader is interested in the institutions and the workings of the American and/or the British economy, a flood of books is available; two recent Pelican Books come to mind: Peter d'A. Jones, *The Consumer Society, A History of American Capitalism* (1965) and Peter Donaldson, *Guide to the British Economy* (1965). S. Brittan's *The Treasury under the Tories 1951–1964* (Pelican, 1964) may also prove useful. The most fascinating book in the field of economic history I know is J. K. Galbraith, *The Great Crash 1929* (1954; Pelican, 1961) though opinions may differ on this.

INDEX

Index

Acceleration Principle, 76, 80; and inflation, 81; and a depression, 82, 122

Agriculture, and protectionism, 101; its changing position, 198, 199

Automation, 32; and the productivity of labour, 35–6

Balance of Payments, origin of the expression, 86–7; its meaning here, 87 n.; the classicists and, 87–90, 96; the Keynesian equilibrium mechanism, 91–3, 96, 97, 228; adverse when more is invested and less saved, 96; the flow of goods and money and, 96; the rate of exchange and, 97–100; and a balanced budget, 110; can its equilibrium be achieved by policy measures?, 229, 238

Bank Credit, an incentive to investment, 49 n., 56, 144; creates money, 128–9; Treasury control of, 151; the central banks and reserve requirements, 151–2

Bank of England, 14, 128, 152 n.

Bank Rate, 28; and credit control, 151, 153; its 19th century influence, 152 n.

Banks, their power to create money, 63, 137–8, 140; claims on accepted as money, 126, 127–8; and the issue of banknotes, 127; create money by overdrafts, 128–9, 137–8; the cycle theory of money and, 138 ff.; Treasury control of their credit, 151; and the Pigou effect, 169

Baumol, W. J., *Business Behaviour*, 201 and n.

Bears, 63, 135; reduce the supply of capital, 136; and created money, 143, 145

Benham, F., *Economics*, 24 n., 135 n.

Bodin, J., 156

Boom, a, government dangers in, 234–5

Boulding, K. E., *Economic Analysis*, 24 n.

Bretton Woods Agreement, 89, 98, 130

Budget, the, its state of equilibrium, 108–10, 114–15, 238; the Keynesian theory, 108–10, 111, 141; what produces a balanced one?, 110; the classicists and, 110–11; Functional Finance and, 111–13, 114; a deficit need not lead to inflation, 113; the Haavelmo effect, 118–21; uses of a deficit to combat unemployment, 121, 153; monetary policy and, 149; a collection of laws, 233; the need for scientific discipline, 233–4

Bulls, 135; and created money, 143, 145

Business, *see* Industry

Business Cycle, Theory of, 23; ascribed to the effect of money, 137, 139

Capital, its productivity does not determine prosperity, 34, 35; importance of its high productivity, 35 n.; savings a preliminary to its formation, 39–40; Keynesianism and, 95, 135, 143; factors comprising, 131; its unproductive

181, 183; his interests not opposed to the employee's, 185–6

Employment, quantitative economics and, 17; investment and, 40; its place in the Keynesian and classical 'models', 65–7, 70, 71, 72; government expenditure and, 112, 141; the Haavelmo effect and, 120–21; the capital sphere of money and, 133; marginal productivity and, 175; effect of wage levels on, 176 ff.; represented in the macro-economic model, 203–8 *passim*; can full employment be achieved by policy measures?, 229–32

Engineering Industry, the savings paradox, 48–9

Entrepreneurs, influence on production, 22, 31, 41, 49, 50–51, 167; influence on prices, 22, 41, 170, 171, 172; and the productivity of labour, 36, 37; and investments, 38–9, 48, 52, 53, 75; dependent on savings for investment, 39, 41–2, 133; and the national product, 47–50 *passim*; and disturbances in the circulation, 61–2; and inflation, 81; and a depression, 81–2, 136; receive money from the bank, 137–8; and the cycle theory of money, 140; a monetary policy and, 153–4; determine the supply of consumer goods, 163–4, 166, 167; government price policy and, 170; and wage levels, 176–7, 186, 187; their changing character, 200–201

Equilibrium, True and False, 71, 73, 111–12, 217

Europe, Western, the need for economic integration, 102, 230; its Payments Union, 130; its economic renaissance, 190, 201; its capital-output ratio, 192; planning techniques in, 219

Exchange, Foreign, reasons for post-war drains on, 97; balance of payments and, 99

Exchange, Rate of, the basis of international trade, 88–9; variations in, 89, 98; and the balance of payments, 96, 97–100, 238; and exports, 98; considerations of the present rate, 98–9; arguments against a free rate, 99–100, 238; and the Gold Standard, 129–30

Exchequer, the, its forms of income, 105 n., 106

Expenditure, the money factor and, 146; expenditure inflation, 168

Expenditure, Total, determines national income, 45–51, 52, 79, 179; in the simple Keynesian 'model', 68–9; in the national income stability 'model', 79–81; Functional Finance and, 112; a balanced budget and, 119; shrinks under a prudent policy, 122; use of National Bookkeeping in accounting, 221–2

Exports, their meaning in this book, 87 n.; and the balance of payments, 87, 89–90, 91–3, 96, 99; income effect of, 90–91, 95, 98, 105; factors governing, 98; affected by cash holdings, 147; rising prices and, 158; effect of wage increases on, 180; represented in the macro-economic model, 203–8 *passim*; their dependent factor, 204, 206; their importance to a balanced economy, 230–31

Finance, Functional, its rules, 111–13, 124; its aims, 113–14, 123, 228, 239; and the national debt, 114–15, 117, 118; and inflation, 123, 171, 217; a form of monetary policy, 149, 230

Fiscal Laws, 107

Fisher, Irving (1867–1947), and the quantity theory, 158–62

Ford, Henry, and high wages, 177, 178

to the national money income,
30–31, 33, 45–51; ways of measuring,
30–31; prosperity and, 34;
determined by total expenditure,
51; the Haavelmo effect, 120; relationship
to prices, 167–8; the
capital-output ratio and, 192; its
production function, 203

Neo-Keynesians, 16, 227; and
Keynes's original theories, 15 and
n., 28; and quantitative economics,
21; process of arriving at
their theory, 26; and 'classical'
economics, 27; general agreement
between, 27; and monetary theories,
28; attitude to economic
growth, 28, 191; accept total expenditure
as the determinant in
the real national income, 51; regard
national income as the equilibrium,
51; and the determinants
of investment, 74, 77; and the
part played by money, 85; and
banking, 129; and government
expenditure, 227, 228, 239; can
their policies achieve full employment,
balance of payments equilibrium,
and stable prices, 229–
32; misconception concerning,
238, 240

Netherlands, the, 58, 151, 167, 183,
218, 236; and financing from
profits, 77; cash holdings in, 84,
147, 150; a free trade country,
101, 168; its unions, 182; its
wage policy, 187; its Central Planning
Bureau, 210 and n., 214, 219,
222; its Central Statistical Office,
222

Neumann, J. von, 182 and n.

Overdrafts, 128–9
Overproduction, the economists
and, 10; the classicists and,
12–13; Say's Law and, 13, 31,
41–2, 50; Keynes's theories and,
16, 31–2; not always the result of
saving, 32; need not lead to a

slump, 32; the growth paradox
and, 195

Patinkin, D., and price stabilization,
169
Petty, Sir William (1623–87), on
'Political Arithmetic', 11
Physiocrats, and the circulation
theory, 29
Pigou, A. C., Keynes and, 12 n.; the
Pigou effect, 169; and the Stationary
State, 189
Planning, its meaning, 215–16; its
technique, 216–19; and government
expenditure, 218–19; in
W. Europe and U.S., 219; and
National Bookkeeping, 222; does
not lead to excessive government
interference, 240
Politics, the economist and, 229;
and the structure of government
expenditure, 233–6
Population, a variable in the consumption
equation, 83; and wage
levels, 173; its growth and national
income, 193
Price system, the classicists and,
42–3; and the Keynesian and
classical 'models', 72; and the
balance of payments equilibrium,
88, 97–8; as a policy instrument,
228; fallacies concerning, 239
Prices, their relation to sales, 18–19,
196; their relationship to production,
22, 32, 42, 196; influence of
the entrepreneurs, 22; textbook
theories of, 22–3; a concern of
the economist, 41; influence of
the consumer, 41; the classicists
and, 42; and the balance of payments,
87, 89; increase under
devaluation, 100; would increase
without taxation, 107–8; and the
value of money, 155–6; inflation
and, 156–7; what does their level
mean to the community?, 157–8;
money theories and, 158 ff., 171;
their relation to costs, 164–5; their

MORE ABOUT PENGUINS
AND PELICANS

If you have enjoyed reading this book you may wish to know that *Penguin Book News* appears every month. It is an attractively illustrated magazine containing a complete list of books published by Penguins and still in print, together with details of the month's new books. A specimen copy will be sent free on request.

Penguin Book News is obtainable from most bookshops; but you may prefer to become a regular subscriber at 3s. for twelve issues. Just write to Dept EP, Penguin Books Ltd, Harmondsworth, Middlesex, enclosing a cheque or postal order, and you will be put on the mailing list.

Some other books published by Penguins are described on the following pages.

Note: *Penguin Book News* is not
available in the U.S.A., Canada or Australia

THE ECONOMIC HISTORY OF
WORLD POPULATION

Carlo Cipolla

This book presents a global view of the demographic and economic development of mankind.

Professor Cipolla has deliberately adopted a new point of view and has tried to trace the history of the great trends in population and wealth which have affected mankind as a whole. For it would have been inadequate to regard such a global history as being merely the sum total of national economic histories, in abridged form.

Among the massive problems that face the human race the author emphasizes the demographic explosion, the economic backwardness of vast areas, the spread of industrial revolution and of technical knowledge. Whilst the statistical approach can help our analysis of these problems, Professor Cipolla believes that they can only be wholly grasped and solved when they are studied in their full historical perspective.

THE GREAT CRASH 1929

John Kenneth Galbraith

Since Lionel Robbins's famous work *The Great Depression* no account of the financial insanity of 1929 has been issued in a form at once so readable, so humorous, and so carefully authenticated as this book, in which Professor Galbraith examines the 'gold-rush fantasy' in American psychology and describes its dire consequences. The Florida land boom, the operations of Insull, Kreuger, and Hatry, and the fabulous Shenandoah Corporation all come together in this penetrating study of concerted human greed and folly. From the cold figures of Wall Street the author wrenches a truly tense drama.

'An intriguing study . . . Professor Galbraith has marshalled and presented his material well . . . What he has done is assuredly worth while' – Roy Harrod in the *Sunday Times*

'Professor Galbraith performed a necessary and useful task in producing a lively and highly readable account of that disaster . . . It abounds in witty remarks' – *Financial Times*

'*The Great Crash*, one of the most engrossing books I have ever read, is also tinged with grim humour' – *Daily Telegraph*

THE ECONOMICS OF EVERYDAY LIFE

Gertrude Williams

'It is a measure of her success that she makes the whole subject sound like very little more than applied common sense, but common sense applied to familiar situations in a way that picks out a consistent pattern and shows the reader that the "economic aspect" is nothing more abstruse than a methodical selection from facts which, in a muddle-headed way, he knows already' – *The Economist*

The title of this book reveals its intention – to analyse in plain, non-technical language some of the important economic issues which affect life today in Britain. Now revised and brought completely up to date to include the National Incomes Commission of 1962, the unemployment crisis of 1963, and other important economic developments, this book deals with matters that are of interest to everybody because they are closely allied to the daily life of the individual. Why do prices go up and down? Who really pays for advertisements? Is monopoly anti-social? These and many other vital questions are discussed in such a way that the reader is able to understand the complex factors involved in trying to reach sensible answers.

ECONOMIC PHILOSOPHY

Joan Robinson

This exceptionally stimulating book begins by showing how
the basic human need for a morality on which the conscience can work has led to the necessity for a philosophy of
economics in any society. It is stressed that economic values
and money values are not identical and it is the task of the
economist to justify the image of Mammon to man 'not to
tell us what to do, but show why what we are doing anyway
is in accord with proper principles'. The relations between
science and ideology over the last two hundred years are
traced from Adam Smith, through Marx and Keynes, to the
dichotomy that exists in current economic thinking and the
pressing fundamental problems which must now be faced.

'It would be difficult to think of a better book than this to
place in the hands of the reader who thinks that economics
is simply a matter of statistics, and who needs to be convinced of its intellectual interest and excitement' – Samuel
Brittan in the *Observer*

NOT FOR SALE IN THE U.S.A.